Breaking Boundaries

Breaking Boundaries

Varieties of Liminality

Edited by
Agnes Horvath, Bjørn Thomassen,
and Harald Wydra

berghahn
NEW YORK · OXFORD
www.berghahnbooks.com

First published in 2015 by

Berghahn Books

www.berghahnbooks.com

© 2015, 2018 Agnes Horvath, Bjørn Thomassen, and Harald Wydra
First paperback edition published in 2018

Library of Congress Cataloging-in-Publication Data

Breaking boundaries : varieties of liminality / edited by Agnes Horvath,
Bjørn Thomassen, and Harald Wydra.
    pages cm
Includes bibliographical references and index.
    ISBN 978-1-78238-766-4 (hardback : alk. paper) -- ISBN 978-1-78533-749-9
(paperback) -- ISBN 978-1-78238-767-1 (ebook)
    1. Liminality. 2. Rites and ceremonies. 3. Philosophical anthropology.
I. Horváth, Ágnes, 1957- editor of compilation. II. Thomassen, Bjørn (As-
sociate professor) editor of compilation. III. Wydra, Harald, editor of
compilation.
    BF175.5.L55B74 2015
    302'.1--dc23
                                                        2014039950
British Library Cataloguing in Publication Data

A catalogue record for this book is available from the British Library

ISBN: 978-1-78238-766-4 (hardback)
ISBN: 978-1-78533-749-9 (paperback)
ISBN: 978-1-78238-767-1 (ebook)

Contents

List of Figures   vii

Introduction
Liminality and the Search for Boundaries   1
Harald Wydra, Bjørn Thomassen, and Agnes Horvath

Part I. Framing Liminality

Chapter 1
Liminality and Experience: Structuring
Transitory Situations and Transformative Events   11
Arpad Szakolczai

Chapter 2
Thinking with Liminality:
To the Boundaries of an Anthropological Concept   39
Bjørn Thomassen

Part II. Liminality and the Social

Chapter 3
Inbetweenness and Ambivalence   61
Bernhard Giesen

Chapter 4
The Genealogy of Political Alchemy:
The Technological Invention of Identity Change   72
Agnes Horvath

Chapter 5
Critical Processes and Political Fluidity: A Theoretical Appraisal   93
Michel Dobry

Chapter 6
Liminality and the Frontier Myth in the
Building of the American Empire   112
Stephen Mennell

Chapter 7
On the Margins of the Public and the Private: Louis XIV at Versailles   130
Peter Burke

Part III. Liminality and the Political

Chapter 8
Liminality, the Execution of Louis XVI, and
the Rise of Terror during the French Revolution   141
Camil Francisc Roman

Chapter 9
In Search of Antistructure:
The Meaning of Tahrir Square in Egypt's Ongoing Social Drama   164
Mark Allen Peterson

Chapter 10
Liminality and Democracy   183
Harald Wydra

Chapter 11
Liminality and Postcommunism:
The Twenty-First Century as the Subject of History   205
Richard Sakwa

Chapter 12
The Challenge of Liminality for International Relations Theory   226
Maria Mälksoo

Notes on Contributors   245

Index   249

Figures

Figure 4.1. The Secret Incantation to Catch Victims   75

Figure 4.2. Being on the Watch, to Observe, Quantify,
and Paralyze Identities   78

Figure 4.3. Alchemical Union   86

Figure 4.4. Hermes in the Egg   87

Figure 4.5. Souls Escaping   88

Figure 6.1. Territorial Growth of the United States   113

Figure 6.2. Territorial Area of the Conterminous United States 1790-1912   117

Liminality and the Search for Boundaries

Agnes Horvath, Bjørn Thomassen, and Harald Wydra

This book concerns comparative applications of the concept of liminality within the social and political sciences. Liminality is a powerful tool of analysis that can be used to explore different problems at the intersection of anthropology and political studies. Social scientists are increasingly sensitive to concepts that advance their ethnographic and historical investigations. Liminality is such a concept—a prism through which to understand transformations in the contemporary world. The objective of this volume is twofold: to explore the methodological range and fertility of an anthropological concept, and to systematically apply this concept to various concrete cases of transformation in social and political environments.

This book illustrates the formative and transformative significance of liminality, presenting some of the most important liminal crises in history, society, and politics. In an ever more interdependent world, globalizing tendencies entail more uniformity and identity within societies and across civilizations. Conversely, the uncertainties created by globalization processes have triggered new divisions and antagonisms. In some cases they spur desperate attempts to recover old certainties; in others, they create new differences. The guiding paradigms of most political and sociological research into these complex processes have been systemic, structural, or normative in nature. Policy makers, public intellectuals, and academics have attempted to "control" or channel crises such as civil wars, terrorist threats, nationalist mobilizations, ethnic cleansing, and economic downturns along the lines of rationalizing and modernizing discourses. But these formal, institutional, legalistic approaches are quite limited because they bypass people's need to make sense of voids of meaning and challenges to their cultural environment.

The escalation of crises demands a new mode of theorizing of the present. It must provide tools for understanding the combination of cognitive, affective, emotional, and "irrational" dimensions of crisis situations. Whereas contemporary social sciences take the dichotomy between order and disorder for granted, this volume problematizes the emergence and crisis of political forms as historically concrete phenomena. A key theme here is dissolutions of order, where experience shapes political consciousness, interpretive judgments, and meaning formation. This book focuses on the ways in which liminal situations can facilitate understanding of the technologies used to shape identities and institutions. What happens when ignoring the irrationality implicit in liminality makes the technological reconstruction of irrational fragments the very principle of rationality? This book's primary aim is to suggest that seemingly irrational conditions of liminality have logics of their own. Its chapters propose various approaches by which to grasp the technologies and tools that can perpetuate liminal moments into "normal" structures.

The two opening chapters by Arpad Szakolczai and Bjørn Thomassen reconstruct and further discuss the concept of liminality. It was developed in social anthropology, first by Arnold van Gennep and later via the works of Victor Turner, as part of the then emerging "process approach." Originally referring to the ubiquitous rites of passage as a category of cultural experience, liminality captures in-between situations and conditions characterized by the dislocation of established structures, the reversal of hierarchies, and uncertainty about the continuity of tradition and future outcomes. Though this book therefore engages an anthropological concept, it does not try to stay within any singular discipline—quite the contrary, this book is an interdisciplinary and theoretically innovative contribution to social science thinking about boundaries and the liminal spaces between them. The central idea of the book is that liminal conditions of irrationality are situations to be studied in their own right. Lived experience transforms human beings—and the larger social circles in which they partake—cognitively, emotionally, and morally, and therefore significantly contributes to the transmission of ideas and formation of structures.

This book intends to gauge cultural dimensions in contemporary sociopolitical processes, especially through the prism of sudden irruptions of existential crisis in people's lives, loss of meaning, ambivalence, and disorientation. As a fundamental human experience, liminality transmits cultural practices, codes, rituals, and meanings in-between aggregate structures and uncertain outcomes. As a methodological tool it is well placed to overcome disciplinary boundaries, which often direct attention to specific structures or sectors of society. Its capacity to provide explanatory and interpretative accounts of seemingly unstructured situations provides opportunity to link experience-based and culture-oriented approaches to contemporary political problems, and to undertake comparisons across historical periods. From a perspective of liminality, the cultural dimension of human experience is not an obstacle to a more rational and organized world but could be creative in transforming the social world.

This discussion has general relevance far beyond the specific setting; indeed, a salient theme in each chapter of this book concerns exactly the modalities through which liminal situations under given conditions tend to perpetuate themselves, replacing by some magical act or alchemic trickery (as Horvath discusses it) the very notion of "normality" or "reality" with a fictive "unreal" state, temptingly inviting people into what Turner often talked about as "life in the conditional." In this vein, many chapters directly or indirectly take up Arpad Szakolczai's famous diagnosis of modernity as "permanent liminality." The difficulty of closing a revolutionary period is also an on-the-spot analytical reflection of what is happening in several Arab and Middle East states right now. Those conditions will change, probably before these lines go into print, but analysis of such revolutionary moments will doubtless retain its significance for time to come.

A note about this book's coming into being is in order. Marking the 100th anniversary of the publication of Arnold van Gennep's *Rites de Passage* in 1909, the then newly founded journal *International Political Anthropology* produced a special issue on "Liminality and Cultures of Change" (issue 2, volume 1, 2009). Since its publication, that special issue has had quite a remarkable readership and has certainly contributed to cross-disciplinary discussions of liminality during the last five years. We would like to acknowledge the support of the Centre for Research in the Arts, Social Sciences, and Humanities (CRASSH) at the University of Cambridge in preparing and coordinating scholarly contributions on this theme of liminality.

Now we wish to carry forward the effort behind the special issue by turning it into the present book, once again situating our contributions with respect to these ongoing and unfolding debates across the social, cultural, and political sciences. Eight of the chapters offered here are elaborated, updated versions of the original articles in the special issue. Four chapters are new contributions, included because they identify crucial dimensions of the liminal that speak to our present age and are also, for obvious reasons, becoming core issues within current academic discussions.

The introductory section with chapters by Arpad Szakolczai and Bjørn Thomassen outlines the analytical dimensions involved in "thinking with liminality." These two chapters also position the concept of liminality within the social sciences with regard to both its almost forgotten intellectual history and its contemporary analytical paradigms and positions. The following two thematic sections engage respectively with social and political dimensions of liminality.

The section "Liminality and the Social" deals with liminality's applicability for social processes. This section thematizes "inbetweenness," critical and fluid junctures, the performative elements of culture and power, and the cultural significance of territorial expansion. Bernd Giesen's chapter "Inbetweenness and Ambivalence" argues that spaces of ambivalence and hybridity are fundamental to sustaining social reality. It suggests that between structuralist and post-structuralist thought lies a third possibility: the space between the opposites, the transition between inside and outside, the "neither . . . nor" or the "as well as . . .". Cultural sociology focuses on something transcending the successful ordering and splitting the world into neat binaries—namely, an inbetweenness that, it maintains, is essential for the construction of culture. Reality itself provides no firm ground for neat classification, so in applying classifications to raw reality there will always be an unclassifiable remainder. In specifying meaning there is no way to achieve absolute clarity while avoiding a rest of fuzziness.

The chapter by Agnes Horvath proposes a genealogy of alchemy, focusing on the conditions conducive to artificial creation and the practices applied in such a craft. It argues that technology can be analyzed as the proposition, and attempted realization, of a genuinely alchemically transformative operation of gaining a new identity, whether in personal, social, or political being. From the perspective of rites of passage and liminality, together with Plato's ideas on imitation and image-making, the essay focuses on the situation when a self-styled outsider, the "Trickster," brings forth this identity change, hijacking the difference-making process.

Michel Dobry's chapter questions the commonly accepted view that critical events like revolutions and political transitions can or should be approached with a specific set of extraordinary methodological and theoretical tools. Approaches leaning on such a "methodological exceptionalism" often assign a whole different set of values to subjective "choices" made by single individuals in critical historical situations, as compared to "normal" politics, where objective structures tend to be in place. Standard approaches to critical events also tend to reconstruct a historical path of such events, leading up to the already known outcome. As an alternative, this chapter presents a "hypothesis of continuity" to account for political crises or transitions from a position of "fluid conjunctures." Dobry's main proposition is not to provide a phenomenological account of the emotions and aspirations active in such liminal moments, but rather to normalize fluid conjunctures with a view to making their study accessible with social scientific tools. Nevertheless, its stress on fluidity of structures or the "desectorization of social space" illustrates elective affinities with social liminality.

Stephen Mennell reexamines the westward expansion of the United States in the nineteenth century, and the central place the frontier often takes in the American national experience, in the light of the concept of liminality. He tentatively draws connections between liminality, stemming especially from the work of van Gennep and Turner, and the famous "frontier thesis" of another Turner, Frederick Jackson Turner. A further element in the discussion is the idea of decivilizing processes, derived from the writings of Norbert Elias. In conclusion, it argues that the frontier, whether as actual liminal experience or as myth, has had lasting consequences for the American habitus and for the United States' position in the world.

Peter Burke's piece stresses the theatrical aspects of identity construction in politics by looking at reconstruction of the everyday life of King Louis XIV at the court of Versailles. Using Erving Goffman's ideas about the presentation of the self in everyday life, this chapter sheds light on the king's rapid passages between different royal roles, identities, and styles of performance. This historical anthropology of daily rituals and everyday performances at the margins of the private and the public offers insight into how a rather small man could become an emblematic political leader, *Louis le Grand*.

The final section concerns liminality's more strictly political dimensions. The contributions focus on various thematic and substantial issues, highlighting the need to examine seemingly chaotic processes of socially intense political transformations in terms of liminality. The chapters thematize revolutionary processes, the liminal sources of the democratic imagination, the challenges of the "cold peace" after the Soviet collapse, and the ways that liminality could become a leading paradigm in a subdiscipline like international relations. Since the special issue appeared in 2009, the world has witnessed a series of revolutions in the "Arab World" that have shattered regimes and broken down existing institutions, paving the way for novelty and radical change. As both Camil Roman and

Mark Peterson argue, political revolutions must be seen as quintessential outbreaks of liminal conditions in a large-scale setting entailing genuine collapse of order and loss of stable reference points.

Roman's chapter focuses on the role of the execution of King Louis XVI during the French Revolution. Though the French revolution is usually seen as overcoming the divine right of kings, the actual execution of the king, the regicide, was not simply an ephemeral event but the centerpiece, the apex of two congruent social processes: the symbolic disincorporation of royal power and the consolidation of a new democratic community of experience. Roman's chapter provides a liminal analysis of the king's trial and execution as well as the creative emotional power emanating from this event.

Mark Peterson carries forward the analysis of revolutions as liminal experience, delving into the detailed, intricate social drama that the Egyptian revolution was and still is. One of Peterson's crucial points concerns the difficulty of "closing" the revolutionary period via some form of ritual reintegration and returning to normality and a certain degree of taken-for-grantedness.

Harald Wydra's chapter takes the question of the authority vacuum in a revolutionary situation a step further. It conceives of democracy as being in dialogue with a condition in which the place of power is empty. In other words, democracy is based on a permanent authority vacuum that, in turn, requires a sacred center of authority to transcend such fractures. Modern democracy has developed bounded spaces—such as territorial states, constitutionalism, or civic collective identity—that check the permanent uncertainty about the place of power. Such bounded spaces and meanings are challenged by the dynamics of political emancipation of individuals and collective groups, which underlies realization of goals of equality and freedom. Contrary to standpoints where democracy is the order of egoism or is an ever stronger appeal to achieve more equality in a global world, this chapter suggests that the democratic imagination is based on the passionate interests in the liminal empty place of power.

Richard Sakwa reflects upon the collapse of the Soviet Union, the end of the Cold War, and the incapacity to achieve more enduring structures of international peace. He argues that the demise of the Soviet brand of emancipatory revolutionism exhausted the great utopian projects for large-scale social amelioration. The new era, though characterized by an unprecedented openness—a type of liminality of political options designated by the term *krizis*—of historical outcomes, is accompanied by political closure throughout the developed world. Although the lack of political imagination imbues this period with potential for novel types of renewal, the agendas of the past have not yet been adequately assessed. In particular, the asymmetrical finish of the Cold War, in which one side claims a victory that the other side sees as a common achievement, generates tensions in the form of "cold peace" that are taking traditional geopolitical forms. Thus, even though liminality is defined as a period of transition from one condition to another, the world today is unable to take advantage of the unique historical situation at the end of the Cold War and risks not only perpetuating its structures but also returning the world to a condition of war of all against all, including through consolidation of elite-driven national politics.

Maria Mälksoo's chapter, covering the analytical challenge liminality poses to the discipline of international relations, crucially opens the discussion of liminality to the larger field of international politics. This addition is both meaningful and consequential, as we are indeed witnessing a constant "permanentization" of warfare and security threats, with "war"—a large-scale liminal experience par excellence—being everywhere and anywhere, all the time.

Into the Liminal and Out Again

Some final words of caution and guidance: Our title refers to the notion of "breaking boundaries." Liminality indeed refers to threshold and boundary experiences. Yet we expressly do not argue that "breaking boundaries" is inherently "good" and necessary with respect to either empirical phenomena or epistemology and the premises by which scholars should pursue understanding and reflection. In fact, a guiding theme in many of the chapters here concerns the problematic attitude or "ethos" so bound up with modernity, namely, that boundary transgressing is a necessary, celebrated aspect of any kind of progress. Precisely this attitude should be questioned and problematized—which also means insisting on the importance of boundaries and limits.

This insistence on limits operates in a very concrete dimension. Today the concept of liminality is used in such diverse fields as conflict studies, international relations, literature, business studies, consultancy, psychiatry, education, theater, leisure, arts, and popular culture. We do not want this book to appropriate or delimit the ways in which this concept can or should be employed in analysis. However, we do wish to signal that any meaningful application of liminality needs to pay due attention to the anthropological and experiential underpinning of the term, and that liminality—despite its communitarian and antistructural appeal—simply cannot be used "freely," without invoking necessary discriminations and analytical-cum-ethical discernments to ground our arguments. Put briefly, this book does not celebrate liminality but instead problematizes the many ways in which liminal conditions have come to shape the contemporary.

Finally, the twelve chapters of this book do not represent any specific "theoretical paradigm" or -ism, nor do they pretend to. Liminality is not a concept that can or will produce "schools of thought." The authors represent an array of different disciplines including anthropology, sociology, political science, history, and international relations. What unifies this volume is a shared engagement with the concept of liminality, and a belief that this concept is indeed central to the social and human sciences, a vital tool for analysis still open to exploration and debate, and still more important for understanding the times in which we all live.

Part I

Framing Liminality

Chapter 1

Liminality and Experience
Structuring Transitory Situations
and Transformative Events

Arpad Szakolczai

Introduction: Liminality in the History of Thought

The term "liminality" was originally developed by anthropologists. This volume's second chapter, by Bjørn Thomassen, covers these origins, so this essay will start by discussing the use of similar terms in philosophy and sociology.

Liminality in Philosophy

Liminality should have been, but was not, among the founding terms of modern anthropology. It was, however, the very first word of philosophy. The Latin "limit" is equivalent to the Greek *peras*, so "liminal," in the sense of removing the limit, is identical to *apeiron*, the famous "first word" of Greek philosophy (Patočka 2002), contained in Anaximander's first fragment. The word became a central category of Pythagorean thought, and Plato and Aristotle discussed it in well-known disquisitions.

The reason the term is little known in modern thought has much to do with Kant, who based modern rationality on the opposite concern: the limit as "boundary" (Gentile 2003; Goddard forthcoming), key to his "critical" philosophy. The great difference between Kant's view of the world and Plato's is obvious in their respective cosmologies, which were essential to the

---

Notes for this chapter begin on page 36.

philosophy of each, though again at opposite ends: Plato's is laid out in one of his last works, the *Timaeus*, whereas Kant's is contained in his first works, devoted to astronomy. For Plato and the Greeks, the world is a cosmos, and any search for knowledge must start by recognizing its ordered, harmonious beauty. This is why Plato is calm, serene, and composed—a beacon of light even after twenty-five centuries. For Kant, however, the world that surrounds us, including our own everyday experiences, is chaotic and impenetrable: the "thing-in-itself" cannot be known.

Hence the consequences: "Kant's life is best described as a heroic struggle to discover order within chaos or, better, an effort to fix human thought and behavior within its proper limits" (Fiala 2004: vii). This statement, and its place in a prominent publication, can be taken as representative. It serves well to indicate the highly problematic "spirit" animating Kant's work. If the world outside is perceived as a chaos, then there immediately emerge fundamental negative and positive basic guiding principles that can never be questioned again. Negatively, it is pointless to try to distill and understand, humbly, the inner structures and beauties of this, our world—an attitude not fully endorsed by Kant but rendered explicit by the subsequent waves of his "neo-Kantian" followers.[1] Positively, Kant argues that the sole ethical position is to take up the challenge and heroically confront this chaos. Such heroism, however, is extremely peculiar and most problematic. Instead of meeting a real challenge encountered in one's concrete life, which requires composure, determination, and courage, it involves an abstract fight against the entire world perceived as chaos. From a Platonic perspective, the Kantian attitude does not lie along an ethical-intellectual axis of courage and cowardice, but rather one of humility and hubris.

The second part of the quote goes a step further that warrants serious consideration, as the author calls it "better." Here, praise of Kant's heroism is transmuted, not simply into an example to be set, but a Law: without the "philosopher" imposing such limits, it implies, we would be lost in the wilderness. The quotation marks above are intentional. Words have their meaning, and Plato, the inventor of philosophy, designated it to mean not abstract thinking, but rather an emotional commitment: love (*philia*) for wisdom (*sophia*). Plato's designation also targeted the Sophists, who did not share such an attitude but instead twisted words to gain fame and money. This was certainly not Kant's aim—yet the attitude of fighting doggedly against a presumably chaotic, hostile, alien world is not philosophical either. It is perhaps Gnostic.

So what exactly does Kant say about the "limit"? This question leads to the heart of Kant's Gnosticism, as Kant performs a series of subtle operations that make it impossible to discuss the "unlimited," amounting to a genuine "revaluation of values."

Characteristically, through a series of steps Kant sketched an attractive agenda concerning the very foundations of thinking that both ignored the classical agenda and concealed the peculiarity of his own way of proceeding.[2] First, Kant identified the limit as purely negative; then, in searching for a positive meaning of limiting, he took the second, crucial step of matter-of-factly taking for granted that "limiting" is a purely mental concern, the limit itself having no reality—one simply could not be "at the limit"; then, in a third step, he defined this positive meaning as a "boundary," something that—in contrast to a limit—"determines what it bounds," so that, "through the act of excluding, a boundary encloses, and determines a completeness and unity" (Goddard forthcoming: 4). The result is an infatuation with limit and law that ignores the fact that Plato's concern with *eidos* (origin of the term "idea", but more explicitly incorporating both words and images) was to restore measure, not to define a completely bounding limit. Thus, although German idealism pretended to revitalize Greek philosophy, it actually misconstrued and thereby betrayed this tradition.

After Kant, the system was immediately felt to be missing something having to do with the reality of human life, society, and experience, but the force of Kant's way of thinking proved practically irresistible. The most important effort to depart from the confines of this legacy came not with Hegel—who remained imprisoned within Kant's problem-setting—but with Friedrich Schleiermacher and Wilhelm Dilthey, founders of philosophical hermeneutics who tried to return to the classical agenda to seek a more secure foundation for studying experience. Dilthey became convinced that Kant was wrong in arguing that experiences are so chaotic that only the "transcendental mind" can "construct" an order among them—an argument that still animates the hubris of "theory" and the various "constructivist" movements in the social sciences. Instead, the task of philosophy is to understand the very structure of experiences.

Dilthey sought this inherent order of experience in the right places—history and biography—but did not manage to identify it and complete his work. This was partly because he was still entrapped in the epistemic limitations of his times, like the reading of Plato as an "idealist" or the lure of "objective science." Consequently he was attacked, even ridiculed, by his most important intellectual opponents, the neo-Kantians, who managed late in his life to marginalize him, just as the Durkheimians marginalized van Gennep.

Nietzsche made parallel efforts, focusing on the personal dimension of experience. However, he was not trained as a philosopher. His most important followers, especially in this regard, were social and political theorists like Eric Voegelin and Michel Foucault, who arguably escaped infatuation with the Kant-Hegelian agenda better than Husserl, Wittgenstein, or

Heidegger. This leads us to social theory, where Dilthey's and Nietzsche's impact was transmitted and rethought by the foremost founding father of sociology, Max Weber.

Liminality in Sociology

The case can be made that even sociology's first word was a synonym of "liminality." Sociology starts with Saint-Simon and Comte, who made the central claim that with the Revolution, France had arrived at a crucial moment of transition. Their work focused on the historical process leading to this juncture, and on the solution that would end the crisis.

However, in conceptualizing situations of transition, the pioneers of sociology followed an Enlightenment logic caught in between two extremes: on the one hand constructing teleological schemes, projecting an inevitable, linear development in history; on the other taking upon themselves the desperate responsibility of "solving" the crisis. The dilemma returned with Marx, similarly caught in between proclaiming the unavoidability of communism and preaching the revolution (Poggi 1972). Anything still relevant and interesting in historically oriented social theory tries to overcome this legacy of Comte and Marx, and of Kant and Hegel; and is mediated through the work of Max Weber.

The two main sources of inspiration for Weber's "method" — here understood in the original sense, as a "way" of proceeding — were Dilthey and Nietzsche. Beyond the early "methodological" writings, Dilthey's impact is most visible in *Economy and Society*, especially the opening chapters focused on the "meaning" of social action as part of a search for "interpretive understanding" (*Verstehen*) beyond neo-Kantianism. His reading of Nietzsche drove Weber's comparative history of civilizations and strikingly informs the opening sentence of his "Sociology of Religion" chapter, which defines its aim as "to study the conditions and effects of a particular type of social action" (Weber 1978: 399). Derived from Nietzsche's *Genealogy of Morals*, this approach was then taken up by the most immediate followers of Weber (not yet afflicted by the impact of Parsons) like Norbert Elias, Franz Borkenau, and Eric Voegelin. Later Foucault labeled it the "genealogical method" (Szakolczai 2000, 2003).

The central issue of genealogical analysis is the exact nature of the "conditions" under which a new phenomenon emerges — a new social practice, political institution, or world religion. In the footsteps of Dilthey and Nietzsche, Weber used several terms to capture these "conditions': "stamping experiences" (Weber 1948: 268–70, 280); the "psychological states" characteristic of major religious figures (ibid.: 270, 277–79); and in particular, their "ordinary" or "out-of-the-ordinary" (*außeralltägliche*) character, a central term in Weber's theoretical framework, and the background foundation for one of his most important theoretical innovations, "charisma" (ibid.: 271–72, 286–95; 1978: 215–56, 41–54, 400–401, 1111ff.). However, Weber never conceptualized out-of-the-ordinary situations and "stamping experiences."

Theorizing the "conditions of emergence," or the fluid, out-of-the-ordinary states with a formative impact on institutions and practices, would remain a primary concern of Weber's most important followers. Elias prominently uses the word "stamp" (Elias 1983: 39; 2000: 268–69, 517–18) and—like Borkenau—returns to the problem of "transition," beyond its trivial Comtean meaning (Elias 1983, 2000; Borkenau 1976, 1981), but even they failed to produce a comprehensive study of the Renaissance as a crucial period of transition (Szakolczai 2007). Just as importantly, clarifying the nature of experience was at the core of the later theoretical work of Nietzsche- and Weber-inspired scholars, most importantly Voegelin, Koselleck, and Foucault. Though none of them were trained as sociologists, they worked in the intersection between philosophy and the social and political sciences, focusing on their anthropological foundations.

Eric Voegelin theorized inbetweenness using the term *metaxy*. He claimed to have discovered it in Plato, but the discovery was probably equally the work of his own interpretation.[3] He emphasized that most key figures in political thought had endured particularly stressful conditions of wars, civil wars, or invasions, arguing that "symbols" are "engendered by experiences" (Voegelin 1956–87, 1997–99; for more details, see Szakolczai 2000, 2003). Similarly, Reinhart Koselleck connected the rise of modern political thought to the religious and civil wars of the sixteenth and seventeenth centuries, introducing the term *Sattelzeit* ("saddle" time) for formative transitory periods, providing a crucial analysis of critique and crisis, and connecting major inflections in the history of thought to such periods with terms like "space of experience" and "horizon of expectation" (Koselleck 1985, 1988, 1989). Finally, Foucault's "archaeology of knowledge" and "genealogy of power" linked epistemic discontinuities with institutional practices, while in his last work Foucault introduced the term "problematization" to analyze the connection between experiencing crises and innovations in thought (Szakolczai 1998, 2000, 2003).

Retrieving Connections

Our line of investigation has delineated the following problem: Modern philosophy, following Kant, drew attention to the "limit" as a heuristic device, reducing formation to limiting, measure to boundary, and *eidos* to idea as "representation," ignoring what happens when somebody is actually "at the limit." Hence, the productive, formative aspects of experience have been played down. The most important late nineteenth-century philosophers, Dilthey and Nietzsche, tried to go beyond the impasse of Kantian thought by focusing on personal lived experience, moving beyond the fixity of the subject and the reduction of experience to objectivity. Sociology, on the other hand, devoted much attention to uncertain, stressful periods of transition. Beyond teleological schemes and titanic attempts to "solve" the "crisis," Weber and his followers were similarly interested in the formative aspects of such periods. The question now is how to connect the two.

This problem was solved by Victor Turner, who in a series of unfortunately posthumous papers argued that "liminality," a concept developed by studying rites of passage or through a processual analysis of unstructured situations, actually solves Dilthey's old problem of the inherent structure of experiences, moving definitely beyond the epistemological horizon defined by Kantian thought.

Liminality as Experience

Turner Meets Dilthey

Victor Turner did not encounter the work of Wilhelm Dilthey until the late 1970s, casually. He immediately perceived an affinity between his own work and Dilthey's, arguing that it takes an anthropologist to understand the significance of Dilthey (1985b: 210). The encounter could not have been more momentous: between continental philosophy and Anglo-American social or cultural anthropology, beyond the dominant rationalist and empiricist paradigms, it opened the way to solving the perennial problem of modern thought concerning the nature of experience.

Dilthey intuited that human experience is not chaotic and random, to be "constructed" and ordered by the abstract categories of the transcendental mind, or by a concrete, hubristic theorist; rather, experience has a structure of its own. However, he never managed to capture the exact nature of this structure. Van Gennep and Turner, on the other hand, tried to place the triadic, sequential, processual structure of rites of passage at the core of anthropology, overcoming the Durkheimian classificatory logic that was further perpetuated by Lévi-Strauss. Turner took up van Gennep's ideas and solved these problems, but his efforts were buried in a few posthumous essays. The solution is the recognition that the sequential order of a rite of passage is the structure of lived experience.

Experience as Rite of Passage

Saying we "had" an experience clearly means something much more comprehensive than merely perceiving an "object" and becoming convinced of its real existence. Having an experience implies that something happens to us—and the word "happen" must be taken seriously, as any experience is above all an *event*.[4] Exactly because it simply happens, an event is unique and fleeting; it involves not just our senses, but our entire existence as well. The consequences are subjectivity and manifoldness. Subjectivity results because existential involvement renders our understanding of our own experiences one-sided and opaque. Manifoldness is due first to our facing so many events in life that they overwhelm us; and second to our participating in events, which pushes us to realize that everyone around us has a similar but also a different viewpoint, which in turn helps us to acknowledge perspective.[5] Thus, the way we assess experiences must not be just subjectively meaningful. Seemingly, we are back to Kant: if we want to go beyond mere fancy and partiality, we have to resign ourselves to a watered-down knowledge of the most important part of our world: human experiences.

Understanding experience as a rite of passage offers a solution to this dilemma. Rites of passage have a simple and clear but by no means trivial structure, according to van Gennep and Turner, who draw on evidence from practically all the studied cultures on the planet. The core substance of Turner's proposition is that this structure is the key to the structure of human experience.

A good example by which to assess this claim is rites of initiation, which van Gennep saw as most typical; and of these, the initiation of youngsters into adulthood, considered most typical by Turner. To become an adult, one must go through a series of crucial experiences. An initiation rite paradigmatically condenses these into the time and space of a single rite. It accomplishes maturity (which Kant assigns to the critical activity of the transcendental mind) without ignoring the participatory aspect, as an initiand must not only understand how to become adult but actually do so.

This transition to adulthood does not simply happen naturally but has a specific structure, which a rite of passage sets in motion and thus reveals. This can be understood through the three phases and their meaning. Van Gennep and Turner characterize the first phase, a rite of separation, as a metaphorical—but not only metaphorical—death. Any child must become adult, but this is a most troublesome process both for the child, who must learn to behave as an adult, and the community, which must adjust its own structure and practices to this new reality. To grow up, a child must first undergo a painful separation from family, literally dying "as" a child.

This suggests that an experience is possible only if one first leaves something behind. It supposes some kind of clean slate, a break with previous practices and routines. We become "children" again when we leave behind a certain fixed role, status, or identity—that is, when we reenter a liminal situation. Maturity is a good paradigm for liminality, but only a paradigm.[6]

The second phase is even more telling. Creation of a tabula rasa via the removal of previously taken-for-granted forms and limits is necessary for the passage to adulthood, both from the perspective of the initiand, who is thereby enabled to make the move across, and for society at large, as the crossing would otherwise be a threatening transgression. However, the resulting situation is just as dangerous as transgression of established customs, as the initiands—and in a way the entire community—are actually moved to the limit. Being "at the limit" is a genuine Alice-in-Wonderland experience, a situation where almost anything can happen. Rites limit this openness, in two ways. First, any rite must follow a strictly prescribed sequence, where everybody knows what to do and how. Second, everything is done under the authority of a master of ceremonies, the practical equivalent of an absolute ruler (Turner 1967: 99–100) whose word is Law—though only during a rite, when there is no law.

Before reaching conclusions about the nature of "experience," we must devote special attention to a key aspect of these initiation rites. Whereas all rituals involve a real element of participation, initiatory rituals contain an extra element of reality in the sense that initiands must succeed in their performance. The rite is not fully scripted: the second phase involves a trial or test by which participants must prove themselves ready to become adults, and they may fail to do so. Moreover, moving to another aspect of reality, successful performance is not restricted to doing or completing something but extends to the person's identity: success means the initiand becomes a new person: a child is "converted" into an adult.

Now to draw a general inference: an "experience" means that once previous certainties are removed and one enters a delicate, uncertain, malleable state, something might happen to one that alters the very core of one's being. In the terminology used emphatically by van Gennep and Turner, "death" is followed by a "birth": the child has died, but only to be reborn as an adult. The third phase, the rite of reaggregation, which celebrates this new birth, is indeed used to mark significant experiences in the life of every human being.

But what exactly happens at the instant in between removing the previous identity and gaining a new one, which lies at the core of "experience," and how does it happen? What is the way in which human cultures try to capture the nature of this experience: the "experience" of "experiencing"? The answer requires us to perfect our magnifying glass by taking Turner's work further, in two senses. First, we must turn to the last page of a related work by Turner, a posthumously published 1980 conference presentation that ventures into the etymology of experience through the proto–Indo-European root *per (Turner 1985b: 226). Second, we also have to go beyond Turner's intellectual horizon, revealed just before the first page of his work related to Dilthey in a likewise posthumously published 1980 seminar note (Turner 1985a: 190). There Turner argues, purportedly following Dilthey, that Plato belongs, together with Aristotle, Descartes, Kant, Hegel, and anthropological structuralism, to a philosophical tradition "hooked on belief in predetermined orderings" (ibid.). Although this might correspond to the interpretation of Plato in the tradition of German idealism, it does not do justice to Plato's ideas. Quite the contrary, Plato (1987) all but advances the Turner-Diltheyan insight in a crucial passage of the *Philebus* (16C), discussed below. Thus, far from representing a break with the legacy of Plato, this insight helps to clarify Plato's notoriously difficult passage about *peras* (the limit) and *apeiron* (the unlimited, boundless, or indeterminate), and perhaps even gives us its proper sense.

Furthermore, at this juncture the Nietzsche-Weberian tradition can also be rejoined, as the passage is one that Eric Voegelin referred to when discussing *metaxy* in "The Ecumenic Age" (Voegelin 1956–87, vol. 4).

Per: The Etymology of Experience

A detailed analysis of the meanings derived from the proto–Indo-European root *per confirms Turner's insight.[7] Its primary meaning is not simply passage, but successful completion of a passage.[8] *Per derivatives also capture the intense emotion that accompanies attempts at such completion, as indicated by terms like "fear" or "peril." A successful passage also assumes a particular order in which somebody goes ahead, showing the way or blazing the trail so that others can follow through imitation, which corresponds to the role of masters of ceremonies in rites of passage or formative experiences. This meaning again survives in numerous modern words — premier, prince, principle, priest, primordial, and primitive, for example. Linguists emphasize that the original meaning implied a concrete spatial, rather than temporal, sequence. Further, *per derivatives capture the idea of birth or bringing into the world, most importantly in "parent" but also in Italian *partorire* (give birth to) and possibly even "father" (pater). Finally, a derivate word, "part," even captures the background horizon of any experience-passage: the home from which and toward which any passage is performed as taking part in something—an experience of participation.

Given Greek's significance as the language of classical philosophy, it is important to note that ancient Greek contains several significant related terms. They include the term "limit" (*peras*) itself, implying that "passage" means going through a limit. However, intriguingly, the central Greek term for experience, *pathos*, from which a series of important terms—passion, passive, pathetic, pathology—derive, does not belong to this group. Rather, it calls attention to another crucial aspect of experience—the passive sense of undergoing or literally "suffering" whatever happens to oneself—alluding to both the destruction of previous stability and the possibility of failure. However, this group also captures a major component of *per derivates, as seen in, for example, the word *pontos*, meaning the sea but only in the sense of crossing it. For the open sea the Greeks used another term (*pelagos*). A series of other terms connect to the Greek *patos* (like path, patio, or passage), but etymologists are reluctant to link these to *pathos*—a connection whose reconsideration the reflections above encourage.

Plato's Philebus

Plato's insights about the limit (peras) and the unlimited or liminal (apeiron) appear in a complex context. Not only is the Philebus a late dialogue, but it was also written outside the originally planned series, after the Statesman and instead of the announced "Philosopher," signaling a conclusive reorientation. Its theme, the link between pleasure and the good life, is highly relevant for the pleasure principle of Bentham and utilitarianism that dominates the modern interpretation of experience. Meanwhile, its central methodological statement concerns the "limit," touching on the core of Kant's theory. Furthermore, Plato's crucial passage in the Philebus, which claims to reveal the very order of the cosmos, fits into a broad time horizon ranging from the remotest prehistory of mankind, when the gods granted insight into the cosmic order as a gift (16c6–7), to Plato's present, where the insight, obscured by the Sophists, has been forgotten (16e5–17a6), thus "bounding" the discussion of the "limit."

The insight has two halves in a paradoxical, tension-like relationship. Whatever exists originates in, or consists of, the one and the many; but the limit and the unlimited are also "inherent" or "innate" to all existing "things" (*Philebus* 16C). This claim is puzzling, as the consistency of things would seem to define their inherent nature. So Plato immediately specifies the link between these two pairs as follows: to state that whatever exists, exists in between the one and the unlimited many is not enough, for it is also important to know "how many" this "existing" is exactly, how it is "formed" between the one and the infinite many. This is where the limit plays its role as formative force (16D–E), and also where Plato places his critique of the Sophists, who fail to pay attention to this "in between" space, moving either too quickly or too slowly between the one and the many (17A). Finally, a few passages later, and after discussing some examples, Plato presents a "general ontology" (Cooper 1977: 714) based on these two key terms, dividing all that exists (23C) into four classes: the limited, the unlimited, their combination, and the causes of their combination. The rest of the dialogue is largely an argument for the superiority of the third, mixed class over the first two "pure" cases. It says little about causes; these are left for the follow-up dialogue, *Timaeus*, which presents Plato's account of the creation of the Universe (as cosmos and not chaos).

The term liminality might shed new light on this puzzling passage. It suggests that the contrast between the one and the many is a problem of perspective, while the difference between the limited and the liminal is a problem of sequence; and that the ambiguity of the latter pair might be due to the complex meaning of *per derivatives in Greek, which express both the limit and its trespass, thus preparing the way for a similarly manifold reading of *apeiron*.

"Perspective" means that the question of the one and many, especially in the context of a dialogue on pleasure, ethics, and the "good life" as part of an overall critique of the Sophists, above all implies a conflict between "internal" and "external" standpoints, incorporating the idea—so dear to relativism—that there are as many internal perspectives as there are human beings on the planet because everyone is the center of a particular perspective: his or her own. If one plays incautiously, irresponsibly, or cynically with such shifts of perspective, as the Sophists systematically did, then the ground in between these perspectives, where agreement concerning the exact "number" of things that exist could be reached (implying norms, practices, traditions), is destroyed.

The relationship between this in-between ground and the limited-unlimited pair can be understood through the dynamic sequential ordering discovered in the study of rites of passage. Plato's discussion of this pair is even more disturbing than that of the previous pair. What kind of poles are the "limit" and the "limitless"? What can be in between them?

Finally, and most perplexing of all, how can they be mixed? Such questions can be answered through the structure of rites of passage and Greek *per derivates.

Rites of passage suggest that the relationship between the limit and the unlimited is a matter of sequential order. The limit has formative powers, this is why terms like limit, idea, form, and *eidos* are so central and linked for Plato. But these formative powers can be activated only if some unformed material is available, that is, if lifting the previous limits creates a liminal situation. The in-between, as a temporary situation betwixt two structured orders, is the *apeiron* itself. At this moment the correct number can be imprinted, again in between the one and the infinite many, because under liminal conditions the contrast between individual perspectives is lifted and the shared experience leaves a common imprint. This enables a group of humans to exist as a community—not as just a bunch of egoistic pleasure-maximizers held together by sententious, abstract talk of "moral obligations."

Greek language is particularly suited to capturing the ambivalence of liminal situations, as terms like *peras* or *peirar* are markers of standards, while *perao* means both "I pass through" and "penetrate, pierce, or drive through with a pointed weapon"; *peira*, "trial" and "attempt"; and *pera*, "beyond" and "further." For the Greeks, the limit as a separating device was inseparable from the idea of actually going through the limit—implying the experience of being at the limit. At this point, we can move from Plato back to contemporary theory and philosophy on the experience of the limit, and the materiality and centrality of this limit.

The Materiality of the Limit

A simple example of a material limit with much relevance for politics and political science is the border between nation-states. This is a legal construct, as a "non-place" (Augé 1995) such as an airport shows; even so, crossing borders can be a very real and taxing experience. Further, it is exactly the constructed nature of modern state borders that can extend them so far in real space that human beings can be stuck on them almost permanently. This idea is embodied by Janus, the two-faced Roman god of warfare, originally the deity of doors and thresholds, whose two faces represent the simple fact that one can see both ways from a door.

The materiality of the limit did not escape the attention of modern philosophers trying to move beyond Kantian presumptions. Jaspers, Wittgenstein, Patočka, and Foucault each reflected on the limit experience. Foucault's example is particularly interesting owing to his related, much misunderstood assertions about the "materiality" of discourse. Foucault had in mind something quite different from the poststructuralist textualism and intertextualism championed by Derrida. Far from claiming the self-referentiality of texts, Foucault pursued a double purpose: negatively, he denied that discourses mechanically copy "objective" reality; positively, he argued that under certain conditions discourses can shape and transform reality. Foucault, however, never mapped these conditions, so it is here that liminality complements his work.

This is particularly clearly illustrated by the theory of "performative speech acts," an approach Foucault used so as to render his ideas more intelligible. John Austin, in his classic *How to Do Things with Words*, introduced his point using four examples (Austin 1962: 5), of which three were rites of passage: a marriage oath; a testament; and a naming (of a ship). Most examples later used to further clarify the theory—baptizing, declaring war, sentencing to death, divorce, desecrating a church, opening or closing meetings—are similar in character. Much debate concerning performative speech acts and poststructuralism can thus be resolved by recognizing that under liminal conditions, discourses form reality and words might become facts, whereas under stable, structured conditions words describe what exists.

The ancients well perceived the physical materiality of the limit. The Latin *limen* originally meant a stone placed at the threshold of a door that physically had to be mounted to cross from one space into the other.[9] This recalls the Greek *herma*, a stone positioned on a borderline to mark the limit. This word has particular interest for the theorization of liminality as the name of the Greek god Hermes, widely associated with ambivalence and liminal activities like language (he is a translator and messenger, but also a liar), commerce (he is also a thief), transport (he guides souls but also misleads them), and sexuality. Another example, discussed in detail in the next section, is the old Hungarian term for a piece of land used to separate two different spaces: *köz*.

This leads directly to the centrality of liminality.

The Centrality of Material Limits

Spatial and temporal liminality have not yet been separated in the present chapter, and one could argue that whereas it is possible to understand the importance of liminal periods, understanding spatial liminality is more difficult. However, the reasoning necessary for the latter is quite similar to that required for the former, and the case is particularly significant.

The theoretical argument is simple and straightforward. In any situation with strongly marked centers and boundary lines, the regions far from the center and close to the border are marginal—irrelevant, local, backward. However, when emphasis shifts to the relationship between two centers, marginal zones become liminal by being situated in between the two centers, thus mediating them. Indeed, they may eventually even become the new center.

England in the sixteenth and seventeenth centuries offers a good illustration. In the medieval period, England, unlike France or Italy, was a marginal country in Europe. The discovery of America altered this situation. Francis Drake was the first to grasp England's new centrality, which explains the lasting controversy between English and Spanish assessments of Drake. A hero to the English but a mere pirate to the Spanish, he was actually both—not simply because things are relative, but because in a liminal situation, and only then, the borderline between hero and villain is temporarily blurred.

The ancients also clearly perceived how the center and the margin can be brought together through inbetweenness, implying the possibility that the marginal, the liminal, and the central may coincide. This can be illustrated through the etymology and semantics of Hungarian words derived from the same root, *köz*.

Starting with semantics, their common etymological root in the Hungarian language unites old words like *közös* (common), *közel* (near), *közép* (middle, center), *központ* (central point), *közben* (meanwhile), *között* (in between), *község* (locality), *közösség* (community), *közönség* (public), or *közönséges* (vulgar) with terms created during the Enlightenment-inspired linguistic renewal, like *közlekedés* (traffic), *közöl* (tell, announce), *közöny* (ennui), or *közömbös* (neutral). The shared meaning of these diverse terms is captured by their common etymology and the original meaning of the root word *köz*, which, going back to the Finno-Ugric heritage (the term *közép* [middle, center] was already a separate Ugoric development), is one of the first recorded Hungarian words, appearing in the first Greek document (around AD 950) in which Hungarian tribes are mentioned. The term originally meant an area that separates persons or things from each other—in other words, the material limit. The insight that this neutral, material separating zone can also be a common central point that brings people together is built into the very structure of the Hungarian language.

Such etymological considerations are not restricted to modern languages. Turner refers to the Ndembu etymology of the ritual unit as "landmark" or "blaze" (Turner [1969] 1995: 15). Archaeologists similarly argue that Neolithic enclosures with still visible boundaries had symbolic (rather than utilitarian) uses strongly associated with the sacred, reinforcing the bonds between the material and the symbolic (Pollard 1997: 30, 41).

Complementary Concepts

Liminality's analytical potential is enhanced by several other terms developed by anthropologists, and similarly ignored by social scientists. Most were coined by "maverick classics": anthropologists who, though trained in the best schools and destined to become carriers of the mainstream, were forced by the evidence they encountered to depart from the theoretical and methodological mainstream of neo-Kantianism, neo-positivism, and Marxist critique. Durkheim and Boas began this tradition; Malinowski, Radcliffe-Brown, and Max Gluckman continued it. Besides Mauss and Turner, the list also includes Lucien Lévy-Bruhl, Paul Radin, Gregory Bateson, and Colin Turnbull. This chapter will discuss three of these terms: "imitation," the "trickster," and "schismogenesis."

Imitation

In marked contrast to classical thought, modern rationalist philosophy ignores imitation. Mimesis, or the imitative aspect of human behavior, was one of Plato's chief concerns. In classical philosophy, Plato's vision of rational thought incorporated resistance to the overwhelming powers of imitation that the Sophists purposefully perpetuated. Imitation, however, had no place in the thought of Descartes or Kant. Descartes emphasized doubt, founding his version of rationalism on the activity of doubting, rendering the study of imitation (the flip side of doubting) impossible. Kant, for his part, bypassed imitation with his emphasis on maturity. In this latter perspective, codified in modern psychology by Piaget and Kohlberg, only children imitate; adults are "mature" and follow solely their reason. This idea, however, confuses liminality and biological maturation around adolescence. Following adolescence, children indeed become adults; but whenever any adult enters a liminal situation, the impulse to imitate again becomes strong. In this circumstance, Cartesian and Kantian rationalism are not only irrelevant but positively misleading, as individuals trapped in a liminal situation cannot follow their "rational interests" for two reasons: first, the structure on which "objective" rationality was based has disappeared; and second, the stressful, emotive character of a liminal crisis prevents clear thinking (Elias 1987: 45–46).

Victor Turner was aware of the imitative aspect of liminal situations and stressed that the middle phase of a ritual was a mimetic enactment of a crisis; Bateson similarly recognized the imitative, even mimic nature of the Naven ritual (Bateson 1958). Not surprisingly, René Girard, the main contemporary theorist of the mimetic aspect of human conduct, considered Turner and Bateson close intellectual allies.

Imitation poses particular problems in liminal situations, the key question being who manages to convince others to follow him or her as a model. This brings us to the contrast between charismatic persons and tricksters.

Trickster

The identification of the obscure, ambivalent, shadowy figure of the trickster is another major discovery by social anthropologists that remains little known outside a limited circle of experts, especially in terms of its significance and potential use. The trickster is a universal, very archaic figure present in the folktales and myths of all cultures. Examples include Hermes and Prometheus in Greek mythology, Loki in Scandinavia, the leprechaun in Ireland, the medieval Flemish Reynard the fox or the early modern German Simplicius Simplicissimus, the Italian Pulcinella and Arlecchino, the Turkish Nasreddin Hodja, the North American Coyote, or the Yoruba Eshu.[10] Tricksters are always marginal characters: they are outsiders, and thus cannot trust or be trusted, cannot give or share, and are incapable of living in a community; they are repulsive, as—being insatiable—they are characterized by excessive eating, drinking, and sexual behavior, having no sense of shame; and they are not taken seriously, given their affinity with jokes, storytelling, and fantasizing. However, tricksters can suddenly become dangerous: in a situation where the community lets its guard down, in an instant the trickster can capture the occasion and institute a lasting reversal of roles and values, making himself a central figure instead of a marginal outcast. The condition that makes such trickster takeovers possible is a liminal situation where certainties are lost, imitative behavior escalates, and tricksters can be mistaken for charismatic leaders.

Tricksters and liminality are closely connected. As outsiders incapable of close, emotional involvement, tricksters can easily preserve their calm under liminal conditions and thus conjure up a cunning and calculative—thus formally "rational"—strategy by which to hook people. When this happens, liminality is not necessarily restricted to a temporary crisis followed by a return to normality, but can be perpetuated endlessly. Gregory Bateson (1958) coined the term "schismogenesis" for such a situation.

Schismogenesis

Bateson developed the concept of schismogenesis in his Cambridge doctoral dissertation, which broke from both structural functionalist and

Marxist anthropology, earning the disapproval of Radcliffe-Brown and Malinowski. Like *ethos* and *eidos*, also key terms in Bateson's book, the word is strongly Platonic in inspiration (Horvath and Thomassen 2008). Closely observing the Naven ritual—characterized by very aggressive behavior combined with mimicking, ridiculing, and cross-dressing—and developing the basic principles of reflexive anthropology half a century before its time, Bateson came to recognize that societies can be stuck for a long time in a state where, although their previous unity is broken, their schismatic components are forced to stay together, producing an unpleasant, violent, harrowing, truly miserable existence.

Transition and Transformation

Based on the previous discussion of liminality, and using the auxiliary concepts imitation, trickster, and schismogenesis, this chapter now assesses the meaning and relevance of its subtitle's two key terms: transition and transformation.

The central problem is that liminality is a concept developed by anthropologists in the context of rituals conducted in small-scale societies, thus combining the experience of noncomplex societies with artificial staging. How can its use be extended to large-scale real-world situations?

Transition, Crisis, and Schismogenesis

The word "transition" repeatedly returns as a key term in social and political analysis. Central to the classics, it was revisited by Elias, Borkenau, and Voegelin, and taken up by political scientists studying the "transition to democracy" after World War II, including recent discussions of the Latin American and South and East European cases. Yet the term itself is rarely analyzed, as if its precise meaning could be taken for granted.

The term implies a short, temporary situation, little more than a theatrical entr'acte. This metaphor seems particularly appropriate, as in theater the "stage"—a word often used in evolutionary accounts of modern history—is set for each particular act and rearranged at intervals. Transitory situations can be quite chaotic, even painful; however, from a stage perspective they are trivial, as the "solution" is given in advance. Contemporary transitologists reject charges of teleology and do not indulge in philosophies of history, but their perspective remains teleological in the sense that the institutional tenets of democratic order provide the solution.

As the stage metaphor indicates, liminality can be particularly helpful in understanding the formative aspects of transitory periods. But this
requires introduction of a further term that is also widely used, though in
different circles: crisis.

Crisis denotes a dramatized version of transition: mainstream sociologists and political scientists talked about the transition to industrial society or to democracy, whereas critical theorists preferred to discuss the
crisis of capitalism or modernity. "Critique" and "crisis" are etymologically related; but as Reinhart Koselleck demonstrated in a classic analysis,
this fact—far from proving the "truth" of critical theory—rather illustrates
the pathogenic nature of the modern world. Meanwhile, the term "crisis"
became so overused that it lost all meaning (Holton 1987). But instead of
discarding the term altogether, it is better to restore its proper meaning,
together with transition, and with the help of liminality.

A real-life situation of transition—unless meticulously regulated by
law, as in political elections—starts with the weakening and eventual sus-
pension of the ordinary, taken-for-granted structures of life. The search
for a solution usually involves an escalating process of imitation. Without
stable institutions, people look to concrete individuals for guidance. If the
crisis is restricted, those involved can look outside of it for stability and
guidance. This is the implicit logic behind the literature on "transitions to
democracy," a solution with its own problems, as indicated by the resistance to Americanization in the 1950s and 1960s, or the "imitation of the
West" in the last decades in Eastern and Central Europe (Wydra 2001,
2007). However, if such models are unavailable, preventing a complete
imitative escalation requires another solution.

The problem was addressed by classic figures of social thought who
tried to escape the limitations of evolutionary and teleological readings
by capturing the nature of an escalating, imitative crisis. Gabriel Tarde,
in the footsteps of Taine and Le Bon, identified imitation as a key concept in sociology, and his work resonated strongly with Simmel, Pareto,
and Freud. Durkheim was an opponent of Tarde, but his work based on
Marcel Mauss's, published originally just before World War I (Durkheim
1995) focused on the study of sacrifice, a practice whose connection with
imitative periods of crisis was demonstrated by René Girard (1972). Finally, though Weber excluded imitative mass processes from his sociology, his term "charisma" helps explain how, in out-of-the-ordinary situations, individuals can emerge and solve the crisis by turning attention to
themselves, thus generating a following.

However, the notion that people in a liminal situation might also follow the wrong kind of individuals was largely neglected. Le Bon alone

was keenly aware of this problem, but in an intellectual world dominated by neo-Kantian rationalism his insight was lost, only to be picked up by great "trickster" politicians of the twentieth century like Mussolini, Hitler, Lenin, and Stalin, mediated through the sinister influence of Georges Sorel. In a confusing situation dominated by erratic imitative behavior, tricksters can literally "steal the show." When trickster figures are mistaken for saviors, emotions are continually and repeatedly incited until the community is reduced to a schismatic state. Societies lacking stable external referent points can maintain themselves in these oppressive, violent situations for a long time without returning to normal order. Indeed, this is why schismogenic societies need to maintain themselves in a perpetual state of war, presumably surrounded by enemies who try to conquer and destroy them—a presumption that, as a performative speech act, can become reality.

Form, Formation, Transformation

Recent literature on "transitology" has often argued that "transformation" is a better term for capturing the active aspects of situations of transition (Stark 1992). Though the discussion of experience has alluded to the problematically excessive importance attributed to activity, choice, and agency—just as problematic as the overemphasis on structure, system, or institution that is the flip side of a schismogenesis—analysis here will be restricted to the new angle provided by transformation.

The term "transformation" denotes part of a series. Something can be *trans*-formed only if it has already been formed, and a formation process implies the existence of a "thing" to be formed: some kind of human "material" that is ready for "typing" or "stamping." Absent undue force and violence, human attitudes, values, and identities can be formed only when previous certainties have been at least partially dissolved by a move "to the limit."

Entering liminality, however, cannot be reduced to postmodern irony, playfulness, or celebration of blank ambivalence. Liminality without masters of ceremonies can easily lead to lasting rule by tricksters. A liminal situation should never be induced without a proper form in hand to impose on the soul of those whose emotions are stimulated by being put at the limit. This stimulation can be effected by a work of art like a Shakespeare tragedy, a Chekhov play, a Puccini opera, a Dostoevsky novel, or a film by Truffaut or Tarkovsky. Emotions, however, are also easily provoked by violence, pornography, or commercials, even though the people who produce such works do not possess measure but just want to make money.[11]

They act assuming that the images they spread do not in reality generate changes in people's attitudes and tastes, but only satisfy their preexisting needs and desires. These assumptions, however, do not correspond to reality—a deficiency explained away by Friedman's positive economics and poststructuralist deconstructionism alike. Experiences cannot be reduced to the perception of pleasure or pain by a fixed subject, in the analogy of Puritan assumptions concerning the predestination of the elect for salvation; for there exist formative experiences, where the subject's identity is altered. Thus, form and liminality, like the limit (*peras*) and the unlimited (*apeiron*) in Plato's *Philebus*, produce together a formative experience, or a formation.

This helps us grasp the nature of transformative events. A transformative event, as a technical term in sociological analysis, is definable as something that happens in real life, whether for an individual, group, or entire civilization. It suddenly questions and even cancels previously taken-for-granted certainties, forcing the people swept up in this storm to reflect on their experiences, even their entire lives, and potentially change not only their conduct in life but their identity. The degree and direction of the change depends on several factors: the surviving fragments of previous identities, the existence of external reference points that remain more or less intact, and the presence or absence of new models, forms, or measures.

The idea of the transformative event is not new; it is even commonsensical. After all, war, revolution, or major economic crisis, just like major illness or a new emotional relationship, changes the lives of all those involved. Liminality, however, leads to understanding that such major events literally and effectively transform the very mode of being of the individuals involved. The formative power of liminality can be well illustrated through the phenomenon of love, which appears not inside one person as a "subject" towards another peson as the "object," but exactly in the "in between." To put it as clearly as possible: it is not the "I" that loves the "you"; rather it is the "it," the love itself that emerges in between two human beings, forming and transforming both, by creating a single unit that cannot be separated without tragedy, that is, a kind of death. The perspective of liminality therefore definitely helps to shift the focus of social and political theory away from fixed subjects "acting" or "choosing" among fixed structures, supposedly maximizing their pleasures and minimizing their pains, which—such theory evidently presumes—is the only reason why we happen to be on this planet. When actually pushed "to the limit" by the force of events, human beings cannot take structures for granted; they need models to follow or "imitate." Under such conditions, people are easily convinced to act contrarily to what is best for them while not apparently acting against their "interests" (a concept quite problematic under liminal conditions, as in the absence of fixed structures it is impossible to objectively define "interest"). Thus they are misled instead of led and, still further, might have their identities altered.

Thus we have again arrived back at Plato. Without the experiential dimension, without consideration of the formative and transformative potential of unsettled, disturbing, and creative but also deeply distressing, suffering-producing liminal situations and events, social and political analysis becomes not only lifeless but useless as well, failing to provide guidance when it is most needed. Precisely this attention to the fleeting, formative, experiential aspect of life helps us realize there must still be something that lies beyond the eternal flux of life, providing guidance in times of change—namely, the eternal Platonic form, measure, or *eidos*. Institutions, laws, and structures will always be deficient, failing us just when we need protection and security most. The form itself is eternal and unchanging but almost distant in situations of dire need, almost just another a utopian ideal. The need, then, is for concrete persons, human beings who manage to embody the measure in their attitudes and personality. Even today, this idea is best expressed through the philosophy of Plato, to which Dilthey and Turner or Voegelin and Foucault lead us to return, rather than through Weber's concept of charismatic leader (though the Weberian perspective can lend aspects of *charis* to Plato's *eidos*).

Ignoring Liminality in Social Life

This last section offers some further examples of the potential use of liminality in social and political analysis, each related to some crucial aspects of social and political life past and present. Here again, only a few examples can be given.

A good starting point is the general downplaying of rituals, which Mary Douglas (1996) identified as characteristic of the modern world. From the perspective of rationalist theory, rituals are mere ceremonies, irrational relics of the past not fulfilling any useful function. But from the perspective of Douglas or Turner, far from "manifesting" or "masking" power relations, they involve the experience of participation and have transformative potential.

Disappearing Rites of Passage: Death and Marriage

The striking receding of rituals in the modern world is nowhere more visible than in rites of passage themselves, the most evidently transformative rituals. Major passages like birth, marriage, and death were once the most important social occasions for any human community. Yet as Philippe Ariès argues in a classic work, in the modern world death has been hidden away, tucked into the recesses of dark, isolated hospital rooms (Ariès 1974, 1977). Perhaps even more importantly, marriage as a rite of passage has yielded its place to mere "living together." This is not simply "rational" behavior in view of skyrocketing divorce rates and legal costs: it is fueled by a Romantic conviction that "true love" does not need ceremonies, a conviction that ignores deep human wisdom about the significance of transformative rituals. The modern world can certainly be proud of its intellectual and technological achievements, but it cannot pretend to have rediscovered the wheel at the level of human relations. The result is a drastic, tragic weakening of the very fabric of society—a genuine trickster revolution erupting at the heart of sociability.

Misunderstood Experiences: Sexuality and Virginity

Just as experience is tightly linked to liminality and rites of passage, ignoring rites and liminality can be correlated with the similarly thorough modern ignoring of experiences themselves. This seems to contradict the general importance modern thought attributes to experience, from Bacon and Descartes onwards. However, modern empiricism and rationalism are interested in experiences only insofar as these can be reduced to sense perception and connected to the search for pleasure. Experiences as genuine transformative encounters, as liminal moments that can change one's life, are systematically ignored.

Sexuality, as an experience particularly closely associated with the modern world, is an apt example. The rise of modernity is widely said to represent the liberation of sexuality. However, Michel Foucault demonstrated that sexual liberation is a modern myth; instead, we have been lured into a tricky game of discursive (and other) incitement of sexuality (Foucault 1976, 1984a, 1984b). Taking Foucault's ideas a step further, one could argue that the "repression" of sexuality was rather part of a general problematization of human experiences, based on fear (and ignorance) of the transformative aspects of human encounters, and their subsequent reduction to the pleasure principle. First, this amounted to a harsh regulation of sexual life, given the intensity of sexual pleasure; second, without changing the underlying perspective, it implied a liberation of the "sexuality" thus created, sanitized and deprived of its transformative aspects— those aspects that make human life worth living, and that make sexual pleasure a cathartic and shared human experience, tying people together for life rather than reducing them to the individualized search for the maximization of pleasure.

The modern neglect of the significance of experience and liminality is most obvious in current attitudes concerning virginity. The issue is not simply that the loss of virginity, a serious event-experience in any time and place, has been trivialized, but that in our arrogant presumption that we are "enlightened," we moderns no longer even understand what is at stake and associate preoccupation with virginity with prejudice, igno-rance, repression, or patriarchy. It is not so self-evident, however, who is "ignorant" here. The loss of virginity clearly, physically implies a first "passage through." For any sane and decent human being it used to matter where and how a young person went through such a passage. It had clear formative and transformative aspects, and was not merely the removal of a strange barrier obstructing the maximization of individual pleasure.

The Ignorance of Evil

The phenomenon of evil is just as significant in human life as marriage or sexuality, though certainly much more sinister. The rationalistic neglect of evil can similarly be connected to schismogenic developments around the Enlightenment, in which—as a reaction to medieval images of the devil—it was asserted that evil does not exist, and that all human prob-lems have purely social origins, rooted in ignorance and poverty.[12] This perspective left a social stamp on rationalism and empiricism, and only af-ter two world wars, the Holocaust, and a series of totalitarian regimes was it shelved as wishful thinking. The origin of evil certainly goes beyond the social sciences, but evil's existence is a confirmed social fact. The task of the social sciences is to analyze the processes by which human beings who possess vicious, evil, demonic qualities—whether they purposefully want to harm others to avenge the misfortunes of their own life, or are simply pathological—manage to exert widespread influence.

Conclusion: Trickster Debauchery and Rationalistic Slumber

This chapter's main aim was to present the case that liminality—devel-oped not by philosophers trained in German idealism, French rationalism, or British empiricism, but rather by social scientists educated in French *ethnologie* and Anglo-American social and cultural anthropology—is not only important for anthropologists but should be a key term of social thought and philosophy. Its potential range of application is comparable

to that of Weberian charisma of Foucauldian discourse, or even such standard vocabulary terms as "institution" and "structure," as liminality aids study of events or situations that involve the dissolution of order but are also formative of institutions and structures.

The applicability of the term is so broad as to be potentially unlimited itself. Anthropologists' frequent claim that it should be restricted to the narrow horizon of small-scale tribal societies where it was originally developed is unacceptable. Concepts are tools for research; they cannot be copyrighted by the discipline in which they were developed.

Apart from being an addition to the social scientist's toolbox, the word also performs an important critical function. For centuries, European thought was not equipped to analyze the effective impact of unsettled situations of transition. This basic weakness at the heart of our own tradition can be traced back to Kant, if not Aristotle. The collapse of Marxism and the weakening of Freud's and Hegel's influence entailed a parallel boost in the popularity of Kant, who has almost become the sacred cow of contemporary social and political theory: one can hardly think of criticizing Kant without risking a considerable loss of credibility. However, as this chapter has demonstrated, Kant's framework cannot accommodate liminality. In his mode of thinking, limits and boundaries are only negative mental ordering devices; it is inconceivable that someone or something could literally be "at the limit." Limit experiences, however, do happen all the time; and with lasting consequences.

That said, this essay does not turn this thorough critique of Kant and German idealism into a postmodern or poststructuralist celebration of relativism, difference, or outright chaos. Quite the contrary, and occasionally even despite Turner's own words or attitudes, it takes the deep-seated ambivalence of liminal situations seriously. "Ambivalence" means that whereas liminal situations and positions can contribute to creativity or renewal of institutions and structures that have become oppressive or simply tired, liminality also implies deep anxiety and suffering for those entering such a stage. The stimulation of creative potentials is inseparable from tragic experiences. The case of war is particularly instructive: though it is evidently true that living through a great war at a particular stage of one's life literally "produces" great thinkers, no rational person would argue for another major war as a way to refresh intellectual life. The point is not to stimulate creativity by promoting tragedy, but rather to recognize that denial of the tragic is at the core of the modern experience and is perhaps the most consequential way in which postmodernism simply carries forward the worst aspects of modern attitudes and ideologies.

Proper attention to liminality implies a move in the opposite direction: a return to and renewal of traditions, including the most classic traditions in philosophy and social thought. In the footsteps of such crucial figures of twentieth-century thought as Voegelin, Kerényi, Patočka, and Foucault, and in search of the antecedents of liminality, this chapter returned to Plato, arguing that a crucial but deeply puzzling passage in the *Philebus* and the term liminality can illuminate one another.

Meanwhile, the significance of liminality, including the grave consequences of ignoring it, goes far beyond academic interests in social theory, philosophy, or education. The deep-seated deficiencies of Kantian thought concern not only academics but every person living in this world. Kant's way of thinking disempowered and neutralized European thought by causing it to ignore the potentially fatal relevance of unsettled, unsettling situations of transition. By conflating the normative and analytical levels of analysis, Kant reduced the task of serious thinking to the setting of abstract limits, boundaries, and classificatory devices, leading astray not just academics but people at large, who thus were helpless to prevent the utter and tragic collapse of order around them, as repeatedly happened over the past centuries in the form of major wars, revolutions, and their aftermath. In such situations tricksters, mimes, and mere clowns seized the occasion, capitalizing on the opportunity to present themselves as compassionate leaders of the sufferers, or as outright saviors of mankind. The tragic consequences of neglecting liminality are particularly noticeable in political science, where "value-free" political scientists regard tricksters like the leaders of various totalitarian movements and parties in the past, and of "catch-all parties" (Krouwel 2003) in the present, as "charismatic" leaders; and where former Marxists of the most irreducible kind flock in large numbers to the camp of "rational choice" theory. Economic theory, however, is not faring much better, having long confused marketing tricks with the care of the self, proliferating an "alchemical" attitude (see Agnes Horvath, this volume) of magical moneymaking (see also Binswanger 1994).

European thought, and Western societies, have been deeply devastated by centuries of schismogenic processes that repeatedly present equally untenable opposites—liberalism and socialism, capitalism and communism, structural functionalism and critical theory, postmodernism and rational choice theory—as the alternatives from which one must "freely choose," if not as sides to which one must morally and existentially commit oneself. To meet the real trickster-induced challenges that we increasingly face, we must necessarily renew our thinking by rejecting such forced choices as tantamount to intellectual blackmail. Liminality belongs among those crucial conceptual tools that are at once innovative and deeply rooted in the most significant historical and anthropological traditions of humankind.

Notes

1. Kant, like Descartes, was not simply a pedant "rationalist" but a strange kind of hermetic-Gnostic mystic who pioneered "rationalist" thinking as a way to solve his deep existential anxieties. The vagaries of academic politics then made this type of thinking socially and intellectually dominant.
2. My interpretation is developed from the excellent essay by Eliza Goddard (fcrthcoming).
3. See Rossbach (2007). Intriguingly, Kant also came to identify in the dynamic between, or in what happens among, substances as the origin of universal interactivity in his early cosmological search for "the divine ground of nature" (Schonfeld 2008), quite close to Voegelinian terminology. What evidently sidetracked him was first the Lisbon earthquake and then his reading of Swedenborg.
4. The two main developments leading to the problematization of "events" in Western thought were Spinoza's attack on miracles and the 1755 Lisbon earthquake.
5. Cartesian rationality is based on this play with experience, claiming that the reality of one's own experience can only be confirmed by others being able to reproduce that experience.
6. This is meant by van Gennep when he strongly—perhaps even excessively—emphasized that the initiation rite is purely social, not biological (van Gennep 1931: 94–100).
7. This section is based on Szakolczai (2008).
8. Even the (Kantian) German word for experience (*Erfahrung*) belongs here. However, *erfahren* has a slightly more passive, receptive meaning, closer to "*pathos*"; another reason why Dilthey insisted on the term *Erlebnis*, taken from Goethe, which connotes "living through."
9. Here I am particularly indebted to the work of Agnes Horvath (2008, 2010, 2013) and Horvath and Thomassen (2008). See also Bright (1993), Dumézil (1986), Kerényi (1976, 1984, 1991), Radin (1972), and Varty (1967).
10. A good example is the clown, in particular the way in which he focuses attention on himself with antics (note the circular structure of the circus). Clowns are harmless when circumscribed in space, but the modern mass media, originally the cinema in particular, provided them with the possibility of escaping such limits. About the figure of the "demonic clown," see Szakolczai (2013), assessing—through the cases of Chaplin, Buster Keaton, Jacques Tati, Giorgio Strehler, and Woody Allen—who is and who is not a "demonic" clown.
11. Though the expression "making money" is part of everyday language, it literally refers to an act of alchemy in the sense developed by Agnes Horvath (see her chapter in this volume).
12. For details, see Castelli (1958), Citati (2000), Masini (1967), Neiman (2002), and Spedicato (1997). The strong presence of Italian thinkers among the best analysts of evil might be due to the sensitivity generated by Machiavelli's impact, not just on political thought but on Italian intellectual life in general, up to Gramsci and beyond. The problem of evil was also central to Voegelin's work; see especially his 1951 exchange with Hannah Arendt (Voegelin 2000).

References

Ariès, P. 1974. *Western Attitudes toward Death*. Baltimore, MA: The John Hopkins University Press.
———. 1977. *L'homme devant la mort*. Paris: Seuil.

Augé, M. 1995. *Non-Places: Introduction to an Anthropology of Supermodernity*. London: Verso.

Austin, J. 1962. *How to Do Things with Words*. Oxford: Clarendon Press.

Bateson, G. 1958. *Naven*. Stanford, CA: Stanford University Press.

Binswanger, H. C. 1994. *Money and Magic: A Critique of the Modern Economy in the Light of Goethe's Faust*. Chicago: University of Chicago Press.

Borkenau, F. 1976. *Der Übergang vom feudalen zum bürgerlichen Weltbild: Studien zur Geschichte der Philosophie der Manufakturperiode*. Darmstadt: Wissenschaftliche Buchgesellschaft.

———. 1981. *End and Beginning: On the Generations of Cultures and the Origins of the West*, edited by Richard Löwenthal. New York: Columbia University Press.

Bright, W. 1993. *A Coyote Reader*. Berkeley: University of California Press.

Castelli, E. 1958. *Il demoniaco nell'arte: Il significato filosofico del demoniaco nell'arte*. Milan: Electa.

Citati, P. 2000. *Il Male Assoluto nel cuore del romanzo dell'Ottocento*. Milan: Mondadori.

Cooper, J. M. 1977. "Plato's Theory of Human Good in the *Philebus*." *Journal of Philosophy* 74 (11): 714–30.

Douglas, M. 1996. *Natural Symbols: Explorations in Cosmology*. London: Routledge.

Dumézil, G. 1986. *Loki*. Paris: Flammarion.

Durkheim, E. 1995. *The Elementary Forms of Religious Life*. New edition. New York: Free Press.

Elias, N. 1983. *The Court Society*. Oxford: Blackwell.

———. 1987. *Involvement and Detachment*. Oxford: Blackwell.

———. 2000. *The Civilizing Process*. Oxford: Blackwell.

Fiala, A. 2004. "Introduction to the New Edition." In Immanuel Kant, *Critique of Pure Reason*, translated by J. M. D. Meiklejohn. New York: Barnes and Noble.

Foucault, M. 1976. *L'histoire de la sexualité*. Vol. 1, *Volonté de savoir*. Paris: Gallimard.

———. 1984a. *L'histoire de la sexualité*. Vol. 2, *L'usage des plaisirs*. Paris: Gallimard.

———. 1984b. *L'histoire de la sexualité*. Vol. 3, *Le souci de soi*. Paris: Gallimard.

Gennep, A. van. 1981. *Les rites de passage*. Paris: Picard.

Gentile, A. 2003. *Ai confini della ragione: la nozione di "limite" nella filosofia trascendentale di Kant*. Rome: Studium.

Girard, R. 1972. *Violence et le sacré*. Paris: Grasset.

Goddard, E. forthcoming. "Kant's Distinction between Limit and Boundary: Charting a Middle Way between Despots and Nomads."

Holton, R. J. 1987. "The Idea of Crisis in Modern Society." *British Journal of Sociology* 38 (4): 502–20.

Horvath, A. 2008. "Mythology and the Trickster: Interpreting Communism." In *Democracy and Myth in Russia and Eastern Europe*, edited by A. Wöll, and H. Wydra. London: Routledge.

———. 2010. "Pulcinella, or the Metaphysics of the Nulla: In Between Politics and Theatre." *History of the Human Sciences* 23 (2): 47–67.

———. 2013. *Modernism and Charisma*. London: Palgrave.

Horvath, A., and Thomassen, B. 2008. "Mimetic Errors in Liminal Schismogenesis: On the Political Anthropology of the Trickster." *International Political Anthropology* 1 (1): 1–24.

Kerényi, K. 1976. *Dionysos: Archetypal Image of Indestructible Life*. Princeton, NJ: Princeton University Press.

———. (1944) 1984. *Hermész, a lélekvezető* [Hermes, the guide of souls]. Budapest: Európa.

———. (1961) 1991. *Prometheus: Archetypal Image of Human Existence*. Princeton, NJ: Princeton University Press.

Koselleck, R. 1985. "'Space of Experience' and 'Horizon of Expectation': Two Historical Categories." In *Futures Past: On the Semantics of Historical Time*. Cambridge, MA: MIT Press.

———. (1959) 1988. *Critique and Crisis*. Oxford: Berg.

———. 1989. "Linguistic Change and the History of Events." *Journal of Mode-n History* 61 (4): 649–66.

Krouwel, A. 2003. "Otto Kirchheimer and the Catch-All Party." *West Europea-n Politics* 26 (2): 23–40.

Masini, F. 1967. *Alchimia degli estremi: studi su Jean Paul e Nietzsche*. Parma: Studio Parmense.

Mauss, M. 2002. *The Gift*. London: Routledge.

Neiman, S. 2002. *Evil in Modern Thought: An Alternative History of Philosophy*. Princeton, NJ: Princeton University Press.

Patočka, J. 2002. *Plato and Europe*. Stanford, CA: Stanford University Press.

Plato. 1987. *The Statesman; Philebus; Ion*. London: Heinemann.

Poggi, G. 1972. *Images of Society*. London: Oxford University Press.

Pollard, J. 1997. *Neolithic Britain*. Princes Risborough: Shire.

Radin, P. 1972. *The Trickster: A Study in American Indian Mythology*. With commentary by Karl Kerényi and Carl G. Jung. New York: Schocken.

Rossbach, S. 2007. "Understanding in Quest of Faith: The Central Problem ir Eric Voegelin's Philosophy." In *Politics and Apocalypse*, edited by R. Hamerton-Kelly. East Lansing: Michigan State University Press.

Schonfeld, M. 2008. "Kant's Philosophical Development." In *The Stanford Encyclopedia of Philosophy*. http://plato.stanford.edu/archives/fall2008/entries/kant-development/.

Spedicato, E. 1997. *La strana creatura del caos: idee e figure del male nel pensiero della modernità*. Rome: Donzelli.

Stark, D. 1992. "Path Dependence and Privatization Strategies in East Central Europe." *East European Politics and Societies* 6 (1): 17–53.

Szakolczai, A. 1998. *Max Weber and Michel Foucault: Parallel Life-Works*. London: Routledge.

———. 2000. *Reflexive Historical Sociology*. London: Routledge.

———. 2003. *The Genesis of Modernity*. London: Routledge.

———. 2007. *Sociology, Religion and Grace: A Quest for the Renaissance*. London: Routledge.

———. 2008. "Sinn aus Erfahrung." In *Erleben, Erleiden, Erfahren: Die Konstitution sozialen Sinns jenseits instrumenteller Vernunft*, edited by K. Junge, D. Suber, and C. Gerber. Bielefeld: Transcript.

———. 2013. *Comedy and the Public Sphere: The Re-birth of Theatre as Comedy a-d the Genealogy of the Modern Public Arena*. London: Routledge.

Turner, V. 1967. "Betwixt and Between: The Liminal Period in *Rites de Passage*." In *The Forest of Symbols*. New York: Cornell University Press.

———. 1985a. "Experience and Performance: Toward a New Processual Anthropology." In *On the Edge of the Bush*, edited by E. Turner. Tucson: University of Arizona Press.

———. 1985b. "The Anthropology of Performance." In *On the Edge of the Bush*, edited by E. Turner. Tucson: University of Arizona Press.

———. (1969) 1995. *The Ritual Process*. Chicago: Aldine.

Varty, K. 1967. *Reynard the Fox: A Study of the Fox in the Medieval English Art*. Leicester: Leicester University Press

Voegelin, E. 1956–87. *Order and History*. 5 vols. Baton Rouge: Louisiana State University Press.

———. 1997–99. *History of Political Ideas*. 8 vols. Columbia: University of Missouri Press.

———. 2000. "The Origins of Totalitarianism." In *Published Essays, 1953-1965*, vol. 11 of *The Collected Works*, edited by E. Sandoz. Columbia: University of Missouri Press.

Weber, M. 1948. "The Social Psychology of the World Religions." In *From Max Weber: Essays in Sociology*, edited by H. Gerth and C. Wright Mills. London: Routledge.

———. 1978. *Economy and Society*. Berkeley: University of California Press.

Wydra, H. 2001. *Continuities in Poland's Permanent Transition*. London: Palgrave.

———. 2007. *Communism and the Emergence of Democracy*. Cambridge: Cambridge University Press.

Chapter 2

Thinking with Liminality
To the Boundaries of an Anthropological Concept

Bjørn Thomassen

Histories of knowledge are shaped by the travels of concepts and ideas, which change meaning and purpose as they migrate from one discipline to another, becoming inserted in new discourses, productively going beyond their delimited empirical beginnings, and opening up new fields of enquiry and spaces of imagination. This chapter is about thinking with the concept of liminality. As introduced in anthropology by Arnold van Gennep in 1909, liminality referred to the middle stage in ritual passages. Here, however, I argue that it should be considered a master concept in the wider social and political sciences. As other chapters in this volume show, it is furthermore a pertinent, even necessary concept for understanding a whole series of contemporary phenomena in a historical period—ours—so variously characterized by constant change, uncertainty, and institutionalized contingency.

This chapter therefore has a dual purpose: to outline the different ways in which liminality can throw new light on processes of change, and to indicate some limits or boundaries to its application. This is a necessary exercise, as the concept currently appears in myriad applications within practically all branches of the social and human sciences, and is now also spreading to social media and popular culture, branding websites and companies, problematically coming to signify everything and nothing at the same time. The exercise is especially necessary because liminality in general has come to assume postmodern connotations of freedom, creativity, and the loosening of modernity's restricting bonds in what amounts to a clearly celebratory attitude toward anything anti-structural and beyond-the-modern (Thomassen 2012b). I will show that at many levels of social and political life, the opposite is so: liminality itself has become the underpinning structure of both attitudes and institutions, and very critically so, in fact cementing some of modernity's most problematic aspects without even remotely representing its overcoming.

Liminality, by Way of Introduction

It is important to stress from the outset that liminality refers to something very simple and universal: the experience of finding oneself at a boundary or in an in-between position, either spatially or temporally. To many people, including my students, "liminality" sounds like a technical term when it is first introduced. Its origins in anthropological studies of ritual passages in what seem to many like exotic cultural contexts ("tribal societies") easily leads them to understand the term as somewhat esoteric and complicated. But nothing could be further from the truth. Human beings go through all sorts of liminal experiences, and quite often at that. Human existence without liminality is simply not possible. Social life would be void without it. Simply put, liminality is about how human beings, in their various social and cultural contexts, deal with change. That "dealing" with change can pertain to something highly personal and deeply intimate like falling in love, or to a collective event, as when a community is forced to cope with a sudden occurrence like a natural disaster. Life is made of routines and repetitions, but life also presents us with situations outside the normal. We require different tools—often unknown ones—to deal with a novel situation.

In other words, liminality involves the experience of inbetweenness itself, as well as how exactly that experience is shaped and structured anew as subjects and collectivities move through the in-between, try to overcome it, and leave it behind—with a difference. Human beings tend to ritualize and symbolize such moments and passages. Indeed, ritual symbolism can largely be understood as frozen representations of a liminal passage or experience, repeated again and again in memory of the importance of that liminal event and how it was dealt with. No doubt, this process lies at the heart of community formation. And here the entire premise of what is argued below can be stated explicitly: the study of ritual passages and ritual-like phenomena is not simply about "form," aesthetics, or the "superficial" ways in which we celebrate ceremonies and give expression to something already there. Ritual is not about how we decorate reality; it is about that reality. Thinking with liminality means to take ritual forms very seriously, for they mold and shape human beings going through liminal experiences. Liminality marks or stamps human beings. The *how* of such going-through—the modalities and the lasting effects of this stamping process[1]—is where analysis starts, long before the *why*. Moreover, as will be discussed, liminal experiences are not always safely embedded within a ritual structure—liminality, applied to a broader social science and historical perspective, can also refer to events that simply happen, and happen *to* us. The analytical challenge to any "thinking with liminality" involves this question: What happens in liminal situations that unfold outside the spatial and temporal boundaries of expert-led ritual passages?

By way of introduction, and so that we may we proceed with an image in mind, let me invoke one particular type of liminal experience, namely, conversion, and one particular example known to most, Paul's conversion on the road to Damascus. As William James long ago argued, conversions are sociologically real, whatever one may think of their religious substance. The letters and Acts documenting the conversion date from years (probably decades) after the event, but there can be little doubt about its abruptness: "I was apprehended by Christ Jesus," Paul says in Philemon. The subject is passive, overcome by a larger force, and transformed. The transformation is radical. Paul had been persecuting Christians, but as of this moment he starts to preach what he once tried to destroy. His preexisting worldview disappears in no time; as James (1902: 217) puts it, "a complete division is established in the twinkling of an eye between the old life and the new." The experience changes the way he sees things and equally changes his conduct of life. The process in question is not a willful act: Paul was on the road to Damascus for another round of persecution against Christians when he was "apprehended" and he had no plans to become a Christian. He was seized, and the experience in question is something he *undergoes*.[2]

I state the obvious with this example: it points to a situation in which the notion of rational actors operating within a known environment does not apply. To be sure, such events are not absolutely random. In religious terminology, being touched by God requires an opening of the soul, but the point is probably more general. For example, it is hardly irrelevant that Paul was "on the road," already situated in an in-between space, moving between two cities. The example, in all its simplicity, indicates how the intimate and the sociologically effective, the personal and the collective, experience and thought, belong together in a processual analysis where a sudden, dramatic in-between experience changes both a person's life and much of the world. No single event, outside the life of Jesus, has changed the course of Christian history as much as Paul's conversion.

Liminality is not just any concept, but a concept with which to think, and it points toward a certain kind of interpretative analysis of events and experiences. Liminality does not and cannot "explain." In liminality there is no certainty concerning the outcome but rather a world of contingency where events and ideas—and indeed, "reality" itself—can be carried in different directions. For precisely these reasons, the concept of liminality also has the potential to push social theory in new directions. Liminality may prove as central a concept to the social sciences as "structure" and "practice," for it serves to conceptualize moments when the relationship between structure and agency is not easily resolved or even understood within the now classical "structuration theories." In liminality, the very distinction between structure and agency ceases to make meaning; and yet, in the hyper-reality of agency in liminality, structuration takes place. Van Gennep's discovery of liminality was tied to an experientially based social scientific project, a "view" still relevant to consideration and elaboration, with and beyond the work of Victor Turner.

Revisiting van Gennep's *Rites de Passage*

Arnold van Gennep (1873–1957) published *Rites de Passage* in 1909 (*Rites of Passage* from now on), having finished the book and written its preface in late 1908. Van Gennep himself considered the book a breakthrough resulting from an inner illumination:

> I confess sincerely that though I set little store by my other books, my *Rites de Passage* is like a part of my flesh, and was the result of a kind of inner illumination that suddenly dispelled a sort of darkness in which I had been floundering for almost ten years. (from a review of Frazer's *The Golden Bough*, here as quoted and translated in Belmont 1979: 58)[3]

Rites of Passage was no doubt van Gennep's most important book. In more than one way, it came to represent a unifying thread in his long but overlooked lifework. Its very structure of identifying ritual passages as they unfold within a human life from birth to death, later served as organizing device for his multivolume work on French folklore (van Gennep 1958). Van Gennep began *Rites of Passage* by suggesting a meaningful classification for all existing rites. He distinguished rites marking an individual's or social group's passage from one status to another from those marking transitions in the passage of time (e.g., harvest, new year), and then proceeded to explore "the basis of characteristic patterns in the order of ceremonies" (1960: 10). Stressing the importance of transitions in any society, van Gennep singled out rites of passage as a special category composed of three subcategories, namely, rites of *separation, transition* rites, and rites of *incorporation*. He called the middle stage in a rite of passage a *liminal period* (ibid.: 11), terming transition rites *liminal* rites, and rites of incorporation *postliminal* rites. Van Gennep also noted that rites of separation, transition, and incorporation are not equally important or elaborated in specific rituals, and that the tripartite structure is sometimes reduplicated in the transitional period itself: in liminality proper, the sequence of separation, transition, and incorporation is often present.

It would be wrong to accuse van Gennep of reductionism. By no means did he try to press all ritual forms into one explanatory framework. He simply noted an underlying pattern in rites that marked a passage from one state to another, without taking away or reducing all the other aspects or "individual purposes" that such rites may also have (ibid.). In other words, van Gennep's work emphatically cannot be used directly either to argue for any specific *theory* of rites or to account for any theory of transition. Meanwhile, van Gennep's work can and must be seen as a reference point for any discussion of transition periods. Van Gennep detected a pattern, a sequential ritual form. The ritual pattern was apparently universal: all societies use rites to demarcate transitions. Van Gennep was right.

The universality of the tripartite structure is not to be underestimated. Anthropological claims to universality have been few indeed, as the discipline's main aim has often been to demonstrate cultural diversity. There were therefore good reasons to expect van Gennep's study and careful classification of rites to become an instant classic. Yet this simply did not happen. Despite rather positive reviews in British and American journals,[4] subsequent scholarship neglected van Gennep's proposed framework. Indeed, Durkheim's most important anthropological work, *The Elementary Forms of Religious Life* (1967, henceforth *EFRL*)—published in 1912, after van Gennep's work had appeared—also singled out ritual as central to the constitution of not just religion but society itself. However, Durkheim did not use the terms and distinctions suggested in *Rites de Passage*. Worse, Durkheim did not even find it worthwhile to *discuss* van Gennep. The disregard of van Gennep's work is even more startling given that in 1906 he had published (in Paris) a book on Australian aboriginal religion entitled *Mythes et légendes d'Australie*, that is, a whole book dedicated to the ethnographic case study that made up the entire argument of *EFRL*. Moreover, *EFRL* carried the subtitle *Le système totémique en Australie*, and van Gennep's first book (published in 1904), *Tabou et Totémisme à Madagascar*, dealt exactly with totemism. Marcel Mauss had proofread and contributed to this book, which contained a theoretical discussion of totemism.

It is outside this chapter's scope to resume this confrontation between van Gennep and the Durkhemians. The point here is that on all salient points, van Gennep's critiques of Durkheim resonated with the objections raised just a few years earlier by Gabriel Tarde (for further detail, see Thomassen 2009, 2012d; see also van Gennep's amazingly pointed, daring critique of *EFRL* [2001]). Suffice it to say that van Gennep lost the battle and was ostracized from French sociology and anthropology [5] Though he authored more than 400 publications, including twenty plus books (see the near-complete list compiled by his daughter, K. van Gennep [1964]), van Gennep never landed a job at a French university, though he did try. The key difference for our purposes here is that Durkheim saw rites as simply the vectors by which individuals became socially determined as acting and thinking beings. But because he distinguished between religion as collective and magic as private, Durkheim overlooked a crucial aspect of rites that van Gennep stressed throughout *Rites of Passage*, namely, that they can act at individual and collective levels simultaneously. Moreover, van Gennep argued, although neophytes undergo a process of undifferentiation to become "annulled" as persons in separation rituals, ritual passages are clearly also crucial moments for a process of differentiation by age group, gender, status group, and personality. He saw the use of specialized languages in ritual as a clear sign of this "differentiating procedure" (1960: 169). In Durkheim's analysis, individuals simply dissipate into the social body. But van Gennep's proposed framework implied a genuine process of change lying at the heart of personal transformation, group formation, and social dynamics write large.

Liminality: The Merits and Limits of Victor Turner

Because van Gennep never became established in French academic life, he also mostly failed to gain traction outside France.[6] He became an important figure in Swiss and of course French folklore, but the discipline of folklore never attained a large outreach. The concept of liminality was entirely absent from post-Durkhemian anthropology and still does not rank as a basic concept in any textbook (indeed, Microsoft Word still does not recognize the term and underlines it with a red zigzag—which, being also a cautionary symbol on high-voltage machinery, is perhaps fitting, given the term's affinities with danger). One of the only prominent anthropologists to discuss *Rites of Passage* before its translation in 1960 was Paul Radin in his *Primitive Religion* (1937). Radin referred positively to van Gennep's work on totemism (1937: 203–4), and Chapter 5 of *Primitive*

Religion, "The Crisis of Life and Transition Rites," was an application of van Gennep's framework.[7]

After the translation of *Rites de Passage* appeared in 1960, van Gennep became known in the context of British anthropologists' renewed interest in theoretical developments within French anthropology. Rodney Needham and Edmund Leach, supported by Evans-Pritchard, undertook to translate the major classics of French anthropologists like Marcel Mauss, Robert Hertz, Hubert and Mauss, and Durkheim. Needham (1967) also translated and introduced van Gennep's *The Semi-Scholars*. This interest in French ethnology was very much due to the high status of Claude Lévi-Strauss and his structuralist approach. Lévi-Strauss had recognized the value of van Gennep's early work in his book on totemism (Lévi-Strauss 1963: 4). As van Gennep had both translated Frazer's book on totemism into French and stated his own position in a publication on totemism (1920; this was the main thesis of his PhD), Lévi-Strauss clearly saw van Gennep as a better starting point than Durkheim. Leach thought likewise. In an overview essay on ritual, Leach stated bluntly that "van Gennep's schema has proved more useful than Durkheim's" (1968: 522). Lévi-Strauss' (partial) recognition of van Gennep is unsurprising, for van Gennep always insisted that ceremonial patterns (as well as myths) should be examined as wholes and that comparison should be based upon similarities in structure rather than upon content. Moreover, by emphasizing systems of exchange, he may have influenced both Mauss and Lévi-Strauss more than has so far been acknowledged, and more than Mauss and Lévi-Strauss themselves ever conceded. Chapter 3 in *Rites of Passage* focuses ritualistic exchange of words, gestures, services, goods, slaves, and wives. Senn concluded that van Gennep "deserves a place as an early and significant structural folklorist" (Senn 1974: 242), a view shared by Belmont (1979).

On various occasions Leach, Needham (1967), and Evans-Pritchard (1960) sincerely wondered why van Gennep was not held in higher regard in French anthropology ("an academic disgrace," Needham said [1967: xi]), but they never went deeper into the question. Lévi-Strauss' "rediscovery" of van Gennep was constrained by his structuralist approach and search for laws of logic, pursuits that were quite distant from van Gennep's own attempt to establish a "biological sociology," a science studying *faits naissants*, that is, cultural phenomena at their moment of occurrence. Lévi-Straussian structuralism used finished texts (myths, kinship terminologies, cooking recipes) as data. Liminality makes sense only within social dramas as they unfold.

It was Victor Turner who rediscovered the importance of liminality. One of Turner's many achievements was to liberate van Gennep's framework from both the functionalist and the structuralist straitjackets and insert his work on ritual passages where it truly belonged: in a processual approach. Having heard of van Gennep in the work of Henri Junod during his fieldwork (Turner 1985: 159), Turner stumbled upon van Gennep's *Rites of Passage* almost by chance in the summer of 1963 at a moment when he was himself in a liminal state. He had resigned from Manchester and sold his house but was still waiting for his U.S. visa, which was delayed because of his refusal to enter armed military service during World War II. The Turners were staying at Hastings on the English Channel, living in "a state of suspense" (E. Turner 1985: 7)—literally at a threshold—when Victor encountered van Gennep. Unlike Lévi-Strauss and his British followers, Turner *experientially* recognized the importance of van Gennep's insight. The reading inspired him, on the spot, to write the famous chapter "Betwixt and Between: The Liminal Period in Rites of Passage," published in 1967 in *The Forest of Symbols*. Turner presented the paper once in the United States, in March 1964, when he had finally taken up his position at Cornell. This was only the first of his explorations into liminality.

In his analysis of Ndembu ritual, Turner (1967, 1969, 1974) showed how ritual passages served as moments of creativity that freshened the societal makeup, arguing against Durkheim (and Radcliffe-Brown) that rituals were much more than mere reflections of "social order." Van Gennep's framework complemented "social drama," a term Turner had already introduced. Turner had been trained in functionalist anthropology, and his early work (1957) largely stayed within this tradition, analyzing schism and conflict as part of the social structure. Van Gennep's book decisively prodded him to redirect his work beyond the functionalist paradigm.

Liminality's travels outside the study of ritual passages in small-scale societies, and thus outside anthropology more narrowly defined, began in Victor Turner's own work. In his ethnographic accounts, he repeatedly identified parallels with nontribal or "modern" societies, clearly sensing that what he argued for the Ndembu had relevance far beyond the specific ethnographic context; yet he offered no systematic analysis or comparison. Toward the end of his life he wrote more explicitly about such links. Turner realized that liminality served not only to identify the importance of in-between periods, but also to understand the human reactions to liminal experiences as they shape personality, suddenly foreground agency, and (sometimes dramatically) bind thought to experience. For these reasons, Turner came to identify his own project with the philosophy of Dilthey (e.g., Turner 1982: 12–19; 1988: 84–97). This intellectual encounter late in Turner's life was important indeed (see also Szakolczai 2004: 69–72).

At the level of empirical application, Turner made two concrete suggestions. First, in a famous article originally published in 1974, "Liminal to Liminoid, in Play, Flow and Ritual: An Essay in Comparative Symbology" (1982: 20–60), Turner suggested that liminal experiences in modern consumerist societies have largely been replaced by "liminoid" moments, when creativity and uncertainty unfold in art and leisure activities. And second, in his work on the Christian pilgrimage (Turner and Turner 1978), he argued that pilgrimage shares aspects of liminality because pilgrims become equal by distancing themselves from mundane structures and their social identities, leading to a homogenization of status and a strong sense of *communitas*.

The suggestions in "Liminal to Liminoid" had far-reaching effects within anthropology and beyond, as several of Turner's students' studies of art, theatre, literature, and "leisure" as liminoid phenomena drew inspiration from Turner. Turner became even more of a reference point in the 1980s and 1990s, when anthropology took a "performative turn" to focus on process. "Process" and "performance" were always crucial terms to Turner.

While recognizing the importance of Victor Turner's insights, I urge hesitation to simply follow him (and his students) here, for four inter-related reasons. First, understanding the liminal as primarily relating to art and leisure in modern society sidelines some of the clearly dangerous or problematic aspects of liminality. It is not irrelevant that Turner's ideas first spread within the "1968 mood" but were not more widely known and used until the postmodernist turn of the 1980s. Turner's (albeit hesitant) self-identification with the postmodernist turn certainly opened up space for this usage of the term. Second, in his discussion of the liminoid, Turner seems to suggest an oversimplified dichotomy between "traditional" and "modern" symbolic systems, arguing that "we must distinguish between symbolic systems and genres which developed before and after the Industrial Revolution" (1982: 30). Third, in contrast to liminal experiences, liminoid experiences are optional and do not involve resolution of a personal crisis or change of status. The liminoid is a break from normality, a playful as-if experience, but it lacks the key feature of liminality: *transition*.

Fourth, by thus delimiting liminality, Turner downplayed the extent to which liminal moments or liminal experiences might be equally present in political or social transformations, that is, outside "culture," in a narrow understanding of that term. Here Turner was probably influenced by the Parsonian version of anthropology as dealing with "symbol systems" or "comparative symbology" (Thomassen 2013: 193–94). Despite Turner's frequent references to "complex society" and allusions to the relevance of liminality for "macropolitics" (1988: 91), and despite his engagement with political anthropology (Swartz, Turner, and Tuden 1966), his work remained largely apolitical in character, at least in an explicit sense.[8] A more promising development in this vein may be found in the Turners' study of pilgrimage, which tentatively suggests that a liminal state may become "fixed," referring to a situation where the suspended character of social life takes on a more permanent character (Turner and Turner 1978). This was in line with an earlier suggestion by Victor Turner, namely, that in the monastic and mendicant states of the world's religions, transition was a permanent condition (1969: 107). I will return to this "permanentization of liminality" further below.

Types of Liminality

In Turner's own words, liminality refers to any "betwixt and between" situation or object. Speaking very broadly, it is applicable to both space and time. Single moments, longer periods, or even whole epochs can be considered liminal. Liminal places can be specific thresholds; they can also be more extended areas like borderlands or, arguably, whole countries situated in consequential in-between positions between larger civilizations. Liminality is also applicable to single individuals, larger groups, and entire societies. These various dimensions of liminality can be outlined very simply:

- Three different types of subject experience liminality:
    1) single individuals
    2) social groups (e.g., cohorts, minorities)
    3) whole societies or populations (perhaps even civilizations)

- The temporal dimension of liminality relates to:
    1) moments (sudden events)
    2) periods (weeks, months, possibly years)
    3) epochs (decades, generations, maybe centuries)

- The spatial dimension of liminality concerns:
    1) specific thresholds (a doorway in a house, a line separating holy from sacred in a ritual, specific objects, in-between items in a classification scheme, parts/openings of the human body)
    2) areas or zones (border areas between nations, monasteries, prisons, sea resorts, airports)
    3) countries or larger regions, continents (meso-potamia and the medi-terranean; Ancient Palestine in between Mesopotamia and Egypt; Ionia in Ancient Greece, in between the Near East and Europe).[9]

The different dimensions of the above three areas can function together in various combinations, as in Table 2.1, which offers examples of liminal experiences according to the *type of subject* and the *temporal dimension*.

Table 2.1. Types of Liminal Experiences

Time	Subject		
	Individual	Group	Society
Moment	-Sudden event in one's life (death, divorce, illness) -Individual ritual passage (baptism, ritual passage to womanhood, e.g., among Ndembu)	-Ritual passage to manhood (almost always in cohorts) -Graduation ceremonies	-Transitions in the passage of time (New Year celebrations) -A sudden event affecting a whole society (invasion, natural disaster, plague) and erasing social distinctions and normal hierarchy -Carnivals -Revolutions
Period	-Critical life stages like puberty or adolescence	-Ritual passage to manhood, which may last weeks or months in some societies -Group travels	-Wars -Revolutionary periods
Epoch (or lifespan duration)	-Standing "outside society" by choice or assignment -Monkhood -Remaining "dangerous" because of a failed ritual passage -Being a twin (twins are permanently liminal in some societies)	-Religious fraternity -Ethnic minority -Social minority -Transgenderedness -Immigrant group membership (betwixt and between old and new culture) -Living on the fringe of "normal structures," often perceived as both dangerous and holy	-Prolonged war -Enduring political instability -Prolonged intellectual confusion -Incorporation and reproduction of liminality in social and political structure -Modernity as "permanent liminality"

To be sure, these analytical distinctions are somewhat arbitrary in nature. There is no absolute way to distinguish "moments" from "periods," and the dimensions invoked could also be thought of as a continuum. Moreover, and as indicated from the outset, this scheme's identification of types of liminal experience by no means implies that all these experiences are demarcated with a transition *rite*—at least, not clearly recognizable, institutionalized rites with identifiable masters of ceremonies, as studied in the work of van Gennep.

As each of the dimensions of subject, space, and time has (at least) three basic subdivisions, a further variable becomes necessary, namely, *scale*, or the degree to which liminality is experienced—in other words, the intensity of the liminal moment or period. Liminal experiences can (and most often do) occur in general settings where much of what goes on stays "normal." Sometimes, however, liminal experiences are intensified as the personal, group, and societal levels converge in liminality, over extended periods of time, or even within several spatial entities. In other words, whereas most experiences of liminality are circumscribed by some kind of *frame*, certain other experiences come closer to "pure liminality," bringing both personal and collective, and spatial and temporal coordinates into play. This neither can nor should be expressed mathematically, but it does seem meaningful to suggest that there exist degrees of liminality, and that the degree depends on how radically the liminal experience departs from persisting structures. Indeed, in his analysis of Weber and Foucault, Szakolczai (1998) argued that liminality becomes particularly intense when personal and "civilizational" liminality converge. Such situations are present in, and in many ways shaped, the lifeworks of the twentieth century's most important thinkers, many of whom happened to go through the decisive years of puberty and passage to adulthood during one of the two world wars.

A final distinction is that liminal experiences can be "artificially" induced, as in rituals, or they can simply happen without anyone planning for it, as in natural disasters or the sudden disappearance of beloved persons. Similarly, individuals can consciously seek out a liminal position outside normality. One could argue that this is exactly what some artists or writers do, and that celebrities consciously seek this embodied position. By contrast, individuals or whole social groups may suffer stigmatizing consequences of being seen or classed as liminal, even if they never asked for such a position.

Societal Liminality and the Collapse of Order: The Challenge to Social and Political Theory

In recent years, the most far-reaching suggestion about liminal situations concerns the wider claim that whole societies can experience them during

crises or the "collapse of order." The importance of such large-scale liminal experiences was perhaps first suggested in Eisenstadt (1995), and
Arpad Szakolczai (2000, 2003, 2008a) has most systematically developed
their applicability to include both personal and collective liminality, temporal as well as spatial (see also Wydra 2000).

This idea stems from a little known dialogue linking anthropology and
social theory, held between Victor Turner and Shmuel Eistenstadt (for
further discussion, see Thomassen 2012d). Eisenstadt's Weberian reading
of the "symbolic anthropologists" strongly influenced his comparative-
historical approach to the study of civilizations, as did his collaboration
with Victor Turner in the early 1980s, when they jointly organized a seminar on "Comparative Liminality and Dynamics of Civilizations" that led
to a series of publications (see in particular Eisenstadt 1995). Eisenstadt
realized that the concept of liminality could re-address the question of
change and continuity in large-scale settings. One may argue, for example, that in a large-scale comparative perspective the Axial Age was a kind
of liminal period (Thomassen 2010) in between two types of worldviews
and two rounds of empire building—a period when certainties and identities were questioned and when, as Jaspers put it, "man asks radical questions" and the "unquestioned grasp on life is loosened" (1957: 3). It was an
age of uncertainty, when possibilities lay open; a period when individuals
were put to the test and new leadership figures arose. Finally, in terms
of spatial coordinates, the axial "leaps" all happened in in-between areas
bookended by larger civilizations, that is, in liminal places neither central nor beyond the reach of major civilizational centers, but exactly at the
margins, and quite systematically so at that.

Following in the footsteps of these discussions, Arpad Szakolczai discussed modernity as a peculiar form of "permanent liminality" (2000:
220ff.), thus conceptually elevating liminality to a diagnostic tool for understanding the modern period as such. If historical periods can be considered liminal, it follows that the crystallization of ideas and practices during this period merits special attention. Once a liminal period has ended,
the ideas and practices established therein tend to assume the qualities of
structure. In this view, history is not a continuous stream of action governed by a structure that changes slowly, if at all. Rather, at some historical moments structure is loose, and at other moments structure takes on
the quality of *doxa*, where it becomes frozen. This accords with van Gennep's view of "periodicity." The playfulness of the liminality period is at
once unstructured and highly structuring: the most basic rules of behavior
are questioned, doubt and skepticism about the existence of the world are
radicalized. However, the problematizations, formative experiences, and
reformulations of being that arise during the liminality period proper feed

the individual (and his/her cohort) with a new structure and set of rules that, once established, glide back to the level of the taken-for-granted. Liminal periods, characterized by wholesale collapse of order and loss of background structure, push agency to the forefront and produce re-orientations in modes of conduct and thought within larger populations. Though this may seem a straightforward suggestion, it opens up a series of questions concerning the liminality concept's applicability outside its original domain of analysis. After all, analyzing manhood rituals among the Ndembu differs from analyzing historical dislocations within wider civilizational contexts, replacing not just a cohort of boys and their identities but worldviews and political structures of state societies or even larger entities.

In anthropological usage the liminal state is always clearly defined, temporally and spatially: there is a way into liminality, and there is a way out of it. Members of a society are themselves aware of the liminal state: they know that they will leave it sooner or later, and have "masters of ceremonies" to guide them through rituals. As applied a wholesale collapse of order affecting an entire society, liminality is distinct from that in ritual passages in two crucial ways: First, the future is inherently unknown (whereas the initiand's personal liminality is still framed by the continued existence of a home society awaiting his reintegration). And second, there are no real masters of ceremonies, as nobody has gone through the liminal period before.

Beyond limiting the application of the concept, these two basic differences seem to indicate a situation where liminal moments become extremely dangerous, setting the stage for various self-proclaimed masters of ceremonies. This raises the question of *leadership* during liminal periods, and the kind of bonds established between leaders and their followers. Agnes Horvath (1998) took up this question directly in her analysis of political communication during communism. In anthropological usage, liminality is closely connected to the development of *communitas*, and for Victor Turner very positively so. How can the link between liminality and *communitas* be understood in mass societies? Which complementary concepts, theories, or approaches are needed to make sense of this connection? Evidently, liminal moments may also generate very negative types of *communitas* dominated by resentment, envy, and hate. How and why does this happen?

As Weber recognized, charismatic leadership can emerge in moments of radical social or political change—"out-of-the-ordinary moments." Yet Weber failed to notice that at such moments—when, as Shakespeare put it, "degree is shaken"—numerous other sinister figures can also appear.

Concerning the role of leadership in liminal moments, it is hardly coincidental that Turner kept returning to the figure of the trickster as one of several (arguably archetypical) liminal figures, although he never subjected them to in-depth analysis. In one of his last essays, "Body, Brain and Culture," Turner even suggested that "slippery" tricksters move between the hemispheres of the brain (1988: 170), creating a real effect while erasing their own traces. Analyzing the trickster as a particularly dangerous type of political leader who may emerge in liminal situations, as Horvath proposed (1998, 2013), may well represent a breakthrough in our understanding of how liminal moments or periods may be taken in dangerous directions (Turner came close to saying this himself [1985: 230]).

Tricksters, as documented in mythologies worldwide, are a particular kind of "joker": non-beings who appear out of blue, inserting an element of novelty and uncertainty into a well-established social situation. Tricksters are outsiders without homes or existential commitments. They are also mimes. The trickster has particular affinities with liminal situations. Under normal circumstances, tricksters are jokers who provoke laughter but cannot be taken seriously. In liminality this changes: as an outsider, the trickster might easily be perceived to represent a solution to a crisis. However, having no home, and therefore no real human and existential commitments, tricksters are not really interested in solving the liminal crisis: they simply pretend. In fact, since they are at home in liminality—in homelessness—their real interest often lies in perpetuating, rather than resolving, conditions of confusion and ambivalence. In this the trickster might succeed, as Lewis Hyde reminds us in a book title: *Trickster Makes the World*.

In a situation of political unrest and a real-world loss of established structures, tricksters present themselves as saviors who claim to have seen the future, but who in reality establish their own position by perpetuating liminality and emptying the liminal moment of real creativity, turning it into a scene of mimetic rivalry (see again Szakolczai 2000: 218 and in this volume). Girard argued exactly so in *Violence and the Sacred* (1976), referring to situations where "degree is shaken" and distinctions cease to be meaningful. According to Girard, once a process of undifferentiation unfolds, the process of doubling threatens to spread and can be halted only via sacrifice. In the last years of his life, Victor Turner came to recognize Girard's theoretical importance (Turner 1988: 34) in the precise context of the ritual structure: crisis is contagious, and sometimes the "redressive machinery . . . fails to function" (ibid.: 35), leading to "a reversion to crisis."

The point here is as simple as it is important: the so-called "charismatic leaders" that so extensively shaped the twentieth century were in fact not charismatic at all. Weber (2004) listed a "matter-of-factness" type of passion, a feeling of responsibility, and a sense of proportion as primary qualities of charisma. He very explicitly described real charismatic leaders as the ones who do not succumb to vanity and self-glorification but instead preserve humbleness and moderation, even as they take on the responsibility of leadership. Political leaders like Mussolini, Mao, and Hitler tick none of the boxes in Weber's presentation of charisma. Far from being charismatic and therefore "gifted," they were rather genuine human failures—outcasts, who in highly liminal moments *somehow* captured power. Tricksters are experts at upsetting the social order by reversing values and deploying their rhetorical and theatrical skills. The trickster is a dangerous clown. The trickster, therefore, is the logical and historical opposite of a truth-telling prophet or *parrhesiast* (Foucault 2001, who in a situation of crisis lays bare the situation, proposes a way out, and takes the lead, exposing him- or herself to the danger this entails.

The Permanentization of Liminality: Modernity as Permanent Liminality

The concept "permanentization of liminality" is close to Weber's concept of "routinization of charisma," a deeply paradoxical but again *real* social process at the very heart of practically any social or political or religious movement.

The institutions constituting a society were created to deal with an extraordinary situation only to later become permanent. In a way this is normal and could not be otherwise, but the experience of being "stuck in liminality" is also highly critical. Again using van Gennep's tripartite structure, Szakolczai argued (2000: 220) that there are three types of permanent liminality imploding within modernity, critically originating in the three phases of the rites of passage. "Liminality becomes a permanent condition when any of the phases in this sequence (of separation, liminality, and reaggregation) becomes frozen, as if a film stopped at a particular frame" (ibid.). Szakolczai invoked a salient example of each type of permanent liminality: monasticism (in which monks prepare endlessly for separation), court society (where individuals continuously perform their roles in an endless ceremonial game; see Burke, this volume), and Bolshevism (exemplifying a society stuck in the final stage of a ritual passage). The first two instances build on the insights of Turner himself, Max Weber (and his study of the Protestant ethic, Weber 2002), and Norbert Elias (and his study of court culture; Elias 1994). The understanding of communism as a specific "third-stage" type of permanent liminality is based on a view of communism as "a regime in which the Second World War never ended" (Szakolczai 2000: 223; see also Horvath and Szakolczai 1992). Rather than healing wounds and looking to the future, communist regimes sustained themselves by playing continuously on the sentiments of revenge, hatred, and suffering, "preventing the settling down of negative emotions" (Szakolczai 2000: 223).

Whereas liminality is "unstructure," a lack of fixed points in a given moment, Victor Turner often stressed that the liminal must at the same time be considered the *origin* of structure, the point of departure for the birth of new forms of cultural and social life. Stated most succinctly, "liminal phenomena are at the level of culture what variability is at the level of nature" (Turner 1979: 95). Seen in this light, the term "permanent liminality" seems paradoxical, for if liminality is the absence of enduring structures—a moment and space of transition—how can it ever become permanent? Yet Victor Turner himself introduced the term "institutionalization of liminality" in reference to monastic orders (1969: 107). Here Turner unknowingly moved his framework closer to Weber's analysis of this-worldly asceticism as a process that moved the continuous "testing" of oneself from the monastery into the secular sphere of professional achievement. Like that self-testing, modernity cannot be pinned down to any specific institutional or ideational structure, as modernity most generally refers to change, transition, and contingency. In terms of historical semantics, it refers to a temporal experience of seeing the "present" as having overcome the past, and the future as an open horizon (Koselleck 1979). As Giesen argued (2009), modernity is a continuous transgression of boundaries and the breaking down of traditions, and therefore involves a deep-rooted sense of ambivalence.

This perspective opens up space for a reading of Western modernity as an institutionalization of liminality. Multiple concrete signs indicate that such a reading, however paradoxical, is indeed meaningful (Thomassen 2012c, 2013). Companies, public administrations, and individuals working within them have come to share the goal of increased "innovation capacity." This call upon individuals to constantly self-assess, self-improve, and self-reform is unsurprisingly attended by several highly ambivalent consequences, including, of course, skyrocketing incidences of stress on the labor market. The introduction of liminality into our political reality is currently visible in the permanentization of warfare and security threats, which are everywhere and anywhere, all the time (Malksöo this volume). The implosion of liminal conditions is arguably increasingly evident in contemporary culture, where "extreme acts" like sexuality, gambling, and violence (mimetic social acts by definition) are increasingly trivialized as part of everyday normality and leisure, and where the very boundary between the ordinary and the extraordinary, between seriousness and play, is systematically becoming more and more porous. It is little wonder that full endorsement of the consumption of such liminal products coexists with rejection of the material world's value altogether. Diametrically opposed self/world-relations oscillating between world-conquer and world-rejection are, as Weber noted, recurring phenomena at historical moments of crisis. Today, at the level of meaningful social life, we clearly have long since reached a kind of limit here—and it is this limit that should signal caution toward our analytical usage of the term. Liminality cannot be posited as the ultimate goal of human existence in limitless freedom, for despite limit experiences' importance, there has to be something to fall back upon. The constant pressures to innovate and transgress boundaries at all levels of social life are in dire need of problematization. In this view, liminality stands as a crucial concept in our attempts to diagnose the times in which we live.

Notes

Parts of this chapter draw on my article on the uses and meanings of liminality published in *International Political Anthropology* (Thomassen, 2009 2 (1)), "The Uses and Meanings of Liminality."

1. It is no coincidence that van Gennep's first publications were on numismatics, and that he retained a vivid interest in marking and stamping techniques throughout his entire career.

2. In fact, we tend to forget the etymological origin of 'subjectivity,' which literally means to be "thrown under" (sub-jectum), in stark contrast to its modernist connotations of autonomy and free will.

3. Van Gennep made this assertion about his work some years after its publication. The "ten years" of darkness most certainly alluded to van Gennep's personal life from 1897 to 1908, when the book was finished. Van Gennep painfully, finally broke with his parents after marrying in 1897. That year he also moved to Russian Poland, starting a new career as a teacher. Upon his return to Paris in 1901, his scholarly work progressed, but without a ritual passage into French academia.

4. Marcel Mauss (1910) published a harsh and extremely unfair review, which certainly made things difficult for van Gennep in France.

5. The only academic position van Gennep ever held was the (first) chair in Swiss ethnography at the University of Neuchatel, a position he took in 1912. But in 1915 he was expelled from Switzerland because he openly criticized the Swiss government and its pro-German attitudes during the war. Van Gennep had an awful habit of criticizing authorities.

6. Upon returning from a lecture tour in the United States and Canada in 1922, van Gennep fell ill and momentarily abandoned all his academic ambitions, settling down as a chicken breeder in Southern France.

7. Turner's own brief overview of the van Gennep reception (1985: 158–59) mentions the work of E. D. Chappell and C. S. Cohn, whose 1942 *Principles of Anthropology* discussed rites of passage. Van Gennep's concept of ritual passage served as the central analytical frame of Volume 1 of Henri Junod's famous *The Life of a South-African Tribe*, originally published in 1912.

8. On the potential Turner's approach holds for the study of political revolutions, see Thomassen (2012a).

9. One could argue a fourth level here also, namely an experience of the whole world as liminal. As an experience, this could pertain to religious or philosophical attitudes of rejection or suspicion toward the world.

References

Belmont, N. 1979. *Arnold Van Gennep: The Creator of French Ethnography*. Chicago: Chicago University Press.

Durkheim, É. 1967. *The Elementary Forms of Religious Life*. New York: Free Press.

Eisenstadt, S. N. 1995. "The Order-Maintaining and Order-Transforming Dimensions of Culture." In *Power, Trust, and Meaning: Essays in Sociological Theory and Analysis*. Chicago: Chicago University Press.

Elias, N. 1994. *The Civilizing Process. Sociogenetic and Psychogenetic Investigations*. Oxford: Blackwell.

Evans-Pritchard, E. E. 1960. "Introduction." In Robert Hertz, *Death and the Right Hand*. London: Free Press.

Foucault, M. 2001. *Fearless Speech*. Los Angeles: Semiotext(e).

Gennep, A. van. 1920. *L'Etat actuel du problème totémique*. Paris: Leroux.

———. 1958. *Manuel de folklore français contemporain*. 9 vols., 1937–1958. Paris: Picard.

———. (1909) 1960. *The Rites of Passage*. Chicago: Chicago University Press.

———. (1913) 2001. Review of (among others), Durkheim's *Elementary Forms of Religious Life* (originally in *Mercure*). Reprinted in *Chroniques de Folklore d'Arnold van Gennep*, edited by J.-M. Privat. Paris: C.T.H.S.

Gennep, K. van. 1964. *Bibliographie des œuvres d"Arnold van Gennep*. Paris: Editions A. & J. Picard.

Giesen, B. 2009. "The Three Projects of Modernity." *International Political Anthropology* 2 (2): 239–50.

Girard, R. 1976. *Violence and the Sacred*. Baltimore, MA: John Hopkins University Press.

Horvath, A. 1998. "Tricking into the Position of the Outcast: A Case Study in the Emergence and Effects of Communist Power." *Political Psychology* 19 (2): 331–47.

———. 2013. *Modernism and Charisma*. Basingstoke: Palgrave MacMillan.

Horvath, A., and Szakolczai, A. 1992. *The Dissolution of Communist Power: The Case of Hungary*. London: Routledge.

James, W. 1902. *The Varieties of Religious Experience: A Study of Human Nature*. New York, London, and Bombay: Longman's Green and Co.

Jaspers, K. 1957. *The Origin and Goal of History*. New Haven, CT and London: Yale University Press.

Koselleck, R. 1979. *Futures Past: On the Semantics of Historical Time*. New York: Columbia University Press.

Leach, E. 1968. "Ritual." In *International Encyclopedia of the Social Sciences*, vol. 1ε, edited by D. Sills. New York: Macmillan.

Lévi-Strauss, C. 1963. *Totemism*. Boston: Beacon Press.

Mauss, M. 1910. "Review of Van Gennep's *Rites de Passage*." *L'Année Sociologique* 11: 200–202 (reprinted in *Œuvres* 1, 553–55).

Needham, R. 1967. "Introduction." In A. van Gennep, *The Semi-Scholars*. London: Routledge.

Radin, P. 1937. *Primitive Religion*. New York: Viking.

Senn, H. A. 1974. "Arnold van Gennep: Structuralist and Apologist for the Study of Folklore in France." *Folklore* 85 (4): 229–43.

Swartz, M. J., V. Turner, and A. Tuden, eds. 1966. *Political Anthropology*. Chicago: Aldine.

Szakolczai, A. 1998. *Max Weber and Michel Foucault: Parallel Lifeworks*. London: Routledge.

———. 2000. *Reflexive Historical Sociology*. London: Routledge.

———. 2003. *The Genesis of Modernity*. London: Routledge.

———. 2004. "Experiential Sociology." *Theoria* 103: 59–87.

———. 2008a. *Sociology, Religion and Grace: A Quest for the Renaissance*. London: Routledge.

Thomassen, B. 2009. "The Uses and Meanings of Liminality." *International Political Anthropology* 2 (1): 5–28.

———. 2010. "Anthropology, Multiple Modernities and the Axial Age Debate." *Anthropological Theory* 10 (4): 321–42.

———. 2012a. "Notes towards an Anthropology of Political Revolutions." *Comparative Studies in Society and History* 54 (2): 679–706.

———. 2012b. "Revisiting Liminality: The Danger of Empty Spaces." In *Liminal Landscapes: Remapping the Field*, edited by H. Andrews and L. Roberts. London: Routledge.

———. 2012c. "Anthropology and Its Many Modernities: When Concepts Matter." *Journal of the Royal Anthropological Institute* 18: 160–78.

———. 2012d. "Émile Durkheim between Gabriel Tarde and Arnold van Gennep: Founding Moments of Sociology and Anthropology." *Social Anthropology* 20 (3): 231–49.

———. 2013. "Anthropology and Social Theory: Renewing Dialogue." *European Journal of Social Theory* 16 (2): 188–207.

Turner, E. 1985. "Prologue: From the Ndembu to Broadway." In Victor Turner, *On the Edge of the Bush*, edited by E. Turner. Tucson: University of Arizona Press.

Turner, V. W. 1957. *Schism and Continuity in African Society: A Study of Ndembu Village Life*. New York: Humanities Press.

———. 1967. "Betwixt and Between: The Liminal Period in *Rites de Passage*." In *The Forest of Symbols*. New York: Cornell University Press.

———. 1969. *The Ritual Process*. Chicago: Aldine.

———. 1974. *Dramas, Fields, and Metaphors*. Ithaca, NY: Cornell University Press.

———. 1979. *Process, Performance and Pilgrimage: A Study in Comparative Symbology*. New Delhi: Naurang Rai.

———. 1982. *From Ritual to Theatre*. New York: PAJ.

———. 1985. *On the Edge of the Bush*. Edited by E. Turner. Tucson: The University of Arizona Press.

———. 1988. *The Anthropology of Performance*. New York: PAJ.

Turner, V. W., and E. L. B. Turner. 1978. *Image and Pilgrimage in Christian Culture*. Columbia: Columbia University Press.

Weber, M. 2004. *The Vocation Lectures*. Indianapolis, IN: Hackett Publishing Company.

Weber, M. 2002. *The Protestant Ethic and the "Spirit" of Capitalism and Other Writings*. New York: Penguin.

Wydra, H. 2001. *Continuities in Poland's Permanent Transition*. London: MacMillan.

Part II

Liminality and the Social

Chapter 3

Inbetweenness and Ambivalence

Bernhard Giesen

Introduction

Social action presupposes a cultural order that—in a structuralist tradition—is generated by applying distinctions and classifications. The two sides of a distinction refer to contrasting or oppositional meanings that, by this opposition, constitute each other: thus inside hints at outside, past at future, equality at inequality, salvation at condemnation, rationality at irrationality, justice at injustice, parents at children, masters at servants. We do not know a concept's meaning unless we can conceive of its opposite. However, our regular thinking tends not to refer to this opposite: it is the excluded or silenced other possibility (Derrida 2010). Thus, reconstructing the excluded other has become the royal path of poststructuralist reasoning. But although this reconstruction of the excluded other of an opposition is widely accepted, mainstream cultural sociology has only marginally theorized a third possibility—the space in between the opposites, the third possibility, the transition between inside and outside, the "neither . . . nor" or the "as well as . . . ," the space of hybridity—despite its centrality for nonsociologists such as Homi Babha, Gilles Deleuze, Michel Serres, and Yuri Lotman.

The following essay deals with this extraordinary space in between the opposites. Focusing on something that transcends the successful ordering and splitting of the world into neat binaries, it maintains that this inbetweenness is essential for the construction of culture. Reality itself provides no firm ground for neat classification. Therefore, in applying classifications to raw reality there will always be an unclassifiable remainder, and in

Notes for this chapter begin on page 70.

specifying meaning there is no way to achieve absolute clarity and avoid a rest of fuzziness. Understanding can always fail, interpretation can be disrupted by surprises and resistance, distinctions can hit indecisiveness, routines can be diluted, rules violated, boundaries between inside and outside crossed by nomads and strangers (Simmel 1996; Lotman 1990), questioned by fools (Deleuze 1992), and disregarded by parasites (Serres 2007). Even when we define and specify meanings extensively, some remainder of uncertainty always exists in the relation between signifier and signified, and this uncertainty cannot be dissolved by linguistic operations alone. Instead it can be overcome by a deictic gesture pointing to the situation at hand (following Schütz (1971): "Me, here, now, this"). Traditional sociology acknowledges the existence of these phenomena of fuzziness and indecisiveness but has treated them mostly as pathologies, disturbances, and crises that require stabilizing repairs and counteracting restorations of order.

The sociology of ambivalence reverses this position. It claims that ambivalences, disturbances, paradoxes, misunderstandings, and exceptions are not critical risks to social order but rather indispensable elements of this order. That is, stability of social order relies not only on neat oppositions but also on the acceptance of the unclassifiable, of surprises and coincidences, ambiguity and fuzziness. Complex cultural orders must have empty signifiers like "God," "nature," or "reason." Even value orientations like "freedom" or "equality" function as such indefinable empty signifiers, which are, by their very semantic porousness, open to cover the unclassifiable and ambiguous.

These phenomena of ambivalence do not simply exist—they drive the process of social communication. Without surprises and disturbances, communication would lack the focus that catches common attention. Without interferences from the background there would be no signal, image, or sign. Without fuzziness there would be neither need nor motive to understand and interpret. Without deviances and breaches there would be no awareness of rules. What was treated as a crisis of social order before, and what actors now mostly see as such a crisis, emerges as the indispensable key to the communicative reproduction of cultural order. The following remarks will address four phenomena of inbetweenness in random order: garbage, monsters, victims, and seduction.

Garbage

The chosen categories of inbetweeness refer to a fundamental ambiguity or indissoluble remainder that resists any attempt at unambiguous

classification. Even though this inbetweenness is inherent and unavoidable in the operation of classifying, ordering, and coding the world, it is
disregarded, invisibilized, and silenced in the order generated by classification. In the natural attitude of everyday life, the world presents itself
as neatly ordered. Cultural classification, however, is somehow weirdly
aware of this elementary but excluded inbetweenness and responds to it
by producing order even in the realm that seems to escape it. It classifies
the unclassifiable, describes different kinds of ambiguity, and delineates
inbetweenness through symbolic figures. It classifies garbage, imagines
monsters, and tells the story of the uncanny behind the boundary.

Our treatment of garbage is a pertinent example of attempts to cope
with this elementary ambiguity. Garbage is not a public health problem
but an offense to the cultural order of things. It is neither sacred nor profane, and this inbetweenness threatens cultural order. Garbage is uncanny:
like the living dead, its pure and absurd materiality compels us to keep
our distance or remove it to avoid contamination by its decay and formlessness. When garbage cannot be removed immediately, its undeniable
existence has to be concealed from our eyes and sealed from our noses.
As long as garbage can be perceived, it remains offensive and dangerous.

But removal into nothingness is only one way to cope with garbage. It
can also be retransformed into something belonging in the realm of usable and classifiable things, as is achieved by recycling, or the realm of the
sacred, as occurs when garbage is treated as collectibles, art, or souvenirs
(Thompson 1979).

The transformation of garbage into usable, profane things follows the
logic of separation and elementarization. Disgusting garbage is removed
to a space beyond our perception. In this enclosed space the decay of
garbage is accelerated until it dissolves into its elementary components.
This elementary stuff, now rid of any memory of its previous form, can be
encountered again as useful raw material that no longer causes disgust.
The realm of profane, consumable things is directed by an increased com-
mandment of presence. Here, any hint at transitoriness, at unavoidable
decay, at the inevitable death by consumption is a scandal that can be
concealed only by presenting ever new, fresh and alluring consumables.
Garbage represents the death of things, which has to be hidden from sight.

Changing garbage into something sacred does not require material
transformation. On the contrary, conservation counteracts its decay and
obvious temporality. Because the sacred is eternal, we must exempt the
objects that embody and represent it from decay. The logic of conservation
is supported by the auratic attraction of the sacred as embodied in useless
things—art, souvenirs, ruins. Even in sacralized form, garbage remains in

an in-between position because it embodies the invisible sacred that represents the whole. We cannot stand the unmediated presence of the sacred, just as we cannot stand the odor and sight of garbage. The unveiled sight of the sacred would blind us as it did Teiresias, who watched the goddess Athena bathing. The blind Teiresias was no longer able to cope with his everyday life but could foresee the future. Whoever has seen the unveiled sacred is lost for everyday business.

Monsters

Another embodiment of inbetweenness and ambivalence is the monster. Sometimes when we encounter abnormal, enigmatic, irregular phenomena, our attempts to assimilate the weirdness into normality fail. When we can neither ignore nor classify these phenomena, we are facing a monster. This encounter is threatening and dangerous because it disrupts the fragile reality of our social order. We feel compelled to reconstruct the boundary behind which we could ban the monstrous phenomena or, this endeavor failing, to try to escape.

Simple cultures interpret the demonic or monstrous as an autonomous source of agency. In this respect it resembles the sacred, but unlike the sacred, it has evil or unclear intentions. It hides its true identity and intentions behind a façade that cannot be trusted. Demons introduce the possibility of deception into the world. Things are not always as they appear. Beneath the surface lies a reality that is stronger than the treacherous appearance. The world is suspect. It is driven by vampires and body snatchers, seducers and tricksters, and we are well advised to distrust the surface (Douglas 1966).

Once they are visible, demons and monsters can be kept at a distance— expelled, ostracized, banned, stigmatized. This holds true also for bodies whose physical features deviate from the regular and normal. In many ancient cultures, disabled or disfigured children were killed immediately after birth or were banned, kept out of sight. Physical distance was maintained between irregular or disfigured persons and the community of normals to prevent contagion and contamination. Later on, disfigured people were interned in asylums that shielded regular everyday society from the shocking sight of them.

A new mode of coping with monstrous disfigurations emerged in the princely courts of early modern Europe, where monsters were increasingly treated as curiosities or miracles of nature—rare objects of the princely collection. The extraordinary monster lost its awful, shocking impact when it was turned into a harmless sensation presented in a frame devoid of all practical considerations: pure extraordinariness. The demonological gaze was replaced by the museological gaze. Dwarfs and giants, disfigured persons or monstrous animals could be watched from a close distance, and the thrill of facing the monsters no longer engendered anxiety or fear but just a pleasing frisson, absent any real danger or risk of contagion. Bars, cages, and chains tamed the monster—we could watch it close up, though we were not to touch it.

To be sure, the logic of collecting and exhibiting curiosities was not confined to princely courts. Traveling circuses, ethnic shows, anatomical museums, and zoological gardens continued this museological gaze at monsters on a more popular level. Quite tellingly, even in the nineteenth century, the museological gaze did not distinguish between disfigured persons and people with a non white skin: both were regarded as different from regular people, and this difference stimulated curiosity and amazement.

Victims

In the twentieth century the museological gaze continued to exist in popular arenas even as a new way to frame monsters emerged. Though still regarded as inferior, the monster was now an object of pity, condescending charity, and emphatic compassion as an innocent victim who could claim our support and aid. Victims embody a special ambivalence between human beings and profane things. They partake in humans' sacred nature, but they have been treated as cattle, whose killing will neither engender blood revenge nor be seen as a sin by the perpetrators. The imagination of victimhood mirrors this special inbetweenness (Agamben 1998; Giesen 2004). In this imagination victims have no face or name. Denied a proper place within the community, they are expelled and displaced to camps on the fringes of human communities, their bodies submitted to violence and killing, their stories silenced, their remains burnt to ashes: nothing should remind the living of their existence. This state of exception from regular civil rights clashes with our conviction that they are human beings like us. Consequently we try to reverse their expulsion from the civil community by remembering their names and stories, compensating their handicaps, and supporting their lifeways. The former expulsion of demonic monsters is thus turned into an emphatic identification and approach: the disabled are like us and we are in a certain respect disabled too.

But public compassion conceals a paternalistic condescension. The victims are not on equal footing with those who advocate their cause. Today, a new class of professionals mediates between common citizens and their uncommon counter images: social workers, medical doctors, welfare officers, and nurses assume the place formerly held, in the demonological gaze, by witch doctors and prison guards. This seemingly inclusive turn does not stop at the boundaries of the human race, for nowadays not only disabled and disfigured humans but also wild animals are identified as victims. What was once a dangerous wild beast is now an endangered species that should not live behind bars but in its natural habitat, eating its natural diet: the dragon is transformed into a pet dinosaur.

Thus the demonological gaze is turned into its opposite, that is, the victimological perspective. It likewise centers on discrepancy between obvious appearance and hidden essence, but the evaluation is reversed: whereas the demonological gaze suspected a hidden evil core behind a harmless façade, the victimological perspective sees a sacred core behind a seemingly abnormal façade. Here too, the ambivalent inconsistency between surface and essence compels us to overcome it, but the evil of the façade no longer frightens or shocks us because our emotions are attenuated by media reports about distant victims that avoid too-abhorrent images showing victims' monstrous deformation. Instead we see faces that differ little from our own. We listen to reporters' voices and see images containing only traces of the evil. Hence we can sit on our sofas and surrender to a mild concernedness: we do not face victims' horror, and we cannot change it. The victimological gaze can unfold only at great distance (Boltanski 1999). Only from a distance can we can opt for compassion or compensate for our inability to intervene. Faced with the actual dying victim, we would weep, be struck dumb, or try desperately to render aid. But victims represented and civilized by the media remain at a distance that precludes shock. The horror is banned by the image.

Seduction

Other forms of inbetweenness are not embodied in figures but instead generated by patterns of interaction. One of the most important is seduction. Seduction is the opposite of blunt violence and naked truth. It relies on ambivalence, equivocality, and inbetweenness; it hints at risk; it lures its targets into a realm beyond the principled world of truth, law, morality, and rationality. Seduction arises from multifarious ambiguities and possibilities, inspired by dreams and fantasies; it is unreasonable and undecided. It occurs in transitory spaces where extraordinary phenomena may occur, but we are able to return from these spaces to familiar everyday life. Seduction crosses

the boundaries between profane sobriety and the imagination of future ela-
tion, the permissible and the forbidden, the safe and the dangerous.

Taking this perspective, the French theorist Baudrillard has portrayed
seduction as the central mode of a symbolic order that differs strictly from
the natural order of law and rationality (Baudrillard 1990). Baudrillard
values seduction and ambivalence as the realm of freedom. However, the
modern imaginary commonly opts for its opposite: natural order, strict
rationality, and naked truth, treated as the proper frame of reference for
social reality. The modern imaginary sees seduction and disguise as an
almost pathological derailing of social interaction attributable to society's
hypocritical pretensions, fake passions, and deceptive promises.

This image of society as the source of deception stems from the Judeo-
Christian tradition. Having lost our original paradise and exchanged it for
a world of sin and violence, we thus, entangled in society, repeat the sin
of Adam that deprived the divine creation of its innocence. Adam's sin
was to be seduced by Eve. Seduction thus marks the loss of paradise and
the beginning of history. After this sin Adam and Eve became aware of
their nakedness. By attempting to cover it, they crossed into a land beyond
the natural paradise: society. Hence society becomes the realm of a false,
treacherous life where distrust prevails, truth is concealed, and lies and
deceptions rule. To escape from this world of deception, one must return
to natural nakedness. Originally this nakedness represented chastity and
liminality, a transgression committed against worldly rule as one stepped
toward salvation to enter the original unity of God and world. Today the
ideology of nudism still hints at this salvational core.

This originally religious transcendence turned into the early modern
epistemology of discovery and disclosure. Instead of searching for divine revelations, the modern scientist plumbs nature for universally valid
knowledge beyond the deceptions and idolatry that veil the truth. Francis
Bacon's *Novum Organum* depicts religious belief, everyday opinion, and
social custom as distortions of this natural truth.

Notwithstanding this widespread image of seduction as the origin of
falsity and evil, the following remarks will present seduction as a constitutive and constructive pattern of social interaction whose values outweigh
its disadvantages. The special inbetweenness of seduction even allows for
major breakthroughs in cultural evolution, starting with female seduction
and the original sin, Eve's sin: the seduction of Adam. Seduction replaces
the paradisiacal merging of men and nature with social relationships. The
female seduction marks the end of mythical prehistory and the beginning
of history, as do the stories of the expulsion from Paradise and of Helen's
seduction of Paris and the mythical Trojan War.

Female seduction's original mark was the savage might of the warrior; later on it targeted the priest's chastity or the citizen's honor. When the warrior stops resisting and surrenders to erotic pleasures, he becomes impotent as a warrior, as the mythical story of Samson and Delilah recalls. Successful seduction terminates not only the natural paradise but also the natural violence between the sexes.

But seduction does not always succeed. Unlike rape and violence, it presupposes contingency. This risk of failure is present in ancient myths: Circe's seduction of Odysseus failed, Salome could not seduce John the Baptist, Joseph resisted seduction by Potiphar's wife, and so on. However, males' resistance to female seduction is not merely a matter of male superiority: another interpretation exists. As Adorno and Horkheimer have pointed out with respect to Odysseus' refusal to succumb to Circe's seduction, such resistance provides the basis for an autonomous personality: a person's closure against external influences creates an inner space where autonomy can unfold because it is driven by resolve and determination not caused by anything external.

Female seduction operates not only through glances and smiles, but also through the intentional or unintentional revealing of parts of the female body—partial nakedness suggests the witness can expect more. Yet seductive unveiling differs strongly from a presentation of complete frontal nudity. The unveiling of only parts of the body maintains an indispensable ambivalence, as it can be taken as either an erotic invitation or an unintentional result of negligence, habits, or fashion. The seductive lady can always withdraw by maintaining that she did not mean to invite the resisting gentlemen, who himself can always justify his refusal by claiming not to have understood the unveiling as an invitation. The unequivocalness of total nudity, on the other hand, violates the ambivalence essential to seduction. By not complying with the unequivocality of total nudity, men most embarrassingly offend those who have exposed their naked bodies. Complete nudity mates well with voyeurism but impedes seduction. It dissolves the realm of allure and temptation, confusion and bewilderment, reducing the situation to sheer rude corporeality. Instead of artful conversation and hints at possibilities, the unconditional and unequivocal presence is in command.

Men do not appear as seducers in grand manner until the seventeenth century (e.g., Duc de Lanson or Casanova). Disregarding certain extraordinary cases such as Abelard or the medieval Minnesingers, we may safely assume that in medieval times, even noblemen relied mostly on speechless violence in sexual matters (Elias 1983). From the seventeenth century on, however, seduction increasingly replaced direct sexual violence, and

speechless corporeality, though not vanishing entirely, gave way to cour-
teous communication about possibilities and contingencies.

The transition that encouraged male seduction was driven by a structural change that turned feudal warriors into courtiers and, in the princely
court, turned close encounters between men and women who were not
married to each other into a permanent experience. Violence and distance
could no longer regulate gender relationships under these conditions, so
they were replaced by dances, ceremonies, letter exchange, and courtesy.
This shift was triggered and supported by a change in the cultural framing of war. After a century of incessant warfare in Europe, war had lost its
heroic aura and was slowly changing into a matter of bodily drill of commoners. Baroque warfare required the mechanical movements of bodies.
In this context, mental qualities like courage and daring decisiveness were
an impediment rather than a propelling cause. Aristocracy, having been
militarily castrated by the princely sovereign, had to turn to new fields
of noble excellence. Thus the court intrigue substituted the battle and the
exchange of erotic letters began to rival the duel.

From then on language was the chief medium of eroticism. Through
speech and dance, promises and confessions, flattery and praise, the courtier had to imagine a tempting and confusing space of erotic fulfillment
and self-growth and thereby bring the seduced one to forgo caution. Ambivalence and unequivocality are of prime importance in male seduction,
too. Whoever presents his erotic desire directly and bluntly immediately
loses his cause, for the desired lady cannot but reject him. Every move that
is made must allow various interpretations, withdrawal and retreat must
be possible, faces must be saved and honor preserved. Seduction is the
opposite of rape, but it is also the opposite of a "safe bet." It presupposes
the courtly civilization of both affects and techniques of indirect communication, in which the literal meaning of speech cannot be taken as the
intended one. Here, seduction becomes a game of possibilities, promises,
and staged authenticity among players who know they might fall victim
to deception and fakery (de Laclos and Pierre 1961).

Thus the ambiguity and ambivalence of seduction generate a very modern mode of sociality: seduction overcomes the unilaterality of the gaze of
voyeurs and rapists alike, and although desire remains the driving motive, reciprocity and recognition of the presence of others are indispensable. Seduction marks the exit from the violent state of nature in much
the same way that, from another perspective, the social contract does.
Both seduction and contract presuppose a mutual recognition of personal
freedom, both exclude violence, and both turn contingencies into binding commitments. Contracting, however, explains society as a normative

order resulting from the pursuit of individual utility, whereas seduction explains social reality as a collective surrendering to the vivid immediacy of a present lifeworld.

From this perspective social integration is possible only insofar as we no longer insist on facing the naked truth, the great totality, the fundamental injustice, or the core of things, but instead accommodate to superficial phenomena of our lifeworld. By contrast, the immediate look at unveiled naked truth is dangerous. If we found out what drives us and what is at the center of the world, we would be lost for everyday life. The mythical figure of Teiresias, mentioned above, was cursed with blindness after watching Athena, the goddess of knowledge, bathe. Unmasked or unveiled knowledge may be as unbearably horrible as the head of Medusa. This horror of immediate, merciless confrontation with the naked truth has to be prevented through disguise and indirect communication. Disguise, irony, and seduction keep us from facing monstrous, destructive truths and allow us to function adequately in everyday life.

What holds for the merciless truth about ourselves and the enigmatic core of the external world holds also for reckless attempts to realize perfect morality and ideal society—attempts that have often ended in monstrous piles of dead bodies. Yet by remaining within the confines of everyday life and keeping on our habitual masks, we can claim to be human and avoid epistemological, moral, and expressive ventures that are destined to failure and catastrophe.

Striving for perfect morality, for absolute truth, and for immediate and unveiled knowledge about ourselves is not only merciless and dangerous but actually impossible: our truth always presupposes a perspective and a language, reflecting on our selves cannot banish masks and background imagery, and attempts to better the world are always doomed to failure. Even if we were able to perceive absolute truth, we would find it completely void. Far from embodying evil, seduction can claim to establish a communicative inbetweenness that opens a space of chances, widens the range of possible interpretations, and allows to switching positions of participants—all on a symmetrical basis and without use of force. In this respect it excels laughter, which also allows us to outdistance the earnestness of regular life, but at the cost of degrading whoever is the butt of the joke.

References

Agamben, G. 1998. *Homo Sacer: Sovereign Power and Bare Life*. Stanford: Stanford University Press.
Baudrillard, J. 1990. *Seduction*. London: Macmillan Education.

Boltanski, L. 1999. *Distant Suffering: Morality, Media and Politics*. Cambridge: Cambridge University Press.

De Laclos, C., and A. Pierre 1961. *Les Liaisons dangereuses*. Paris: Garnier.

Deleuze, G. 1992. *The Fold: Leibniz and the Baroque*. Minneapolis: University of Minnesota Press.

Derrida, J., and A. Bass. 2010. *Writing and Difference*. London: Routledge.

Douglas, M. 1966. *Purity and Danger: An Analysis of Concepts of Pollution and Taboo*. New York: Praeger.

Elias, N. 1983. *Die höfische Gesellschaft*. Frankfurt: Suhrkamp.

Giesen, B. 2004. *Triumph and Trauma*. Boulder, CO: Paradigm.

Lotman, J. M. 1990. *Universe of the Mind: A Semiotic Theory of Culture*. London: Tauris.

Schütz, A. 1971. *Collected Papers, vol. 1, The Problem of Social Reality*, edited and introduced by M. Natanson. The Hague: Martinus Nijhoff.

Serres, M. 2007. *The Parasite*. Minneapolis: University of Minnesota Press.

Simmel, G. 1996. "Koketterie." In *Gesamtausgabe*, vol. 14, *Hauptprobleme der Philosophie*. Frankfurt: Suhrkamp.

Thompson, M. 1979. *Rubbish Theory: The Creation and Destruction of Value*. Oxford: Oxford University Press.

Chapter 4

The Genealogy of Political Alchemy
The Technological Invention of Identity Change

Agnes Horvath

Introduction: Breaking Boundaries

This chapter aims to put the in-depth human, social, and political impact of technology on the agenda in a novel manner. Though technology is widely considered a mere tool, and technological growth the highway to prosperity and a key to progress, a significant stream in social theory and political philosophy (Heidegger 1967, 1969; Mumford 1967; Foucault 1974, 1982) has long argued that technology's impact on social life is broad and deep, and that the transformation of nature and use of its forces through technological means are often modeled on the similar organization of human forces. Taking these ideas further, and in a direction not explored previously, I argue not only that technological processes take "technologies of the self" (Foucault) or the "human megamachine" (Mumford) as models, but that parallels between technological processes and social and human transformations are even stricter, incorporating the destruction and reconstitution of identity. The hypothesis that a precondition of any technological growth is prior destruction of the resistance of beings—whether inorganic or living, animal or human—has not yet been properly investigated, and neither have the implications of this destruction been properly drawn.

Any academic work requires prior distancing. Given the complex character of this problem, however, the distancing necessary to render visible the problematic nature of technology, a central value of the modern world,

---

one must proceed with extreme care. It requires a double approach, even a "meta"-distancing. Thus I offer a joint temporal and spatial distancing from current, taken-for-granted practices by way of historical and conceptual analysis. Historically, I propose a genealogy of transformative technology, tracing back such ideas to the practice of metallurgy and also exploring the connections with alchemy, its supposed theoretization (about alchemy, see Albertus 1958; Chikashige 1936; Linden 2003). Conceptually, the chapter suggests social and political transformations be seen from the viewpoint of technological processuality, arguing that rites of passage and thus liminality (van Gennep 1960; Thomassen 2014; Turner 1967, 1969) reflect the theorization of metallurgy and thus are themselves technologically inspired. It proposes a genealogy of mechanization through technology that aims at identity transformation. To achieve this purpose technology breaks up, antagonizes, and polarizes identities, making them suffer pain and violence, doing anything that helps to dissolve entities' resistance and facilitate their reconstruction into a new identity.

The genealogical reconstruction of alchemy as the source of identity change also addresses the question of why awareness is lacking about the identity-transforming, even integrity-destroying, aspect of technology.

The assumptions and language of most contemporary theoretical approaches render it impossible to even pose the question of identity change, as illustrated by the case of "rational choice" theory. As Alessandro Pizzorno (1987, 2007) convincingly argued, this theory assumes the identity of the individual is constant over time and thus cannot deal with situations when identity is altered. Rational choice theory is only one of the theoretical approaches incapable of posing the problem of identity change as a condition of possibility for technological growth. This incapacity involves a foundational paradox in thought that is traceable to the origins of classical philosophy. Parmenides, a major pre-Socratic, famously argued that one should deal only with Being and ignore non-Being as the hole of the irrational. Yet Plato claims in his late dialogues, particularly the *Sophist*, that due to the activity of the Sophists' conjuring up of non-Being, this is no longer a possibility.

Non-Being, or unreality had another name in Greek thought: *arrheton*, or "a type of knowledge that cannot be uttered." The technical knowledge connected to identity change is associated with initiation rites, magic, and metallurgy (Gell 1988; Parr 1958), visible in the Cabeiri, sons of the smith god Hephaestus, who is also linked to initiation (Kerényi 1980). This knowledge was unnamable: as a violation of the limit, it infringed the intactness of beings, ruptured identities, and destroyed reality, starting an accelerating spiraling movement of fragmentation continuing into infinity. Because this infinite, mechanical process of growth destroys the very possibility of harmonious proportionality or *ratio*, it suggests that technology is by definition irrational; and as it implies a shared breaking (co-rupture) of intact units, it promotes corruptness. The knowledge of non-Being was bound to cancel out unity, driving out the perfection of Being.

In contemporary times this process is demonstrated in the tight affinity between three characteristics shared by modern thought and the alchemic way of thinking. The first, known as dichotomization, dualism, or bipolarization, proceeds by breaking a phenomenon to be studied into diametrically opposite poles. The second can be called "apocalyptic," as it insinuates a decisive, conclusive end to history as a process. This is illustrated by the various political utopias, whether liberal (see Fukuyama's "end of history" thesis), or socialist (as in the revolutionary song the *International*): once the proposed and inevitable ideal state is effectively realized, "history" will reach an end. The third is constructivism, which claims that nothing is natural or given, as every aspect of social and human life is "socially constructed" and thus freely altered at will by the "autonomous" subject. Further, at the level of deconstructionism, any meaningful aspect of social life can be "deconstructed," explicitly propagating an alchemic transformation that results in the dissolution of given identity (natural or social), and its willful recomposition.

This chapter thus pioneers a comparative political anthropology of transformative technology, focusing on the conditions conducive to artificial creation and the practices applied in such craft. It argues that technology can be analyzed as the proposition, and attempted realization, of a genuinely alchemical transformative operation meant to shape a new identity, whether in personal, social, or political being, through the sacral processuality of an alchemical opus—sacral, because based on incantation. To this end I will first introduce the figure of the smith, who is master of the ceremony of identity change. Secondly, I will show some phases of the alchemical opus that leads, finally, to the conclusion that will attempt to bridge the gap between the figure of the smith as a sacred transformer or a kind of trickster, and the role alchemy plays in the theorization of identity change (Blakely 2006; Kieckhefer 1998; Popov 1933).

The Smith: Agent of Identity Change

Figure 4.1 is taken from Agricola's technically detailed sixteenth-century textbook on metallurgy. The illustrations, in all of their naïveté, show us a distinct type: the smith/metallurgist. These agents, who undertake to search out, mine, and smelt ores into metals, have particular rules, strange

Figure 4.1. The Secret Incantation to Catch Victims.
Source: G. Agricola, *De Re Metallica* (1950: 434)

customs, and a commanding power over nature. The smith hunts down nature: stones are burnt; things are made to suffer. This new power transforms the earth according to his own designs. The images portray hooded men, masked faces, a sickle in hand for mutilating, pits dug, pots stuck in the earth. Stones are burned, matter hunted down. The curved legs of the smith allude to magic circles: see the furnace and other enclosed spaces;

see also the Phrygian cap, sign of demons of death (Kerényi 1930, 1986). Mask and hood, the traditional fool's uniform (Pizzorno 2010), suggest a subhuman dexterity, a sureness of the eyes: feeling the way. Note the smiths' hood of invisibility (called the cap of Hades), their sickle sword (an aspect of magic), and the mask, attributes that deform or disintegrate anything because they are equally at home in the world of reality and the world of imagination, their unreality designated by the mask and hood, whereas their self has no order or rank.

Though we certainly do not know how this forbidden knowledge of the irrational that causes infinite growth escaped from its hiding, we can at least perceive its effect mechanism and direction. Indeed, there is even a guiding thread to assist onlookers in this historical investigation of the identity mutilation that comes from the mechanical processuality of the sacral, technological knowledge of metallurgy. In trying to locate this tradition, the name of the Greek smith god Hephaestus, with his emblematic, problematic smithery skills, inevitably arises. A relevant myth has him spending nine years at the bottom of the sea, mastering metalworking in the company of Thetis (Détienne and Vernant 1978: 300). Several motifs entwine here: gaining a craft out of chaos, with the sea as the primal element, a shapeless yet material essence; the cunning, shape-shifting Thetis/Metis; the character of mimesis. Each left its mark on the ever changing, bisexual, half-deity smith figures associated with metalwork, like the dwarfs of the mountains, the Dactyls, the Telchins, or the Cabeiri (Kerényi 1980). Hephaestus yearns for a transcendental change, approaching the continually growing mass with unlimited desire. His escape from reality to spend nine years secretly inventing an unknown, probably forbidden craft extracted from nature has violently parasitic elements that combine with a possessive power able to bind and enchant. This power is comparable only to that of Aphrodite—not accidentally his wife, though the couple of the lame dwarf smith and the beautiful goddess of love has always consternated interpreters. His hypnotic, fluid, fungible power works like a net that could paralyze its catch with surprise, as happened in the myth of Ares and Aphrodite. Hephaestus keeps tight control of Aphrodite and explicitly makes her the final basis of his incantation, according to the interpretation that Yates based on Bruno's *Thirty Seals* (Yates 1964: 283). "Sexsmith" is thus not just the chosen name of a contemporary singer, but a convenient allusion to the smith-like parasite Eros (Horvath 2013; Horvath and Szakolczai 2013), who transforms desire into the basic source of hostility and strife. Via Helen and Paris, such desire was also the origin of the Trojan War, which explains why Ares ended up being part of the story.

Here I advance the following proposition: If rites of passage contain a fluxional, chaotic, void-like liminal stage, then something or somebody must be set apart from it to guide participants out of it. That is, to set the effect mechanism in motion, there must be somebody who infringes upon the causes of liminality, imitating the creative law and order. This figure is the master of ceremonies, with the possibility that its role can be usurped. Therefore this chapter incorporates the figure of the imitator—the trickster (Radin 1972) who hijacks the idea, thus playing the same role as the smith. In other words, alongside the already disintegrated "limit" and the invading "unlimited" (Plato 1987, *Philebus*)—this irrational black matter— there stands a third figure: the learned, experienced blacksmith trickster, who has the "equipment" to provide the invaded with guidance and can generate a new form out of the formless liminality. Yet these liminal figures do not crave mere possession—to command power over matter, instructing and ordering it to reach the desired form, embodying free will in contrast to the underlying structure of tyrannical holism with its priority of the whole over its parts—for they themselves are servants who have no order, rank, or self-discipline, but only a pernicious will to devour and dissipate limits by inserting a new, different identity. They are themselves the desire, and they desire everything that they can achieve. Their role is parasitic. My aim now is to illustrate how these "universal consumers" trap, poison, and smother their victims to deprive them of self-support.

The figure of the smith is prominent in this inquiry because the one who desires and achieves everything—shaping stones first by hammering, cutting, and grinding, and then by using heat to obtain metals that, when molten, can be cast—is the one who obtains knowledge about the secret manipulation of nature. The smith is a craftsman, an intellectual luminary who knows from concrete experience that everything in the world is a reflection of and an analogy for other entities in the various domains of nature, clothing itself in a body and unifying its properties with matter; yet he does not have a real idea of the extent to which the smith's actions are blended together. His operation on nature seems rational to him because the efficiency of his operation is promptly demonstrated and actually works, repeatedly producing wealth, progress, and prosperity. The metallurgical process is governed by principles and broken into automatic sequences, mirroring creation through the iron rules of logic. The identity of the metals can be changed artificially by recombining or altering the proportion of composing elements, literally making them die and thus suffer by violating their previous proportions, pulling them into a state of desire to escape from deprivation. Moreover, the whole process can cycle within a tightly sealed vessel: more deprivation brings more desire, and more desire results in more deprivation.

In other words, the smith is a parasitic figure. Yet the same holds true for alchemists, and still more visibly so, as they merely imitate the smith's invention. The alchemists came to see identity transformation processes as an imitation of nature, where matter both disintegrates and is created in the middle, liminal phase of the metallurgical process, when the previously stable quality of the elements is dissolved by various machinations: heating, burning, sublimation, descent, distillation, calcination. Their will is oriented to make matter suffer from disintegration and then please it with reintegration. In this bottomless pit, the elements first lose their character, becoming mortified as all distinctions between them are eliminated; second, any new form can be printed on them, so they become ready for copying; and finally, they are reaggregated into a new unity, occupying a new space in reality. The Greek term "metallurgy" itself, according to one etymological interpretation, means "one after one," alluding to the rite of passage that stones are subjected to in being transformed into metals: the technique of purifying metal alters the character of the original ores, first by weakening and then by mounting them, imposing on them a new property that now has an eternal battery for growth in its deprivation of self-support. This growing imitation of creation provides the ultimate justification for alchemy, as it attempts to assert itself against boundaries and break free of constraints toward new desires and expanding possibilities.

Figure 4.2 illustrates the element of searching out the loosely unified. The hooded and cloaked figures look like manikins. The one behind is searching with a device in hand, while the figure in the front is hidden inside shafts and tunnels. A smith is often described as a hobgoblin or homunculus. Always on the watch for an occasion where the outcome is never certain, with an agile mind, he examines matter, concentrating his gaze on particular marks of weakness in matter. Again, hoods and caves indicate secrecy and illicitness.

Figure 4.2. Being on the Watch, to Observe, Quantify, and Paralyze Identities. *Source:* G. Agricola, *De Re Metallica* (1950: 105)

Metalworking with smelted stones is a new craft; it did not exist when the only known metal was gold. The first metal to be recognized and utilized, gold could be obtained in a pure state without violent operations and is easily shaped, so its manufacture cannot be considered a technical practice. The Bronze Age takes its name from the first metal obtained through mechanical techniques, which were later continued with alchemy. Copper was first smelted and mixed with tin around 4000 BC in a procedure that changes the reddish-orange, flexible copper and the soft pale tin into a third substance: the hard, brown, enduring alloy bronze. The transformation leaves the underlying matter intact, as it remains metal, but smelting transforms the character of both the copper and the tin to the third metal, bronze—an expanded identity. Copper, like gold, could be found in pure form, but the conversion process of smelting it and mixing with about 10 percent tin made the result, bronze, the first metallurgical product. It is certainly no accident that the biggest mercantile center for bronze, Troy, is associated with the first significant examples of liminality: the Trojan War, the first identifiable world-scale liminal crisis and the origin of "world history"; and the travels of Odysseus, the origin of "world literature"—an entire series of trials and testing, including separation, shipwreck, and encounters with monsters, titans, nymphs, and witches (which are not always easily distinguished from each other), until the hero's eventual return. Here Paris appears as a thief, a parasite on friendship who subsumes the treasure and pride of the Spartans—Helen, the daughter of Zeus—while he is the guest of the Spartan king Menelaus. The Greeks associated the similarly greedy, lascivious reputation of Crete, another major center of bronze production (in Greek mythology Talos, the bronze giant of Crete, was created by Hephaestus himself), with the story of Pasiphae's illicit love for the bull and the resulting offspring: the Minotaur hungry for young sacrificial victims. From the very beginning, metallurgy combined warlike aspects with peculiar, forbidden, sexual connotations. The sex smith does not simply confuse borders but dissolves resistance to his superhuman transforming will, invalidating most ideas about reality.

Invented in the late Neolithic, the new craft of metallurgy differed greatly from all other arts, as it explicitly solicited incantation. The manmade invocation of a god's power, the manipulation of this power to achieve a practical effect, was embodied in the technology of metal making, a knowledge that seemed to pass through the eye of a needle, the hole of the *arrheton*. The smith's art requires mysterious skill and cunning; its task is to evoke and intensify divine interference, and then to command and master it. The smith swears to the gods, sings songs in their honor, makes prostrations, observes chastity out of respect for cosmic powers, fasts and scourges the flesh to gain their favor, and sacrifices beasts and his own blood for their pleasure so that in the next stage his turn might arrive, and with it the opportunity to gain power over the gods (Kieckhefer

1998: 71). Smiths' connection with sinister powers is known, so although they are sometimes despised, they are always feared. Cursing or insulting them is considered unwise. Regardless of any responsibility they hold for the fractured world, they catch and embody powers themselves, in their own bodies. Their ambivalent status reflects the perilous nature of their work, situated in between the unreal and the real worlds—harmful action invoking forces in forbidden ways. The smith's work does not do violence to identities alone, for the limit that represents unity and order to man is also beaten, buried, heated, and crushed. Smiths, however, undergo self-divinization, making their bodies into offerings to divine powers.

Bipolarities direct the smith, who on the one hand commands and exploits the forces but on the other dedicates himself to the same power. Despised and outcast, sacred and untouchable, he is always a dark figure. Working apart from the community, he observes strict sexual taboos during his labors with the elements, closing himself off from the human world and opening himself to irrational interference. His helpers are dwarfs, considered magic, fearful, disturbing creatures; he is visited by dark forces and is under their patronage. His power derives from an alien world of gods with whom he is in constant, undefined contact. The smith has the power of a medicine man, the one who tries to convince the gods to help him (by promising obedience and dedicating himself to them with various sacrifices), though always with a view to further possessing and abusing them.

Gods are conjured in various ways. First, the smith's metallurgical operation interferes with the harmonious growth of the elements; second, he steals their properties during an imitative operation that symbolizes submission by subordinating properties to each other so that they might imitate each other; third, the *prima materia* are afflicted with violent passion until they yield to the will of the smith, whose disintegrative energy is now reinforced by the god's and thus burns indissolubly, like a storm or a disease. In all, the smith makes the material worse than it was at the start, by opening up an otherworldly space. He never loses his apocalyptic outlook, as he builds up terror from the outset, a terror that in different form—now crushing to unite rather than dividing to dismember—necessarily returns at the end and starts the cycle again. This forceful unity offers neither solution nor solace—indeed, quite the opposite. He creates an obscure situation that necessitates his intervention, either because the elements are too weak to survive on their own, or because the overall confusion accelerates in liminality. The smith's general practice is to offer a sacrifice to compensate for the diverted identities, the conjured gods, the disintegrated nature, and the induced state of flux—and also, finally, for the deception that invites the gods into man's consuming affairs (Forbes 1950).

Secret manipulation of magical powers, theft of properties by embodying them, dismemberment of identity, phallic fertility features, and the wicked, harmful nature of tortuous procedures are all attributes of the Trickster—the versatile demigod of both material abundance and disintegration into death. The smith and the Trickster face one another as if playing chess, as in the folktale about the devil who wants to bring the smith to Hell but always fails because the smith manages to outwit him and ultimately remains in his smithy, still able to unleash further wickedness on mankind. As in divination, the crucial overall motif is sacrifice, an act that guarantees the involvement of gods (subjects that we know nothing about). Furthermore, all other techniques developed out of this founding, primordial technique—geomancy, necromancy, the invocation of spirits, and so forth—evoke this original, sacrificial technique of offering a body for exchange (Girard 1977, 1989). When stealing a piece of property, the Trickster gives himself up to be possessed, or sometimes offers a third party in exchange. Most often, he is the only survivor.

Pleasing gods with confusing diversions, from music and dance to the offer of sacrificial victims, the smith uses all things that nourish the spirit and help build sufficient strength to compel and channel cosmic energies according to his will. He calls upon divine aid for creation, with the guaranteed result of material multiplication (Walker 1958). A more recent example is Blake's Preface to *Milton*, where the command "Bring me my bow of burning gold," as the "New Jerusalem" will be built "among these dark Satanic mills" (Blake 2007), implies absolute acceptance of whatever happens to oneself on the voyage toward making gold (or toward becoming gold, as alchemy came to imply not just the transformation of matter but self-transformation, expressing total subordination to events higher than oneself for the sake of reaching the stage of enlightenment) and also, significantly, directly links the old and new "industrial revolutions." This subservient will is deconstructive, tossing identities into an erratic, wobbly liminal nothingness. It intensively cultivates technology as an end and beginning in itself. The point where beginning and end touch is by definition the apocalypse, and in fact technology operates inside the apocalypse, stressing from the start the outlook toward the end, thus implying a necessary return to the beginning.

Man-Made Liminality: The Alchemical Opus

It is often taken for granted that splitting, breaking, denominating, or fracturing identities aids the pursuit of growth, multiplication, and wealth.

Classical Antiquity considered this knowledge forbidden, for it necessarily launches an infinite reproduction of identity splits in a chain reaction, as an actor continues to generate residual splits into identical units, into infinity. Leading to a self-propagating spiral, or setting in motion a schismogenic process, this chain reaction of identity splitting releases more energy than any other action taking place in reality, where lines, borders, and constraints exist. The problem is that whereas growth and wealth are at once perceptible, the corresponding sense of dissolution is not. The technological development of identity split machinery first appeared with metallurgy in industry and with alchemy in philosophy. Chinese philosophy from its inception developed in tandem with alchemy (Chikashige 1936; Needham 1983; Sivin 1968) via the connection with concrete performance of a ritual technology, helping to transform matter and ignoring the Greek concern for *arrheton*. Comparable only to the Babylonian case, Chinese thinkers attributed a vast cosmological significance to this technology, believing they were purging the natural world of its impurities and thereby redeeming it (Riesebrodt 2009; Asad 1993). Around 600 BC in China, alchemists, a peculiar class of image-makers, came to see transformation processes as an imitation of nature.

As a new discipline, alchemy later passed through many transformations, but identity change remained at the forefront. Gold was considered a paradisical metal, and its successful production, or the artificial creation of a like image, necessarily evoked its connotation with the promised land flowing with milk and honey, the land of youthfulness (*ver*, virile, virtue, *virgo*; see also Hungarian *ver* [beat], *vér* [blood], *veres* [red], *férfi* [man]), the blossoming green garden full of virtuous men and virgins. As Hesiod (2006) said about the golden race: they "lived like gods, with carefree heart / remote from toil and misery" (*Works and Days*, line 109–13). The alchemic operation for achieving this real or metaphoric golden state consists of forcing the participating elements to undergo a repeated cycle of dissolutions and coagulations, leaving the elements to die in solitude. The transformation dissolves the original identity into the *prima materia* that alchemy defined as the original chaos; continuing with the alchemical vocabulary, this material is then "coagulated" into a new, purer form. Each cycle of dissolution and coagulation further purifies or sublimates the substance so that opposites are reconciled, or their differences united, through a cycle of separation and conjunction.

The addition of alchemy to the discoveries of metallurgy gave this technical enterprise a theoretical underpinning. Not only does the transformative process make the imperfect perfect, in the alchemist's view, but the inanimate metal also acquires the qualities of growth—a multiplication achieved by marrying male and female ores, whereby new metals are born. Such bipolarities have been an obsession in the sciences in the last several centuries, along with the contemporary fads of deconstructivism and its mate constructionism. Thus the oppressed and the ruling class, the raw and the cooked, the female and male, the savage and the civilized, purity and danger compete for the attention of the scientifically oriented mind, which quantifies and restructures their identities. This cultivation of reason has probably the same effectivity as its metallurgical model source: it diverts attention away from the real, proliferating an "unreal class of image making craft" that evidently proved (e.g., see Marxism as a "scientific method") that reuniting opposites after death produces only matter that is ignorant, deluded, and wasteful not only of knowledge.

The wholeness of identity, with its decency and agreeable appearance, cannot be compromised by an alchemical multiplication at a mass level where creation is a product of inflicted pain. Alchemically, during the liminal stage matter loses its properties and longs to become equal with its opposite. This is possible because a natural communion binds the elements of the world together: "All is one," as Heraclitus said. René Girard (1977) theorized this type of regression, where differences gradually diminish until a complete leveling takes place, as a mimetic crisis, introducing the concept "undifferentiation." In this stage, understandably, the elements are without their identity. Matter has lost its form, disturbing the relationship between form and matter and generating the conditions for the successful imitation of another, new model. Yet how exactly this pain/suffering motif is a side effect of metallurgy—that is, an artificial, man-made creation—was never really realized. The first creation evidently involved neither division of elements or bipolarities, nor death, rebirth, union, or transformation, as there was no matter before creation. Consequently, pain and suffering are needed only when the creation is secondary (artificial, manmade, constructed, modeled, forced, or imitated), in order to form a relationship with the divine, which produces identities through emptiness and has a handicapped mind that does not work normally, being deprived of agreeability.

This is why alchemists, despite referring frequently to Plato, hardly hint at the pain of being (and still less at the fact that Plato authored no dialogue concerning alchemy). The other frequently cited author, Hermes Trismegistos, was considered very ancient during the Renaissance, but in the sixteenth century the *Corpus Hermeticum* was identified as an eclectic mix of Egyptian, Greek, Roman, and Gnostic thought dating to the first few centuries of the Common Era. The philosophical schools amalgamated in the hermetic writings included Neoplatonism, Gnosticism, and

Stoicism, each influenced by the problem-setting of Plato's *Timaeus* (itself a beautiful conglomerate of pre-Socratic ideas) concerning the pattern of all living creatures having body and soul, the four element theory, the circle characterized by conversion under the influence of heat, the world soul or *anima mundi,* and the relationship between form and matter. Aristotle's ideas about the natural subterranean formation of metals and minerals — as espoused in his *Meteorology* — became popular with alchemists who, believing that their art imitated creation, established Aristotle's treatise as a text on the artificial production of metals and other related matters. Therefore the most widely accepted theoretical account of the multiplication of metals and minerals is traceable to the pre-Socratics, Plato, and Aristotle, who also discovered the metamorphosis of interacting elements (e.g., smelted vapors or exhalation), even though the Greeks before Archimedes had rejected the artificial fracturing of identities. Complementing such concerns in the parallel development of alchemy was the idea of the Earth's womb as a furnace for creation, which inspired the development of the "sulfur-mercury-salt" theory that every living thing consists of these three elements. However, this theory did not mention ancient authors' lack of reference to pain and suffering as the supposed underlying structure of everything living.

Pain and suffering was instead a new invention, one that followed the practices of metal making. Its procedures were theorized as follows. Alchemy attached a methodological significance to each particular ore, which was thought to receive its particular character from a particular planet linked to heat, cold, moisture, or dryness: the Sun is linked to gold, the Moon to silver, Jupiter to tin, Venus to copper, Mars to iron, Saturn to lead, Mercury to quicksilver. But the most common elements of all metals are Sulphur (male, the planet Saturn — the damp, cold, and slimy) and Quicksilver (female, the planet Mercury), whose union produces a child: the metallic stone. Alchemists speculated on and interpreted pre-Socratic notions for their own needs. For instance, "the whole is eternal . . . and homogenous, and has no space within it," or "for it is not possible for anything to exist for ever unless it all exists" (Melissus, as in Kirk and Raven 1957: 299–300).

Moreover, in Anaxagoras, according to Theophrastus, "the solid things come into being out of their own form;" "warm becomes cold and what is cold warm; that which is hard turns soft and what is soft hard;" "A thing that is as cold or as warm as we are does not either warm us or cool us by its approach, nor can we recognize sweetness or bitterness by their like; rather we know cold by warm, fresh by salt and sweet by bitter in proportion to our deficiency in each" (Kirk and Raven 1957: 394). Furthermore, "if they were real they would not change" — or, as Zeno of Elea stated, "there will always be other things between the things that are, and yet others between those others" (Fr. 3, in Kirk and Raven 1957: 288) — right up to Leibniz, the inventor of infinitesimal calculus (Yates 1976), and his reflections on why things exist, rather than not.

This thinking is a fairly honest outcome of a state of mind focused on suffering in existence, on alienated living in a fractured world that over-whelms existence with an ever increasing terror of eliminating identities and generating new differences. Deception, cheating, lies, hatred, desires, and vilification became the customary attributes of initiation rituals that form and transform the senses through enclosure in a nursing bottle. Such rituals play with feelings as subservient agents, selling the bogey-man's sack about the quintessence of being in sensuality, and treacher-ously reducing the power that maintains things' integrity. As the *Corpus Hermeticum* cynically put it, "there is no necessity that every living being should conserve its identity" (quoted in Yates 1964: 243). Hence liminal-ity alone will reign over an imperialism where fabricated harmony and peace are indifferent to self-support. This space recalls the Habermasian public sphere. Recognizable within it are not only Durkheim's social facts and social solidarity but the alliances of Lévi-Strauss as well, all striving to fulfill the immense potential for the united, universal union that looked very impressive in a delirious enthusiasm.

Figure 4.3 illustrates the "alchemical marriage of the opposites." Hermes/ Mercurius stands in the middle, clothed in women's garments to reveal the perfect alchemical union: his incarnation as Hermaphrodite. He is surrounded by six figures representing the planets and thus compos-ing a cosmic order. The planet Mercury is the closest to the Sun, hence to gold; but as quicksilver, Hermes/ Mercurius dissolves gold, extinguish-ing its sun-like brilliance. Mercurius is also the servant of the opus: *servus* or *cervus fugitivus*, the fugitive slave or stag. Mercurius is base as *prima materia* (chaos), but also sublime as *lapis philosophicum* (the philosopher's stone): he is the *psychopompos* (guide of souls) and the guide for good luck, but also for ruin, being dual-natured (see Goethe's *Faust*; Goethe studied Paracelsus). He is *aqua permanens* (eternal water), or *argentus vivum* (the water); he is also the serpent *mercurialis*, as with the help of the caduceus, Mercurius unites two natures (male and female, sun and moon) in the alchemical vessel. From this vessel emerges the *filius hermaphroditus* (their hermaphrodite son).

There is no surprise in an initiation ceremony or a wedding (Augé 1995), which always goes through the same levels, steps, and stages. Like-wise, the alchemical opus of the chemical wedding (Yates 1972) also goes through the same mechanical steps: separation, or sublimation, descent,

Figure 4.3. Alchemical Union. *Source:* C. G. Jung, *Psychology and Alchemy* (1989: 64)

and distillation; liminality, or calcination, solution, coagulation, and fixation; and reaggregation, or creation. The process of purifying or refining a precious metal has affinities with the creation of the philosopher's stone (*basanos*; see Foucault 2001), that is, the effective gold or divine love essence that can transform mere mortals into divine beings. The most important aspect of this transformation is the benefit derived from the divine or from the acquisition of divine powers during unification with the void (the nothing). Postclassical Greek terms this *anastasis* (resurrection), the turning of human savages into full humans in the manner of, for example, the Egyptian sun god Seth, who brought water, light, and life to the world. The alchemists were ultimately concerned with the unification of different substances, which was often called the "marriage" between feminine and masculine qualities, or the reconciliation of opposites. This "marriage"of opposites would ultimately attain the goal of the opus, namely, the production of gold and its metaphysical equivalent. However, such a wedding need not always take the form of a direct union; it can also occur through a third, mediating principle. This is mercury, the *prima materia* or seminal matter, again composed of both female and male (androgynous, hermaphrodite). The god Hermes is the personification of the metal mercury, and in fact alchemy catches and imprisons the god, intending to make him enter into the transformation process to serve the master of ceremonies. The entrance of the divine brings about a new unity, one truth again, participating in an eternal machine based on pure, lucid calculation of sacrifice and tricking beneficiaries out of benefits.

Figure 4.4 depicts the god Hermes, reborn after the successful accomplishment of the alchemic process. After the liminal phase, in which the god was conjured, hunted, caught, imprisoned, and made to suffer, comes the stage of reconciliation, the return to order. Here Hermes/Mercurius is caught in the circle, unable to escape: in the egg, in his new existence, he stands on the sun and the moon. Birds betoken spiritualization; the Sun warms the vessel. The god's mobility is reduced, he appears to exist in a state of queasiness in a tyrannical "tower."

Mercury/Hermes is known as the glue that bonds the female and the male together. Alchemists and neo-Platonists denoted the union, reconciliation, or reaggregation of such basic substances (male and female, fire and water) into an "ultimate love" using a particular word: "conversion," defined as a new interpretation of qualities (Hadot 1993). In conversion, the forces within previously divided properties are reconciled in a new state that can, through an epiphany, heal all the diseases of the

Figure 4.4. Hermes in the Egg. Source: C. G. Jung, *Psychology and Alchemy* (1989: 64)

world (Agricola 1950). As shown by the imprisoned god who serves man through his own death, pain, and suffering, as in the Hermes in the Egg motif, this is not simply an alchemical symbolism. It has further significance in crosscurrents of knowledge such as gnosis, where we encounter the idea of salvation from the tormenting radical dualisms of existence. In salvation, god and man unite through a further turn: the release of the inner divine from the bonds of the world, and his return to its native realm of light. Though already present in Gnostic thinking (Jonas 1963; Voegelin 1987), this idea received its full theoretical statement in Enlightenment philosophy, which proffered morbid mental excitement to the paradoxically irascible and enslaved. Voltaire, Diderot, Lessing, and Rousseau offered a new model to follow in the mean-spirited misanthropy of the revolutionary, the sensualist who saves the world. As Koselleck (1988) has shown, their relentless critique undermined the sociopolitical order and its norms, turned the private into the public and, thus out of tune, created a new syncretism, as captured in Tarde's concept of "passionate interests" (Latour and Lépinay 2009).

The small illustration in Figure 4.5, again from Jung's book, illustrates the alchemist-made encapsulated unity. Souls escape from a serpent's burning body yet remain in the vessel, thus readied for stamping. The matter is heated and cooked in an abnormal, timeless, ambiguous, sacred liminal state. Going a step further than before in examining the way artificially induced liminal situations can facilitate the technological shaping of identities, this image becomes crucial. It shows how the irrationality (death) implicit in liminal incommensurability is ignored by the contemporary

Figure 4.5. Souls Escaping. *Source:* C. G. Jung, *Psychology and Alchemy* (1989: 240)

recognition of liminality, and therefore also by the technological reconstruction of irrational (fractured, as in mathematics) fragments, where precisely the dead matter becomes the very principle of rationality. At this moment, regarded as liberation and enlightenment in *gnosis* (Jonas 1963), existing knowledge is revaluated. The self is left on its own to obtain a new identity that is indifferent to the traditional one, free of prejudice and on the cusp of a new life that is in fact a return to the native realm of light and understanding. However, this secret knowledge from beyond is gained processually, through a technicalized knowledge machine, so its value is commensurable. As an intellectual luminary, the smith extracts as much as he desires from reality, utilizing the knowledge gained through the hole of *arrheton* to make all of us rich and prosperous, though at the price of transforming reality into unreality. Curling up space is surprisingly simple and does not require any quality: it is enough to follow the technological knowledge of extraction of the self-governing capabilities of healthy life.

Conclusion

This chapter has taken one of liminality's most classic applications in a previously unexplored direction. The term liminality was introduced in analysis of rites of passage, rituals that help human beings and communities pass through major moments of transition in their life cycles. Such transitions, especially in the case of initiation rites, can be seen as changes of identity: an adolescent becomes an adult; a single person a spouse; a mere candidate a doctor. Analogous to these rituals, major unstructured moments in the life of a human being or a collectivity can be conceived of as liminal situations. The experience of a particularly significant event can cause an identity change, prepared by the fluidity of the liminal situation.

Such a liminal moment is "unforced," emerging within the context of everyday life as a sudden challenge, crisis or opportunity. However, once knowledge is acquired about the transformative power of liminal situations, that knowledge can also be deployed to purposefully create liminality, undermine a previous, intact identity, and then literally manipulate the human beings entrapped in this precarious state to acquire a new, ready-made identity. This essay argues that this kind of knowledge is characteristic of metallurgy, where the solidity of stones is destroyed to obtain a liquid ore that can then be molded into a fixed shape, and on a massive scale. Given that the theoretical discourse developing around early metallurgy was alchemy, such identity transformation can be considered an alchemical operation. Thus this chapter has explored the genealogy of political alchemy as a transformative technology.

Unlike inanimate stones, human beings put up strong resistance to external efforts to forcibly alter their identity and destroy their integrity. But this resistance can be overcome by manipulative stimulation of the strongest human affective impulse, Eros. Human beings whose desires are artificially stimulated enter a state of deprivation and longing to regain their previous state of unity. Thus they become ready to unify or mingle in ways their previous state of integrity or intactness would not have permitted.

Therefore manipulation of affectivity is a key aspect of liminality, the central way to elicit human beings' willingness to give up previous identities and acquire new, ready-made, homogenized forms. In our times, this mode of transformation dominates and has radically altered the world, all but eliminating the borderline between nature and technology. Every aspect of nature has become technologically copied and mimed, and the strongest moving force of these changes, at once managing and hiding them, is the incorporation of Eros into the mechanism. Thus love is transformed into a technological trick. Eros is the secret of soft, "democratic" technology: it separates, takes away, imitates, substitutes, and steals the genuinely real.

References

Agricola, G. 1950. *De Re Metallica*. Edited by H. C. Hoover and L. H. Hoover. New York: Dover.

Albertus M. 1958. *Libellus de Alchimia*. Edited by S. J. Linden. Cambridge: Cambridge University Press.

Asad, T. 1993. *Genealogies of Religion*. Baltimore, MD: Johns Hopkins University Press.

Augé, M. 1995. *Non-Places: Introduction to an Anthropology of Supermodernity*. London: Verso.

Blake, W. 2007. *The Complete Poems*. Edited by W.H. Stevenson. Harlow: Longman.

Blakely, S. 2006. *Myth, Ritual, and Metallurgy in Ancient Greece and Recent Africa*. Cambridge: Cambridge University Press.

Chikashige, M. 1936. *Alchemy and Other Chemical Achievements of the Ancient Orient*. Tokyo: Rokakuho Uchida.

Détienne, M., and J.-P. Vernant. 1978. *Cunning Intelligence in Greek Culture and Society*. Brighton: Harvester Press.

Forbes, R. J. 1950. *Metallurgy in Antiquity*. Leiden: Brill.

Foucault, M. 1974. *The Order of Things: An Archaeology of the Human Sciences*. London: Routledge.

———. 1982. "The Subject and Power." In *Michel Foucault*, edited by H. Dreyfus and P. Rabinow. Chicago: University of Chicago Press.

———. 2001. *Fearless Speech*. Los Angeles: Semiotext(e).

Gell, A. 1988. "Technology and Magic." *Anthropology Today* 4 (2): 6–9.

Gennep, A. van. 1960. *The Rites of Passage*. Chicago: University of Chicago Press.

Girard, R. 1977. *Violence and the Sacred*. Baltimore, MD: John Hopkins University Press.

———. 1989. *The Scapegoat*. Baltimore, MD: John Hopkins University Press.

Hadot, P. 1993. "Conversion." In *Exercices spirituels et philosophie antique*. Paris: Institut d'études Augustiniennes.

Heidegger, M. 1967. *The Question Concerning Technology and Other Essays*. New York: Harper.

———. 1969. *Identity and Difference*. New York: Harper.

Hesiod. 2007. Theogony; Works and Days; Testimonia. Cambridge, MA: Harvard University Press.

Horvath, A. 2013. "The Fascination with Eros: The Role of Passionate Interests in Communism." *History of the Human Sciences* 21 (5): 79–97.

Horvath, A., and A. Szakolczai. 2013. "The Gravity of Eros in the Contemporary: Introduction to the Special Section." *History of the Human Sciences* 21 (5): 69–78.

Jonas, H. 1963. *The Gnostic Religion*. Boston: Beacon Press.

Jung, C. G. 1989. *Psychology and Alchemy*. London: Routledge.

Kerényi, C. 1980. "I misteri dei Kabiri." In *Miti e misteri*. Turin: Boringhieri.

———. 1986. *Hermes, Guide of Souls: The Mythologem of the Masculine Source of Life*. New York: Spring Publications.

Kieckhefer, R. 1998. *Forbidden Rites: A Necromancer's Manual of the Fifteenth Century*. University Park: Pennsylvania State University Press.

Kirk, G. S., and J. E. Raven. 1957. *The Presocratic Philosophers*. Cambridge: Cambridge University Press.

Koselleck, R. 1988. *Critique and Crisis: Enlightenment and the Pathogenesis of Modern Society*. Oxford: Berg.

Latour, B., and V. A. Lépinay. 2009. *The Science of Passionate Interests: An Introduction to Gabriel Tarde's Economic Anthropology*. Chicago: University of Chicago Press.

Linden, S. 2003. *The Alchemy Reader*. Cambridge: Cambridge University Press.

Mumford, L. 1967. *Technics and Human Development*, vol. 1, *The Myth of the Machine*. New York: Harcourt.

Needham, J. 1983. *Science and Civilization in China*, vol. 5, *Chemistry and Chemical Technology*. Cambridge: Cambridge University Press.

Parr, G. 1958. *Man, Metals, and Modern Magic*. Cleveland, OH: American Society for Metals.

Pizzorno, A. 1987. "Politics Unbound." In *Changing Boundaries of the Political*, edited by C. S. Maier. Cambridge: Cambridge University Press.

———. 2007. "Rational Choice." In *Handbook of the Philosophy of Science: Philosophy of Anthropology and Sociology*, edited by S. P. Turner and M. W. Risjord. New York: Elsevier.

———. 2010. "The Mask: An Essay." *International Political Anthropology* 3 (1): 5–28.

Plato. 1987. *The Statesman; Philebus; Ion*. London: Heinemann.

Popov, A. 1933. "Consecration Ritual for a Blacksmith Novice among the Yakuts." *The Journal of American Folklore* 46 (181): 257–71.

Radin, P. 1972. *The Trickster: A Study in American Indian Mythology*. New York: Schocken.

Riesebrodt, M. 2009. *The Promise of Salvation: A Theory of Religion*. Chicago: University of Chicago Press.

Sivin, N. 1968. *Chinese Alchemy: Preliminary Studies*. Cambridge, MA: Harvard University Press.

Thomassen, B. 2014. *Liminality and the Modern: Living through the In-between*. Farnham Surrey: Ashgate.

Turner, V. 1967. "Betwixt and Between: The Liminal Period in Rites de Passage." In *The Forest of Symbols*. Ithaca, NY: Cornell University Press.

———. 1969. *The Ritual Process*. Hawthorne, NY: Aldine de Gruyter.

Voegelin, E. 1987. *The New Science of Politics*. Chicago: University of Chicago Press.
Walker, D. P. 1958. *Spiritual and Demonic Magic: From Ficino to Campanella*. London: Warburg Institute.
Yates, F. 1964. *Giordano Bruno and the Hermetic Tradition*. London: Routledge.
———. 1972. *The Rosicrucian Enlightenment*. London: Paladine Books.
———. 1976. *The Art of Memory*. Chicago: University of Chicago Press.

Chapter 5

Critical Processes and Political Fluidity
A Theoretical Appraisal

Michel Dobry

ritical events and processes, such as revolutions, political crises, breakdowns, or transitions, seem at first sight to elude the analytical grasp of "normal" social science. Puzzled by their liminal characteristics, their unexpectedness, and the unpredictability of their outcomes, scholars tend to assign a special epistemological, if not ontological, status to these events and processes. Such scholars see critical events and processes as simultaneously requiring both special methodological treatment and "appropriate" theoretical tools and perspectives. This essay rejects that position as a major impediment to understanding such critical phenomena or processes. The purpose of this chapter is to outline an alternative approach whose methodological orientation, as I have called it in preceding works, is the *hypothesis of continuity*. This alternative approach suggests that to grasp phenomena and processes that we spontaneously tend to regard as extraordinary (i.e., outside the universe of ordinary objects of the social sciences), we actually have to think about them, despite their liminal characteristics, with the same viewpoint, questions, and intellectual instruments that we apply to critical social phenomena that a priori seem much more "normal."

The hypothesis of continuity is a principal basis of the theoretical perspective that the following discussion relies on: the theory of fluid conjunctures (Dobry 1983, 1986). The aim of this discussion is twofold. First, I will elucidate why and how mainstream approaches to critical events or

Notes for this chapter begin on page 107.

processes lead to real dead ends at the level of understanding—or, from another angle, why we need radical transformation in the perspective we adopt when analyzing such phenomena. Second, I will lay out the content of this transformation as well as several of its implications. This should make clear that the continuity perspective, far from being paradoxical, is a necessary condition for understanding what can be considered specific or particular to such seemingly extraordinary phenomena.

The Temptation of Methodological Exceptionalism

To start, I will examine two intellectual pitfalls that the social sciences encounter when they approach empirical fields of the type described above. The more significant of these pitfalls lies in the traditional opposition between objectivist and subjectivist or phenomenological approaches to the social world and its multiple variants. In particular, I have in mind the opposition between "structures" on the one hand, and "events" or "action" on the other, independent of the detailed meanings attached to each of these diverse notions. When confronted with critical events and processes such as "revolutions," "political crises," or "transitions," the social sciences are constantly deluded by what I have called the *heroic fallacy* (Dobry 1983). Roughly, this fallacy is that the normal social sciences approaches—that is, approaches combining analysis of social structures and their effects with causal or "deterministic" explanations—are naturally pertinent, suitable, or "adapted" to contexts, situations, or periods of stability of political regimes or institutionalized configurations; whereas critical events and processes, revolutions, or political crises, by their nature, require a completely different type of approach focused on actors' choices, strategic calculations, or decision making.[1]

Although advocates of this position do not necessarily regard such events and processes as social or political pathologies (though the idea lingers in social science discourse), they do not hesitate to associate the rejection of "normal"—that is, structure-oriented—social science methodology with phenomena that are perceived and conceived as being outside the realm of "normal" life or "normal" workings of the political and social systems in question. Furthermore, as this position's reliance on methodological discontinuity seems to attribute some essence or nature to such phenomena, it is permanently burdened with a range of essentialist assumptions about the social world.

The heroic fallacy has been a central feature of the immense bodies of literature on the "great revolutions," crises of "political development," and transitions to democracy since the late 1980s. Its ascendancy is most puzzling, however, especially given the great variety of sociological "traditions" or "paradigms" said to inform the works it appears in. It is remarkably tangible in writings that define themselves as objectivist, such as those following different variants of "structural functionalism" (e.g., Chalmers Johnson 1964; Almond, Flangan, and Mundt 1973), as well as in works focused on action or rational choice based on methodological individualism and game theory, as in the case of the seminal "transitology" conceptualizations of O'Donnell and Schmitter (1986), or Przeworski (1986). Perhaps even more significantly, the heroic fallacy is also found outside the academic realm. It is in fact the ordinary viewpoint or rationalization of modern revolutionaries such Lenin and Trotsky, who saw revolutionary situations and their own role in them through the lenses of a taken-for granted opposition between objective and subjective factors of revolution,[2] and conceived of revolutionary situations as moments where subjective factors dominate.

Such imagery may certainly constitute a useful and perhaps necessary illusion for actors' practice. But in terms of knowledge—which, I suggest, should obey a different social logic—the intellectual attitude of the heroic fallacy leads to a methodological decision burdened with momentous, uncontrollable consequences (which, as we shall see, are not exclusively methodological themselves). Dealing with critical events and processes, the scholar will deliberately abandon any sustained empirical and theoretical interest in "structures" and what they are, potentially become, or could produce during critical periods.

Complementarily, and in line with the above, such a scholar will simultaneously conceive of actors' choices and decisions as somehow "underdetermined" and, most often, as simply eluding the causalities or determinations of "normal social science methodology" aimed at accounting for actors' actions or behavior. To put it differently, the heroic fallacy is fatal to intelligibility of the social word, as it entails a double loss: it first leads to ignorance about the fate of "structures" in critical periods, the transformations structures can be subjected to, and these transformations' possible effects; and second, it precludes identification of the distinctive features of actors' choices, decisions, and calculations, and their relation to "normal" periods. Is it absolutely certain, for instance, that in critical situations actors' calculations are much less determined, socially constrained, or shaped than in "normal" periods?

The Attraction of Outcomes

The second intellectual pitfall differs considerably from the first, at first blush: it refers to the immediate aspect that seems to link the "event" to its outcome. This connection seems a priori beyond doubt, so it becomes natural for the scholar to approach political crises, revolutions, or transitions by considering the peculiarities of the results of such events or processes as the point of departure of the *explicandum*, or what is to be explained. But as I will show, thinking of critical events and processes from the perspective of their outcomes is a mistake whose effects damage the understanding of these events at least as much as the heroic fallacy does.

It is easy indeed to understand one reason for social scientists' and historians' fascination with the outcome: once it has happened (and only then, *after* its occurrence), an outcome—for instance, the Nazis' seizure of power—"matters." Given its significant impact on the fates of individuals, groups, or even societies, the outcome can produce not only dramatic and momentous effects in the short run, but also long-term consequences that the scholar may be induced to promote to the dignity of "structural effects." Though at first sight this may appear somewhat plausible, it is nonetheless impossible to accept the claim that an outcome and its particularity can constitute the explanatory key to the processes or events in which it originated. In other words, we have to avoid the illusion in which outcomes summarize, mirror, or encompass the processes that produced them. Yet this is not only the standard thought process but even, I dare say, the "normal" procedure used by scholars. The outcome casts a spell on interpretation, in ways both irresistible and legitimate. Both the consequences and the forms of this intellectual pitfall are multiple.

The outcome most often governs the construction of historical intrigue:[3] more precisely, it suggests how to cut out—to select—the facts, which are arrived at by regressive analysis starting from the peculiarities of the outcome (e.g., a great revolution, the seizure of power by fascists, or the victory of democracy). Careful examination reveals that the selection of facts is always a way of making these facts converge on the outcome. This is especially so for approaches involving the "natural history" of revolutions, of the type provided by Crane Brinton (Brinton 1965). Here, the revolutionary event or process is connected to a particular historical trajectory, a sequence of successive phases that eventually entail a "great revolution" such as that of 1789 or 1917. Thus, "preliminary signs" betoken the revolution to come (whose "symptoms" stretch from accelerated economic growth to intellectuals' "transfer of allegiance"); an ensuing phase of "fever" corresponds to the seizure of power by "moderates"; in the subsequent phase of "crisis," the radicals come to power, unleashing the Terror; and in the final phase of stabilization (convalescence), society reaches a kind of acceptable status quo, a Thermidor. An analogous analytical scheme operates when scholars aim to explain the differences between different outcomes. For each category of outcome (e.g., the break-down or emergence of democracy, the rise of fascism, or the extrication from communism), they try to identify a single trajectory, historical path, or one sequence of phases that would be specific to this category of out-come.[4] A further difficulty arises from the intention to elucidate historical trajectories—similarly presupposed to be specific to peculiar outcomes such as democracy, fascism, or communism—that cover periods of not just several months or years, but several centuries (see, e.g., Barrington Moore's very illuminating—though quite problematic, from the perspec-tive applied here—*Social Origins of Dictatorship and Democracy* [1966]).

Thinking about critical events or processes from the viewpoint of their outcome is less innocuous than it seems, mainly because such an attitude relies upon more or less robust historicist presuppositions (Popper 2004). Essentially, this perspective refuses to accept that within the event, the unfolding of processes can turn toward one outcome or another only at the margin. Since the outcome is supposed to ascribe its very meaning to the event, this position cannot admit that very "small causes" can result in very "big effects" and may even reverse "structural trends." The scholar's focus on the outcomes of events leads simply to ignorance of the—very frequent—contingency of these results. Thus it is forgotten that such out-comes emerge from unnecessary, accidental co-occurrences of multiple series of determinations and causal chains that are separate, heteroge-neous, and very often autonomous with regard to each other. The intellec-tual logic of this historicist perspective posits that processes or events that entail particular outcomes have a similarly particular "nature," different from the "nature" of events or processes that resulted in other types of outcomes.[5]

Accompanying these errors is a further problem: our common vision of different outcomes and differences between them is nothing but a stylized systematization of the scattered remainders of reality embedded or in-scribed in categories of ordinary language. Obviously, these categories—revolutions, political crises, and breakdowns, as well as mutinies, revolts, and so on—interest us because they are meaningful for actors involved in such events (and also central to the struggles to name or label these events). However, it is hazardous to see these categories as starting points and principle determinants in the selection of facts, and to thereby allow them to become a privileged instrument of research, as the mainspring of the identification of causal links. To do so is to borrow the haziest elements of ordinary language: unclear frontiers, implicit intellectual schemes, and confused typologies. Furthermore, we are tempted to presume that behind nouns we can discover corresponding substances, essences, or "nature," and to associate each noun designating a type of outcome with a "nature" that we suppose to be particular to the processes that have resulted in this outcome. Finally, one should note, these ordinary taxonomies and categorizations most often proceed from the outcomes entailed by the processes or events thus categorized. This circular movement contributes to the persistent hold such taxonomies and categories have, not only on mundane representations of social reality, but also—and with far more serious consequences—on scholarly representations.

Laws *of* History and Laws *in* History

Here we are dealing with the manifestation, in Bachelard's (1967) terms, of an authentic *fonds d'erreurs* or set of fallacies—a dense and systematic (in terms of its effects) but also incoherent network of representations, presuppositions, and causal imageries. The only solutions are radical: to account for critical events and processes, scholars have no choice but to discard the entirety of this set of fallacies. The remedy I propose to overcome the fascination with the outcomes of "great historical events" (and probably also not-so-great events) may surprise many, but I cannot see another: as a methodological decision, we have to try to forget or set aside the outcomes of critical events or processes, for the time being. In other words, to explain such events we must never undertake to "explain" their outcome but should instead construct the "enigma" to be solved differently.

To this end, the theory of fluid conjunctures (Dobry 1983, 1986) deals with "the event" by replacing the focus on its outcome with sustained attention to, so to speak, what the critical events or processes are made of. To cope with the inextricable, complex tangle of junctions and collisions among multiple and heterogeneous historical causal chains, this theory attempts to identify classes of situations or configurations of interdependence, enabling us to think about systems of constraints that constitute different types of logics of situation (or situational logics) that impose themselves on the perceptions, anticipations, calculations, and practices of actors who act in the "event," thereby shaping it.

In the intellectual climate of "postmodern" blurring or softening of the social sciences' critical requirements, talk of classes of situations or different situational logics might appear provocative. Indeed, in face of the chaotic historicity of "social facts," it might—rightly—be taken to signal the very possibility of identifying (and explaining) certain regularities or sets of regularities. Here, however, we are not dealing with any kind of regularities: despite the ever-present temptation to formulate "laws *of* history" (i.e., laws of historical development—precisely the type that are propagated willy-nilly by those who aim to "explain" the outcomes of critical processes or events), this perspective pursues the entirely different ambition of identifying the workings of "laws *in* history" (to put an alternative spin on Paul Veyne's [1971] terminology).[6] Discussing the premises or presuppositions of this perspective in the social sciences is of little use; ultimately, it will be judged by its fruitfulness, in which respect my strong impression is that pessimism is unwarranted.

Some particular lines of this perspective are well illustrated by referring to an author who may appear somewhat "exotic," and to a class of events quite dissimilar from those I have outlined so far. The social sciences should be interested in Clausewitz's thought primarily because the specific object of *Vom Kriege* (*On War*) consists of a particular class of situational logic. By no means is Clausewitz's famous formula "war is the continuation of political relations by other means" the key element in his conceptualization. It lies rather in the combination of this somewhat trivial formula with another, more forceful, proposition that can be restated as follows: once war, or armed confrontation between two political units, has broken out—once it is here, and regardless of the political determinants that have brought it about—its protagonists are caught up in a particular logic of situation whether they like it or not, and whatever their aims or intentions. This logic, which Clausewitz calls the grammar of war, envelops and constrains the protagonists. Its central feature is that it confronts them with the possibility of a rise to the extremes of violence. Clausewitz identifies this characteristic by means of an explicit idealization, namely, "absolute war," which, though it never actually exists, helps to explain reality (Clausewitz 1955). In Clausewitz's perspective, the possibility of the rise to extremes constrains not only the protagonists of wars intended to destroy the enemy, but also the protagonists of wars of a "second kind," that is, wars with limited objectives or aims, despite precisely these limited objectives. This particular dynamic cannot be found in other classes of "critical" processes or events.

The Autonomy of the Event

Clausewitz's way of thinking can also help us to grasp another aspect of the discussion at hand: if war is, as he argues, a simple continuation of political relationships, then it emerges out of the very diverse political aims pursued by states or their governments. Yet, as I pointed out, the essential aspect is not the isolated formula. Because of the situational logic that engulfs its protagonists, war tends to develop logics of its own, independent of its original political end, cause, or determinant. In other words, war tends to take off, to become independent from the conditions of its genesis. Thus the "grammar" of war burdens its protagonists with a constraining social logic, regardless of the diverse causes, political ends, motives, and historical paths that lead to each particular war. Clausewitz's intuition is, in my view, highly consequential. This is so primarily because this intuition effectively undermines one of the bases of all forms of historicist reasoning, in that it encourages us to reexamine all that the social sciences—in both recent developments and older research traditions— could expect from the elucidation, unveiling, or rediscovery of the historical conditions of the genesis of the phenomena in question. Trying to unveil what was hidden or repressed by the "amnesia of the genesis"—a banal type of social process whose existence is evidently undeniable—is often considered an attempt to decipher the sociological truth of the event that allegedly resulted from it.

This is why extreme prudence is warranted regarding the often taken-for-granted idea that "explaining" an event comes down to identifying its etiology. To put it bluntly: the etiological illusion provides the characteristic shape for the designation *before* the event—be it a political crisis or a revolution—of some vaguely plausible "cause," whereby the event is explained by some frustration (relative or absolute), disequilibrium, suffering, anomie, exploitation, alienation, discontent, or the like. What is to be discovered in crises is not what occurred, for instance, in the clashes between police and Parisian students in the week of 6–11 May 1968, or in the demonstrations in Leipzig and Prague in the autumn of 1989. These "facts" are perceived and conceived as transparent, free of mystery. In other words, they constitute the "surface" or "froth" of the events. The goal of discovery is supposed to reside in more profound, less visible facts deemed more important—more "determinant"—that would explain precisely "what actually happened." These factors or causes are presumed to be located ahead of such events and also, most often, to be external to these very events.

My argument here is not to contest that such types of "facts" may exist before our events (though it would be wrong to assume that they can be solidly established in all cases: this is certainly not the case for the "causes" that are generally attributed to May 1968 in France or to the "revolutions" of 1989 in Eastern and Central Europe).[7] It concerns primarily, at least as to my immediate purpose, the construction of the research enigma. This refers to the lack of scholarly interest in what actually "happens" in the event and, simultaneously, in the event's—possible—autonomy in relation to what actually made it emerge—that is, in the event's own internal dynamics.

The Plasticity of Structures

At this point, I must return to the opposition or polarity between structure and action. The heroic fallacy prevents identification of precisely the plasticity of structures—their sensitivity to mobilizations or actors' tactics and moves. This is indeed a major contribution of the theory of fluid conjunctures, for what is at stake is the possibility of thinking about certain classes of events and processes in terms of specific conditions or, better, specific states of structures of the social system in which these mobilizations spread.[8] Today everyone agrees that matter is found in different states (solid, gas, or liquid). The phenomena that we call social "structures" and more generally institutions and social relations, even though they may be strongly "objectified" or institutionalized, are not necessarily more solid or stable than matter. Structures and social relations can likewise experience transformations of their states and therefore experience different states.[9]

Let me go into more detail. The theory of fluid conjunctures stresses one fundamental feature, which is undoubtedly the one with the most fruitful empirical and theoretical implications. I call this feature the process, or the tendency, toward the *desectorization* of the social space. To understand it, we have to remember that complex systems (which constitute the domain of "validity" or pertinence of this theory, and which, as is well known, have not existed at all times), in their routine state or condition, are differentiated into multiple social spheres, "fields," or sectors that are autonomous with regard to others and strongly institutionalized. Furthermore, complex systems are endowed with social logics that are specific to each of them—that is, with logics different from those that are specific to other sectors—and that also tend to be auto-referential. "Crises" associated with multi-sectoral mobilizations (meaning competitive mobilizations that are localized simultaneously in several social spheres) must be analyzed as processes of desectorization of the social space, given that these conjunctures tend strongly to reduce sectoral autonomy (and sometimes even bring about autonomy's collapse), at least for the sectors affected by the mobilizations. This desectorization is particularly tangible in the collapse of sectoral borders and increasing vulnerability to tactical actions and stakes that are external to the local social logics. Similarly, it also implies that previously closed enclaves of arenas of competition and regulation (e.g., parliamentary arenas) are now open to the different social sectors or fields. In these situations, the noticeable mobility of stakes—so disconcerting for both the protagonists of such crises and their observers—stems largely from the loosening of the strong connection that, during routine conjunctures, underpins the relationships between certain sectoral arenas and certain types of stakes.

Desectorization is also evident in sudden, visible breakdowns of institutionalized temporalities or sectoral rhythms (sometimes leading scholars to analyze these phenomena carelessly in terms of the "synchronization" of such rhythms). Modifying the angle of observation only slightly, we discover that sector-specific social logics cease to function as reference points, tools of perception, evaluations of the efficiency of different lines of action, or definitions of situations for the actors present in these social sectors. In other words, sectoral logics' ascendancy—their hold on the calculations of these crises' protagonists—ebbs away. I shall return to this discussion below, after first introducing two other features of fluid conjunctures that strongly influence these calculations. The first is the abrupt occurrence of what we may, for want of a better expression, call processes of *de-objectivation*, in which previously stable parts of social reality and particular institutions lose "objectivity." The second feature corresponds to the emergence of a broader scope of interdependence that takes the place of the political or social games characterized, in routine conjunctures, by forms of interdependence that are much more local, sectoral, partitioned, and separate from each other.[10] By identifying and explaining these transformations of the states of social and institutional systems (transformations that are, strictly speaking, conjunctural), we dismiss several respected research traditions that—notwithstanding subtle rhetorical precautions—reify "structures" and thus fail to conceive their transformations as anything other than effects or by-products of long-term evolutions.

How to Think about the Calculations of Actors

Having identified the characteristics of fluid conjunctures, we may now measure the intellectual reach of an analysis carried out from the perspective of situational logics. These characteristics, which clearly situate themselves at the macro-sociological level, have multiple implications and effects at the micro-sociological level.[11] For instance, I have shown elsewhere the extent to which these conjunctural transformations of the social space could affect even the identities of actors who are much less "stable" than we usually think (Dobry 1986). A very interesting phenomenon appears at the conjunctures most intensely marked by the irruption of political fluidity, the desectorization of social space, the opening up of sectoral arenas, and the collapse of multiple forms of support that routine sectoral logics provide for our identity constructions: a clear tendency toward making identities unidimensional eventually reduces what Goffman (1961) called the "multiple self" to one single dimension of an individual's social definition, the quality of "aristocrat," "worker," or "true believer." For the purposes of this chapter, I nevertheless view the calculations of individuals, and the way the characteristics of fluid conjunctures tend to shape them, as most useful in illustrating the relationship between the macro- and the micro-sociological.

Here again, it is hardly surprising that the opposition between structures and action emerges as the major intellectual obstacle to comprehension of "what happens" in critical events or processes. We know that certain sociological traditions dislike this question of calculations. Some deny or choose to ignore actors' calculations by caricaturing them, whereas other traditions—no less distortingly—subscribe to a simplistic philosophy of the "decision" or the "free choice." Both actually miss the main point, which becomes clear when the question is reformulated as "How do social actors calculate, when they calculate?" (thus acknowledging that we do not always calculate). "How?" directs our intellectual and empirical curiosity toward intellectual and cognitive tools, instruments of evaluation, markers, clues, and indices, as well as the "rules of the game" that the protagonists of our revolutions, political crises, transitions, or breakdowns resort to when they calculate. This encompasses situations when they evaluate what is worthwhile, risky, or probable; when they tend to anticipate the effects of their own moves and the effects of the actions of their adversaries or competitors; or even when they seek simply to understand or define the situation in which they are caught and must act. From the perspective of the theory of fluid conjunctures, this means above all that it is difficult to dissociate this interest in the tools and the materials of the actors' calculations from the situations, "contexts," configurations, conjunctures, and so on in which these tools are mobilized—or more precisely, from the situational logics that are nested in and that structure these conjunctures.

Here, differences count. Take, for instance, the ideal-typical opposition between routine conjunctures and conjunctures of strong political fluidity. The former concerns political games characterized, in particular, by their sectorization, and the actors' calculations are constrained by social logics that are specific to political fields. The instruments and materials of these calculations derive extensively from such logics: the actors' tactical activity is carried out according to sectoral rules of the game (which are "pragmatic" as well as "normative" or "official"[12]), stable categories of locally legitimate resources, local stakes, and institutionalized temporalities, all of them proper to these different fields or sectors, and also familiar to the actors. The irruption of political fluidity, the desectorization process, and the passage toward a situation of extended interdependence tend to introduce resources, indices, and markers that are external to the logics of such political fields into the calculations while also depriving actors of their routine instruments of calculation and anticipation. Therefore we can acknowledge an element of *structural uncertainty*. In no way does this indicate that actors no longer calculate, or that they are less rational in times of political crisis than in routine conjunctures. It simply means that they are constrained to other ways of managing the ways they calculate. These conjunctures of crisis are characterized especially by an increased importance of *focal points* or situational "saliences" in the formation of their diverse protagonists' anticipations and interpretations.[13]

This property of the fluid conjunctures can help us, firstly, to account for certain seemingly atypical configurations of charisma theoretically conceptualized by Max Weber (1965) and, secondly, to propose a reformulation of this conceptualization. The key point is that charisma can be situational and, therefore, needs to be understood as rigorously relational. For example, in the French political crisis of May 1958, the source of the charismatic quality usually attributed to General de Gaulle apparently was not the "extraordinary qualities" of a charismatic leader that are supposed to attract members of his or her "emotional community." De Gaulle's peculiarity served as a good focal point for antagonistic actors who, though pursuing highly diverse purposes, were also caught in a process of strategic interaction. He represented a point of convergence of these actors' anticipations—a possible solution, but a purely *conjunctural* one that was able to work in that way only at certain moments of the historical episode in question. In contrast to Weber's conceptualization, here the leader's personal acts do not "testify" to his charisma: remarkably, de Gaulle's tactical activities in May 1958 consisted above all in caution, prudence, and silence. Moreover, his emergence as a focal point in the course of the May 1958 crisis did not primarily depend on his followers but was rather the outcome of competitive tactical activities by actors who were entirely external to his "emotional community"—on one side, Algerian militaries or, of course, the rioters in Algiers (who, significantly, were often linked to the anti-Gaullist extreme right), and on the other, socialist leaders, who are no longer true followers of the "charismatic" leader. In reality, the quality at issue here should be analyzed as a genuine *situational charisma* (Dobry 1986; Gaïti, 1998; François 1996).[14]

Some Implications

To conclude, I would like to go beyond the field of critical "events" or processes to tackle some aspects of the impact of the theoretical perspective outlined here. The question of situational charisma touches upon the first of these aspects, which is that the theory of fluid conjunctures invites us to revisit several knowledge attainments that the contemporary social sciences currently take for granted and to shift their understanding quite radically. To illustrate this point I will refer briefly to the case of our conception of political legitimacy and of processes of legitimization. This conception, which I call the standard paradigm (and whose foundations also hark back to Weber), tends to favor a *normative* vision of legitimacy. It locates legitimacy in beliefs, values, or feelings that are held to be products of individuals' socialization; it interprets political legitimacy as a vertical relation between the governed or "dominated" and the governing; and it assumes that a political system's survival or reproduction depends primarily on a high level of legitimacy so defined, and that therefore the delegitimization of this system can only be a long-term process. The perspective outlined above allows for significant modification of this picture. The details are beyond this chapter's scope, so I shall limit myself to certain elements. The perspective introduced in this essay renders intelligible what may be called horizontal forms of legitimization, routine processes of legitimacy production through exchange, or better yet, collusion between multiple elites localized in differentiated, autonomous sectors, spheres, or fields. The mainspring of these exchanges is not necessarily any adhesion to common values or common beliefs. It may be linked to the actors' calculations.[15] Thus, this perspective offers a means to understand why, in defiance of the standard paradigm, political systems can survive weak levels of normative legitimacy among the "dominated." Similarly, within the "crisis" conjunctures one can also identify sudden, very broad processes of delegitimization as sub-products, so to speak, of mobilizations and of the desectorization of the social space. To sum up, this perspective enables us to question an ignored or misunderstood foundation of the standard paradigm that lies in the Weberian opposition between legitimacy and rationality (Dobry 2002).

The second aspect to be tackled concerns somewhat similar implications. The perspective set out here demands—and simultaneously makes

possible—a systematic reorganization of various series of phenomena
dealt with by the social sciences. More precisely, it enables us to bring
closer together, or line up, phenomena and social processes that ordinary
language (and the more or less scholarly typologies and categorizations
that espouse their delimitations) separates or opposes, while also assign-
ing them radically different "natures" or "essences." This remark applies
foremost to understanding most of the phenomena that we call revolutions, political crises, breakdowns, or transitions, as well as to multiple
forms of mobilization and collective action. Yet it also concerns events, historical epochs, or processes with phenomenal appearances or façades that
contrast strongly with those of political crises, and for which a hypothesis
drawing on their specific essence appears to be a priori inevitable, as is
the case with political "scandals," for instance (Dobry 1983; Briquet 1996,
2007; Roussel 2002). Overall, the perspective outlined in this chapter implies alternative construction of the enigma to be solved. It means—contrary to common sense (and, most often, to scholarly common sense) and
to the essentialism it bears—choosing to compare the incomparable (that
is, what is spontaneously perceived and defined as such).

The third aspect concerns what I referred to above under the notion of
situational logics. This is hardly a new intellectual tool in the contemporary social sciences. At first glance, the approach outlined here can appear
quite germane to one of Karl Popper's propositions, despite its mainly
programmatic and epistemological intent. Trying to grasp what exactly
could be a social science—or a sociology—that would approach a reasonably demanding conception of the scientific process, Popper sketched out a
particular procedure, that of "objective understanding." Methodologically
this procedure centered on the need for scholarly reconstruction of what
Popper called logics of situation and, at least in principle, their characteristics. He intended this way of thinking, which he also called situational
analysis, to explain behavior without concessions to psychological factors
while also safeguarding the principle that only concrete, individual actors
can act effectively. Situational analysis consists, in Popper's own terms, of
showing how the individuals' actions are "objectively appropriate" to the
situations in which they act (Popper 1973, 1976). A major weakness in this
conception of situational logics and actors' practices is the very serious or
even insurmountable difficulties that attend any idea of "appropriateness"
or "adequacy" between individual actions or the ways they are produced
on the one hand, and the situations or contexts of action on the other.[16] Yet
I argue that another flaw is more pertinent to the discussion in this chapter.
I refer to the role that Popper, in explaining actors' behavior or observable
practices, assigns to the aims or purposes that actors set themselves, and

to their knowledge and information; or to the aims and purposes that he ascribes to them when he wants to understand or explain—that is, to "rationally reconstruct"—their actions and behaviors.[17]

Actually, Popper's conception tends to divert scholarly interest away from identification of the characteristics of a given class of situations—characteristics that constrain not only the perceptions and actions of individuals but also, in my view, the goals they pursue—and toward the quest for scattered historical elements that could fit the well-known outcomes of the effectively observed actions. The perspective of this essay urges a break with the intentionality at work in Popper's conception of situational logics. My argument is that exploration of situations, their characteristics, and their logics loses a great deal, probably even the essentials, by focusing on goals or purposes pursued by the actors or imagined by the scholar. In fact, reducing the analysis of situational logics to the a posteriori reconstruction of the intentionality of actors—"objective" though it may be—deprives research programs that want to take situational logics seriously of any interest. Such problems of understanding situational logics result also from the temptation—which in principle is perhaps not entirely and consciously Popper's, but which is generally encouraged by the modus operandi he advocates—to abandon any ambition to tear oneself away from the ambiguous and mostly sterile delights of pure description of a unique historical configuration of actors' purposes or interests[18] (and sometimes also, despite Popper's proclaimed principles, of their "motivations"). From this essay's theoretical perspective, analysis of situational logics refers primarily to what these logics are made of—namely, the typical configurations of constraints (and, some would say, opportunities) that impose themselves on the actors caught up in such situations and shape their perceptions and interpretations, regardless of these actors' objectives or the state of their information or knowledge. Only under this condition can situational analysis perhaps achieve its aim of accounting for entire classes of historical situations, processes, events, or phenomena.

Notes

1. A quotation from an early work in "transitology" exemplifies this scholarly attitude: "Normal science methodology does not apply to regime crises and regime transitions in general. Structural explanations for behavior and performance become, as it were, suspended" (Di Palma 1990: 34).

2. Analysis of transition to democracy explicitly takes up this opposition of objective and subjective factors of revolution, most often in the Gramscian variant (see, e.g., Przeworski 1986).

3. For this notion see Veyne 1971.

4. One set of studies on the breakdown of democratic regimes had a major impact on the entire field of contemporary political science (Linz and Stepan 1978). Significantly, the authors of a seminal study in "transitology" (O'Donnell and Schmitter 1986) concluded that they had at least partially failed in their undertaking, in that they were incapable of realizing the central objective set up by Linz's (1978) perspective. Originally, their understanding of transition had been guided by the "theoretical" model of the conceptualization proposed by Linz and Stepan (1978), who talked about processes of breakdown of democratic systems. But from this perspective, O'Donnell and Schmitter failed to identify a sequential pattern that referred to successful processes of transition to democracy. Given the authors' self-assessment, this "failure" constitutes a stimulating result that could even be considered the most important result of O'Donnell and Schmitter's work

5. In some variants, this essentialist understanding of critical events from the viewpoint of their outcomes produces outright vagaries. All the possible mistakes are tidily condensed in the example of the interpretation of the February 1934 crisis of the Third Republic, which French historians until recently considered the dominant one. The birth of the crisis is linked to the Stavisky scandal, a financial crisis that resulted in a month of massive, violent street demonstrations orchestrated by the extreme-right *Ligues*. On 6 February, when the demonstrations targeted the Chambre des deputés (Lower House), the response of the forces of order killed fifteen people and injured another 1,400. The government constituted by the radical (left-moderate) leader Daladier—who on the very evening of 6 February was voted leader of the government by a clear majority in the House—resigned and gave way to a government representing the *Union Nationale*, led by Gaston Doumergue, in which leaders of Rightist parties were heavily represented among the Radicals. This outcome of the crisis enabled the political regime of the Third Republic to survive several more years. The outcome of the regime's survival underpins conclusions historians have drawn on both the "nature" of this event itself and its significance for the "nature" of the authoritarian right in interwar France. Crucially, they have claimed that French society was "allergic" or culturally immune to fascism. Based on the outcome of the crisis, historians deduced in particular that participants in mass mobilization eschewed *Ligues* radicalism in favor of steadfast conservatism and moderation, and that they lacked seriousness (because only "authentic" fascisms—like those in Italy and Germany, where fascists enjoyed political success by managing to seize power—deserved to be taken seriously). But historians also presumed the *Ligues* leaders' political weakness and lack of charisma, the inconsistency of their programs, the absence of any structured ideology, the unreality of their ambitions, the "marginality" of their social bases, and the simulated character of their fights. Overall, this ensemble of "facts" is highly doubtful. The central thrust of this historical interpretation was that neither the event nor the mobilizations it produced held anything at all that substantiated a relationship or even a vague kinship with processes that elsewhere entailed the establishment of fascist or authoritarian regimes. For a critical analysis of this historical interpretation—which came close to a sort of official history but by now has been discredited in scholarly circles—see in particular Dobry (2005) and Jenkins (2005).

6. The spin aims to avoid reference to any effects of "natural laws" (e.g., physical laws) within history. Such effects would be pointless in the context of this chapter, which deals exclusively with sociological regularities.

7. I wish to stress the extreme fragility—which is a weak formulation—of the causal explanations present in etiological reasoning. A minimum of control of his or her own procedure should prompt the scholar to highlight the fact that most "causes"

or "determinants," such as those in the pseudo-explanations drawing on frustration, alienation, discontent, and so on, are very often found in our societies or in vast social segments without actually sparking critical events of such magnitude (on this point see Dobry 1983 and Aya 1990). To paraphrase Barrington Moore, the pertinent question for the social sciences may well be not why men rebel, but rather why do they not rebel much more often (Moore 1978: 49)

8. For the plasticity of structures and the analysis of critical processes through the transformation of social structures, see Dobry (1983, 1986); for similar reasoning focused mainly on ideational structures, see Sewell (1996).

9. This perspective compromises the incapacity of an important part of contemporary social science to emancipate itself from the old sociological tradition that posits the doubtful equivalence between critical conditions or states of social and political systems, and *social pathologies*; it is hardly necessary to stress that it is precisely this imagery (the opposition between "normal" and "pathological") that underpins the methodological exceptionalism criticized above.

10. See Dobry (1983, 1986); also see, in relation to the collapse of communist systems in Eastern Europe or the Soviet Union, Wydra (2007) and Sigman (2009).

11. This is also another way of evaluating or "testing" the fruitfulness or the "validity" of the theory of fluid conjunctures.

12. For this distinction see Bailey (1969).

13. For focal points, see in particular Schelling (1960) and Goffman (1970).

14. Kershaw (1991) comes close to the perspective expounded here; for discussion see Dobry (2006).

15. Significantly, this perspective is applicable to observations in democratic and contemporary authoritarian systems alike. The processes that have led to the collapse of authoritarian systems in Central and Eastern Europe and in the Soviet Union can hardly be otherwise explained. These processes have largely been nurtured by very broad crises of collusive transactions between different "elites" in these systems.

16. For a more detailed analysis see Dobry (2007).

17. This role relies on Popper's position regarding psychology. The procedure consists in systematically substituting psychological categories—motivations, needs, desires, etc.—with categories that the author sees as typically sociological (above all, precisely any goal or "objective" purpose pursued by the actors, and their knowledge and information).

18. I see a very strong link between this drift toward a fully detailed reconstruction of a unique historical situation and a central point of Popper's epistemological thought, specifically the importance he attaches, when trying to understand the scientific approach and scientific discovery, to the rational reconstruction of the problem situation that confronts a given scholar, a situation that is then thought of in terms of historical uniqueness. Actually, concerning situational logics, Popper's conception often oscillates between the nomological ambition he explicitly attributes to the "theoretical social sciences" (sociology, economics, linguistics), and the very different task of showing that historical methodology, which seeks to explain the unique, can nevertheless gain in rigor and understanding when one applies situational analysis, particularly in order to "test" (strangely, Popper uses this notion himself) its singular statements.

References

Almond, G., S. Flanagan, and R. Mundt. 1973. *Crisis, Choice, and Chage: Historical Studies of Political Development*. Boston: Little, Brown.

Aya, R. 1990. *Rethinking Revolution and Collective Violence*. Amsterdam: Het Spinhuis.

Bachelard, G. 1967. *La formation de l'esprit scientifique*. Paris: Vrin.
Bailey, F. G. 1969. *Stratagems and Spoils: A Social Anthropology of Politics*. Oxford: Basil Blackwell.
Brinton, C. 1965. *The Anatomy of Revolution*. New York: Vintage.
Briquet, J.-L. 1996. "Mobilizzazioni politiche e congiuntura critica. Ipotesi per l'analisi della crisi politica in Italia." *Teoria politica* 12 (1): 15–30.
————. 2007. *Mafia, justice et politique en Italie. L'affaire Andreotti dans la crise de la République (1992–2004)*. Paris: Kathala.
Clausewitz, C. 1955. *De la guerre*. Paris: Minuit.
Di Palma, G. 1990. *To Craft Democracies*. Berkeley: University of California Press.
Dobry, M. 1983. "Mobilisations multisectorielles et dynamique des crises politiques." *Revue Française de Sociologie* 24 (3): 395–419.
————. 1986. *Sociologie des crises politiques*. Paris: Presses de la Fondation Nationale des Sciences Politiques.
————. 2002. "Valeurs, croyances et transactions collusives. Notes pour une réorientation de l'analyse de la légitimation des systèmes démocratiques." In *A la recherche de la démocratie*, edited by J. Santiso. Paris: Karthala.
————. 2005. "February 1934 and the Discovery of French Society's Allergy to the 'Fascist Revolution.'" In *France in the Era of Fascism: Essays on the French Authoritarian Right*, edited by B. Jenkins. Oxford and New York: Berghahn Books.
————. 2006. "Hitler, Charisma, and Structure: Reflections on Historical Methodology." *Totalitarian Movements and Political Religions* 7 (2): 157–71.
————. 2007. "Ce dont sont faites les logiques de situation." In *L'atelier du politiste. Théories, actions, représentations*, edited by P. Favre, O. Fillieule, and F. Jobard. Paris: La Découverte.
François, B. 1996. *Naissance d'une constitution. La Cinquième République 1958–1962*. Paris: Presses de Sciences Po.
Gaïti, B. 1998. *De Gaulle prophète de la Cinquième République (1946–1962)*. Paris: Presses de Sciences Po.
Goffman, E. 1961. *Asylums*. New York: Anchor Books.
————. 1970. *Strategic Interaction*. Oxford: Basil Blackwell.
Jenkins, B., ed. 2005. *France in the Era of Fascism*. New York and Oxford: Berghahn Books.
Johnson, C. 1964. *Revolution and the Social System*. Stanford, CA: Stanford University Press.
Kershaw, I. 1991. *Hitler*. London and New York: Longman.
Linz, J. 1978. *Crisis, Breakdown, and Reequilibration*. Baltimore, MD: Johns Hopkins University Press.
Linz, J., and A. Stepan, eds. 1978. *The Breakdown of Democratic Regimes*. Baltimore, MD: Johns Hopkins University Press.
Moore, B., Jr. 1966. *Social Origins of Dictatorship and Democracy*. New York: Oxford University Press.
————. 1978. *Injustice: The Social Bases of Obedience and Revolt*. London: Macmillan.
O'Donnell, G., and P. C. Schmitter. 1986. *Transitions from Authoritarian Rule: Tentative Conclusions about Uncertain Democracies*. Baltimore, MD: Johns Hopkins University Press.
Popper, K. 1973. *Objective Knowledge: An Evolutionary Approach*. Oxford: Clarendon Press.
————. 1976. "The Logic of the Social Sciences." In *The Positivist Dispute in German Sociology*, edited by T. W. Adorno et al. London: Heinemann.
————. 2004. *The Poverty of Historicism*. London and New York: Routledge.
Przeworski, A. 1986. "Problems in the Study of Transition to Democracy." In *Transitions from Authoritarian Rule: Comparative Perspectives*, edited by G. O'Donnell, P. C. Schmitter, and L. Whitehead. Baltimore, MD: Johns Hopkins University Press.

Roussel, V. 2002. *Affaires de juges. Les magistrats dans les scandales politiques en France*. Paris: La Découverte.

Schelling, T. 1960. *The Strategy of Conflict*. Cambridge, MA: Harvard University Press.

Sewell, W. H. 1996. "Historical Events as Transformations of Structures: Inventing Revolution at the Bastille." *Theory and Society* 25 (6): 841–81.

Sigman, C. 2009. *Les clubs politiques informels à Moscou et la désintégration du régime soviétique*. Paris: Karthala.

Veyne, P. 1971. *Comment on écrit l'histoire*. Paris: Seuil.

Weber, M. 1965. *Essais sur la théorie de la science*. Paris: Plon.

Wydra, H. 2007. *Communism and the Emergence of Democracy*. Cambridge: Cambridge University Press.

Chapter 6

Liminality and the Frontier Myth in the Building of the American Empire

Stephen Mennell

W e—Americans and Western Europeans—have all grown up on the mythology of the Wild West, depicted in a thousand Hollywood films, not to mention spaghetti Westerns from nearer home. Both the movies and American national mythology depict the frontier as the boundary between "civilization" (that is, "us") and something else: the "Indians," the "Mexicanos," and wild men of all origins (in other words, "them"). In this light, it is easy to view the famous frontier as a distinct line moving steadily westward—the advance of "civilization"—over the course of a century or two. The story of the United States' westward expansion is an interesting study in social liminality, historically as well as mythologically. There is, as Peter Burke notes (see Burke in this volume), some danger of overextending the concept of liminality so that everything is made to seem liminal. Nevertheless, the advancing western frontier did constitute—both geographically and temporally—a situation in which (to paraphrase Szakolczai in this volume), in order to facilitate a 'passage through' a particular limit all limits were removed, and thus the very structure of the society was temporarily suspended. In this essay, I will discuss the extent to which social limits *actually* were suspended in the course of America's westward expansion. But I shall also emphasize the importance of Americans' later *perception* of westward expansion as a national *rite de passage* culminating in the "successful completion of the transition" to a new

---

Notes for this chapter begin on page 128.

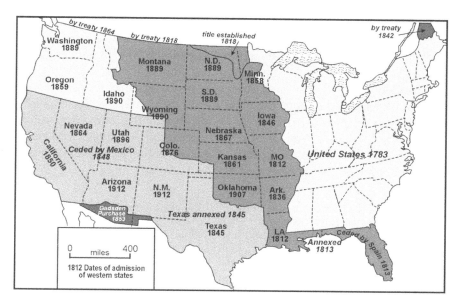

Figure 6.1. Territorial Growth of the United States. *Source:* Stephen Mennell (2007) The American Civilizing Process, Cambridge: Polity, 189. The map was redrawn by Stephen Hannon, the cartographer in the School of Geography at University College Dublin.

"phase of the [national] life-cycle" and tentatively argue that it has played a part in legitimizing the United States' pursuit of world dominance.

The Frontier

The frontier was not a steadily advancing line, even though a simple map of the expansion of the United States can make it appear so. Figure 1 shows the expansion of U.S. sovereign territory between 1783 and 1864, and the more gradual incorporation of territory into states of the Union between 1812 and 1912. In its report on the 1890 national census, the U.S. Bureau of the Census famously declared that the western frontier—which over the course of a century had moved steadily from the Appalachians to the Rockies, where it met the Pacific states—had been "closed" by the spread of unbroken settlement from the Atlantic to the Pacific. More exactly, the Superintendent of the Census wrote: "Up to and including 1880 the country had a frontier of settlement, but at present the unsettled area has been so broken into by isolated bodies of settlement that there can hardly be said to be a frontier line." This was a somewhat arbitrary judgment, statistically based on there being no territory that fell below a certain population per square mile.

A United States of America stretching from Atlantic to Pacific had seemed a far-fetched idea at the time of Independence, but Thomas Jefferson, the third president (1801–09), had advocated it and done much through the Louisiana Purchase to make it possible. He also had a clear vision of what it meant in terms of the then conventional ideas of civilization and barbarism. Near the end of his life, he wrote:

> Let a philosophic observer commence a journey from the savages of the Rocky Mountains, eastwardly towards our seacoast. These he would observe in the earliest stage of association living under no law but that of nature, subsisting and covering themselves with the flesh and skins of wild beasts. He would next find those on our frontiers in the pastoral state, raising domestic animals to supply the defects of hunting. Then succeed our own semi-barbarous citizens, the pioneers of the advance of civilization, and so in his progress he would meet the gradual shades of improving man until he would reach his, as yet, most improved state in our seaport towns. This, in fact, is equivalent to a survey, in time, of the progress of man from the infancy of creation to the present day. I am eighty-one years of age; born where I now live, in the first range of mountains in the interior of our country. And I have observed this march of civilization advancing from the seacoast, passing over us like a cloud of light, increasing our knowledge and improving our condition, insomuch as that we are at this time more advanced in civilization here than the seaports were when I was a boy. And where this progress will stop no one can say. Barbarism has, in the meantime, been receding before the steady step of amelioration; and will in time, I trust, disappear from the earth. (Letter to William Ludlow, 6 September 1824, in Jefferson 1907: vol. 16, 75)

By the 1840s, a United States stretching from the Atlantic to the Pacific seemed inevitable to many Americans. Justifying expansion into Texas, Mexico, and Oregon, the journalist John L. O'Sullivan (1845: 5) wrote that it was "by right of *manifest destiny*" or the United States 'to overspread and to possess the whole of the continent which Providence has given us," both for "the development of the great experiment in liberty and federative self-government entrusted to us" and for "the free development of our yearly multiplying millions."

Yet westward expansion was not driven by ideas or ideology, but rather by people's hunger for land, which the government could not control. The sixth president, John Quincy Adams (1825–29), admitted defeat: "My own system of administration, which was to make the national domain the inexhaustible fund for progressive and unceasing internal improvement, had failed." His successor, President Andrew Jackson (1829–37), "formally recommended that all public lands should be gratuitously given away to individual adventurers and to the States in which the lands are situated" (both quoted in F. J. Turner 1947: 26). This largely unplanned advance of settlement into the "wilderness," ahead of the apparatus of government, administration, and the forces of "law and order," is in marked contrast with the contemporaneous eastward expansion of Russians into Siberia or, closer to hand, the westward expansion of Canada (Mennell 2007: 196–97). "A system of administration," Frederick Jackson Turner (1947: 26) pithily commented, "was not what the West demanded; it wanted land."

It was the announcement of the 'closing of the frontier' in the report of the 1890 census that caused Frederick Jackson Turner to write his celebrated paper, "The Significance of the Frontier in American History," which he delivered at a meeting of the American Historical Association in 1893 (1947: 1-38). This remarkable paper is still debated among American historians today; I can think of no other academic essay that is still actively discussed 122 years after it was written (though Max Weber's *The Protestant Ethic* comes close among sociologists).

There is much in Turner's vocabulary that jars in modern ears. When Turner wrote about "civilization," he used the word in the accustomed nineteenth-century sense redolent of "progress," with the implication that "white" European and American society at the time represented the leading edge of human history, and the opposite of 'civilization' was "barbarism." Perhaps most startling is his assertion that "the most significant thing about the American frontier is that it lies *at the hither edge of free land*" (1947: 2-3; my emphasis). Of course, what lay beyond it at any one time was not a desert devoid of population. It was not "free land" in that sense. Americans viewed their hinterland in the same way that Australia, upon the arrival of the First Fleet in 1788, was regarded as *Terra nullius*. The Australian aborigines and the American Indians, as they were then called, did not count—not because they were not there, but because their occupation of the land did not take the form of anything that Europeans or Americans could easily recognize as an established territorial government. Turner knew that, of course, but did not pay it much heed. His own student, Herbert E. Bolton, pointed out in his book *The Spanish Borderlands* (1921) that Turner's model of a steadily advancing frontier certainly did not do justice to the "borderlands" of the formerly Spanish and Mexican territory of the United States. They had always been populated by a mixed population not just of "native Americans" but also Hispanics, blacks, and others. (One thing one doesn't see in the Western movies is the fact that historically a large proportion of cowboys were black.)

In any case, even Turner did not think of the frontier as a single advancing line. "The American frontier," he wrote, "is sharply distinguished from the European frontier—a fortified boundary line running through dense populations" (1947: 2-3). In particular, he distinguished various phases of the advancing frontier of European-American settlement: first came the traders' frontier (led by the trappers), then the miners' and ranchers' frontier, and finally the farmers' frontier. The battles between Cain and Abel on the Western frontier sometimes do find their way into the Westerns, and, as in the Bible (Genesis 4:1–8), Cain won. The cowboy phase lasted only a couple of decades or so.

When allowance is made for the passage of time and our very different vocabulary, even Turner's severest critics usually acknowledge there still remains something of interest and value in his thesis. He certainly had a point about the steady advance westward of the apparatus of the U.S. state. In Figure 6.2, the gap between the upper and lower lines represents an area and a phase of internal colonization—or, for present purposes, a zone of potential liminality. Or, to use a later coinage by another Turner, Victor Turner (1967), it might be said to be a *liminoid* zone for those who had actively chosen to participate in the process.

It is entirely reasonable to consider the effect of this process of state formation on the old and the new inhabitants of the Territories and then States of the Union. It can be considered as a *process of diminishing liminality*. And Frederick Jackson Turner's thesis remains an impressive starting point for considering this process.

The Turner Thesis

Turner contended that the existence and expansion of the frontier from the earliest settlements to the 1880s had introduced a decisively different "evolutionary" influence into the development of American society. The kernel of his argument runs:

> We have . . . a recurrence of the process of evolution in each western area reached in the process of expansion. Thus American development has exhibited not merely advance along a single line, but a return to primitive conditions on a continually advancing frontier line, and a new development for that area. American social development has been continually beginning again on the frontier. This perennial rebirth, this fluidity of American life, this expansion westwards with its new opportunities, its continuous touch with the simplicity of primitive society, furnish forces dominating American character. (1947: 2-3)

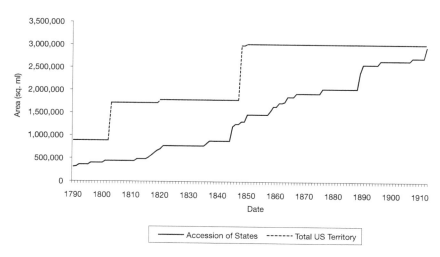

Figure 6.2. Territorial Area of the Conterminous United States 1790-1912. *Source:* U.S. Department of Commerce and Bureau of the Census (1975) Historical Statistics of the United States: Colonial Times to 1970. Washington, DC: U.S. Government Printing Office.

Turner distinguished three phases of the advancing frontier: the traders' frontier, the miners' and ranchers' frontier, and the farmers' frontier. He (1947: 22-38) listed a number of specific ways in which the experience of the frontier fed back into American society in the more settled east. I shall mention only the ones that are most relevant to the present context.

First, the frontier had "promoted the formation of a composite nationality for the American people." It diluted the predominantly English character of the eastern seaboard. "In the crucible of the frontier . . . immigrants were Americanized, liberated, and fused into a mixed race, English in neither nationality nor characteristics. The process has gone on from early days to our own" (1947: 22, 23). That can be translated into the terms used by Victor Turner (1967): he might have said that the frontier promoted a *communitas*, in which conventional differences of social class and ethnicity were played down in favor of a common quality of Americanness.

Second, the most famous of the consequences of the frontier that Turner discerned for American society was its promotion of "rugged individualism":

> The frontier is productive of individualism. Complex society is precipitated by the wilderness into a kind of primitive organization based on the family. The tendency is anti-social. It produces antipathy to control. The tax-gatherer is viewed as a representative of oppression. (1947: 30)

How prescient that has sounded with the rise of the extreme right in the late twentieth and early twenty-first century. Hostility to the tax gatherer can be seen in many facets of American politics: Republican faith in tax cuts as the universal panacea for all economic problems from boom to bust, in Proposition 13 adopted by California in 1978, which makes it impossible for any state tax to be raised without a two-thirds majority vote in both houses of the state legislature.

Third, and in Turner's own opinion most important, frontier individualism had from the beginning promoted "democracy," By that, he mainly meant the extension of the franchise. Turner, however, also sounded a note of warning:

> So long as free land exists, the opportunity for a competency exists, and economic power secures political power. But the democracy born of free land, strong in selfishness and individualism, intolerant of administrative experience and education, and pressing individual liberty beyond its proper bounds, has its dangers as well as its benefits. Individualism in America has allowed a laxity in regard to government affairs which has rendered possible the spoils system and all the manifest evils that follow from the lack of a highly civic spirit. (1947: 32)

If even Turner could enter such a reservation, later writers, less sympathetic than he to the romanticization of the pioneer, underlined how individualism undermined the civic spirit. Lewis Mumford (1957: 26), noting how on the frontier "social man could become an 'individual,'" spelled out how that was linked to what would later be called environmental depredation: "Uninfluenced by peasant habits or the idea of an old culture, the work of the miner, woodman, and hunter led to unmitigated destruction and pillage . . . backwoods America turned the European into a barbarian."

Decivilizing Processes on the Frontier?

A central part of Turner's thesis was that, over a long period, elements of the American population were returning to conditions of greater autarky and to much higher levels of danger in everyday life, and thus—in Norbert Elias's terms—to a continuous source of *decivilizing* pressures. To quote one of Elias's most important *obiter dicta*,

> the armor of civilized conduct would crumble very rapidly if, through a change in society, the degree of insecurity which existed earlier were to break in upon

us again, and if danger became as incalculable as once it was. Corresponding fears would burst the limits set to them today. (2012: 576)

The pattern of people's fears responds to changes in the dangers they face. Changes in people's fears are in turn likely to be associated with wider changes in their typical behavior, emotions, and beliefs. Elias thinks of civilizing processes as involving a change in the balance between external constraints and self-constraints, the balance tilting over the generations toward the latter in the steering of behavior in the average person. "External" constraints include both natural forces and constraints imposed by interdependence with other people. The lengthening chains and more extensive networks of interdependence, through which people exert more demanding but also more indirect constraints over each other, play a principal part in the tilting of the balance. Now, if these chains break and the networks shrink, as Turner contended they did for people on the frontier—if people are "precipitated . . . into a kind of primitive organization based on the family"—the pattern of external constraints will be changed.

It follows that the operation of self-constraints will not remain unchanged if changes take place in the pattern of external constraints. There are two broad reasons for this. First, calculation of the external constraints always plays a part in the steering of conduct, and so if the calculations suddenly or gradually yield different outcomes, behavior will change. To put it more directly, at the margin people's behavior will change if they discover they can get away with pursuing their advantage in ways that were not worth the risk before. Secondly, however, behavior will change still more if the calculations become more difficult, if the changes become more "incalculable," if life is lived in face of greater uncertainty and unpredictability. It is quite likely that the greater fears corresponding to higher levels of danger will produce in some people, or perhaps eventually all, behavior that may be described as 'more emotional' or 'more impulsive,' in which the gradually acquired apparatus of self-constraints is undermined.

On the face of it, many of these conditions would appear to have been met for white settlers on the frontier. They lived on scattered homesteads in relatively self-sufficient small groups. They were more at the mercy of natural forces—fire, flood, wild beasts—than they would be in a city. Far from medical help, minor injuries and infections were more likely to be fatal. Violence from human enemies, white or Indian, was a greater threat outside the daily beat of the forces of "law and order" within the boundaries of an organized state. Fears rise when control of natural forces and social events declines. Rising fears make it still more difficult to control events, notably to stand back from an escalating and self-perpetuating cycle of violence—such as that between whites and Indians and, through a detour via detachment, find the means to bring it under control. Such rising fears make people still more susceptible to wishful fantasies about means of alleviating the situation.

But is all this true of what actually happened on the frontier?

Although Turner considered that the "primitive conditions" of the frontier had left their mark on the settlers and that in turn had made a large imprint on American culture and (what we now call) habitus more widely, he did not perceive any general collapse of civilized standards on the frontier. It was not a situation of "liminality" in the extreme sense that van Gennep was to define some years after Turner wrote his essay; that is, it was not the case that "ritually and temporally *all* limits were removed [and] the very structure of society . . . suspended" (Szakolczai 2009: 149).

Turner was correct. Decivilizing pressures (in Elias's terms) were always in tension with quite strong civilizing pressures too. One reason was that those who moved west were not tabulae rasae: they had, by and large, been raised in more settled and (again in Elias's technical sense) more civilized circumstances. They took with them a vast inheritance of knowledge, beliefs, and feelings into which they had been socialized and enculturated in the more settled East (or Europe). In most people, most of the time, this inheritance precluded any abrupt abandonment of "civilized" self-constraints in their usually temporary return to "primitive conditions." A second reason is that, although the first generation of settlers' offspring might indeed be raised amidst a relatively high and incalculable level of danger, the process of internal pacification of territory, accomplished by the forces of the state together with economic development of many sorts, was rarely more than a generation behind the first settlers in their movement west.

The upshot is that the more lurid manifestations of what we might call "frontier decivilizing processes" did not happen on the farming frontier, or certainly not widely or for very long if they did at all. Ray Allen Billington (1903-81), one of Turner's most distinguished students, pointed out that most of the settlers "had some wealth, for the frontier was no place for the penniless" (1967: 10); Billington gives further details on the costs of setting up a farm even on cheap land in the West in the mid nineteenth century). Moreover, Billington concluded that nearly all the settlers were determined to transfer the cultural institutions of their homelands to their new communities, and that, although most were people of small learning, most pioneer settlements contained an educated group that assumed the functions of leadership. Nevertheless, such ambitions were rarely fully attained, since every effort to create carbon copies of eastern seaboard or European patterns of life was doomed by social and economic conditions on the frontier. Reiterating the central point of Turner's thesis, Billington contended that "both these environmental conditions and the determination of the pioneers to duplicate accustomed patterns help to explain the unique western culture that did emerge" (1977: 56).

On the other hand, in a fine study of surviving memoirs of fur trappers at the extreme forward edge of the traders' frontier in the Rockies in the period 1825–45, Billington produces some vivid evidence of their lowered threshold of repugnance in relation to eating, drinking, sex, violence, and cruelty (1977: 19-50). This appears to be an effect of adaptation to a situation of extreme danger and the extreme measures necessary to survival. They faced the dangers of freezing winters in the mountains, of grizzly bears and rattlesnakes, and (even though many of them took wives from tribes such as the Crow) especially from hostile Indians.

> The mountain men had to adjust themselves completely to the wilderness world about them. Their primitive existence revolved about three things: beaver, buffalo, and Indians—or, as they would have phrased it, fur, meat, and ha'r, or their own scalps. To secure fur and meat, they had to risk their ha'r; to keep their ha'r, they had to develop forest skills superior to those of their principal antagonists, the Indians. Of the red men with whom the trappers carried on a constant battle, the Blackfeet of the Three Forks country were most feared; it was understood in the mountains that when a trapper saw a Blackfoot or a Blackfoot saw a trapper, shooting started at once. Yet even such friendly Indians as the Crows could never be completely trusted, for few could resist stealing a carelessly watched horse or pouncing on an unwary white man. Constant vigilance and superb skill were necessary just to stay alive in such a country. (1977: 27-28)

If the term "decivilizing process" is considered too contentious, an alternative way of describing what was happening would be to say that such men in such an environment had to re-acquire skills that would have been "second nature," essential to survival, for all human beings in the long millennia when hunter-gatherer societies were the sole form of human social organization, but which had since been lost to most people living in the commercial, agrarian, and industrial society that the United States had become by the nineteenth century. The kind of constant vigilance needed to survive in the mountains was a polar opposite of the kind of vigilance that Elias depicts as necessary for aristocrats' social survival in French court society (Elias 2006). Both situations demanded foresight, but for the courtier an extreme curbing of the impulses was necessary, whereas for the mountain trapper (more like the medieval warrior) a capacity for the unrestrained venting of impulses . Billington speaks of the trapper Edward Rose, who had joined the Crow:

> A fellow trapper saw Rose lead his tribesman to victory against a Blackfoot war party in 1834 then whip his followers into a bloody frenzy as they hacked off the hands of the wounded enemy warriors, pierced their bodies with pointed sticks, and plucked out their eyes. (1977: 29-30)

"Liminality" hardly seems the right word to describe what was happening here: such people appear, upon leaving the kind of society in which they had grown up, to have passed through a liminal zone, and then—instead of returning through "rites of reaggregation"—exited on the far side of the zone into something quite foreign to their earlier experience.

These accounts in Billington's book date from a period when the trapping frontier was nearing its end. They describe an extreme situation. But in long-term perspective they are rather interesting. They depict extremes of violence and cruelty in combat that are reminiscent of Elias's (2012: 186–98) account of *Angriffslust*—the "joy in attacking"—among early medieval warriors in Europe. And the element common to both of these otherwise very different times and places is the very high everyday level of danger. The ability to give unrestrained vent to aggression had survival value in both instances. Equally, it became a liability on the more complex battlefields on which organized armies came to fight.

The Frontier as Continuing State Formation

The classic status of "The Significance of the Frontier" and the other writings in which Turner elaborated his thesis is beyond dispute, although the "frontier hypothesis" has remained the subject of controversy among historians for more than a century. Until the 1920s it was the dominant interpretation of American social development. Then, in the 1930s and 1940s, it was the target of extensive criticism. After a period of more evenly balanced debate and detailed research to test particular aspects of the original hypothesis, controversy flared up again in the 1980s, notably following the publication of Patricia Nelson Limerick's brilliant book *The Legacy of Conquest* (1987).

Limerick began by very cogently undermining the image of the self-reliant and individually responsible pioneer, at any rate on the farming frontier. Even the dietary self-sufficiency of settlers had been greatly exaggerated: *The Legacy of Conquest* opens by citing the recollections of a Virginian woman, Nannie Alderson, who married and went to live in Wyoming in the 1880s. She remembered that "everyone lived out of cans," and outside every farm in the 1880s stood a great mound of empty food cans, steadily growing from year to year (1987: 17). The consumption of canned food is evidence of the long chains of interdependence stretching back east (although the fact that the garbage collectors never called is a reminder that differences remained between life in west and east). Limerick also showed vividly how the supposedly self-reliant pioneers fell into the habit of blaming everyone but themselves when things went wrong. Farmers encroached on areas of semi-aridity, and felt betrayed when rains proved inadequate. Mechanized farming caused dust bowls. Where crops did not grow, weeds were introduced that did. The promoters of farming or mining on the frontier were often blamed for failure. Increasingly, so was the federal government: "In effect," she writes, "Westerners centralized their resentments much more effectively than the federal government centralized its powers" (1987: 44).

The rhetoric of heroic independence, says Limerick, has begun to sound anachronistic in our own complex times of global interdependence—but in fact "the times were always complex." "There is nothing wrong with human interdependence," she wrote in words reminiscent of Norbert Elias: "it is . . . a fact of life" (1987: 78).

> A recognition that one is not the sole captain of one's fate is hardly an occasion for surprise. Especially in the American West, where the federal government, outside capital, and the market have always been powerful factors of change, the limits on personal autonomy do not seem like news. And yet humans have a well-established capacity to meet fact of life with disbelief. In a region where human interdependence has been self-evident, Westerners have woven a net of denial. (1987: 95-96)

Nowhere is this denial more evident than in what Limerick called "the idea of innocence." One of the virtues of the "new Western history" has been its capacity to deal with multiple points of view. And a characteristic of the "white" point of view has been blindness to any "white" motives other than the most innocent. The dominant motives are seen as improvement and opportunity rather than to "ruin the natives and despoil the continent":

> Personal interest in the acquisition of property coincided with national interest in the acquisition of territory, and those interests overlapped in turn with the mission to extend the domain of Christian civilization. Innocence of intention placed the course of events in a bright and positive light. (Limerick 1987: 36)

It is impossible to resist the parallel between the frontier story in the nineteenth century and the formation of the American empire in the twentieth century. The "idea of innocence" was deployed on all fronts, no matter how many natives were ruined and continents despoiled. So—as we saw once more after the attacks on New York and Washington, DC on 9/11 (Mennell 2007: 23–25)—was the idea of "civilization" in all its uncritical nineteenth-century European glory. Charles Jones (2007) has offered a corrective to these myths, arguing that the United States is a lot more like Latin American and a lot less like Western Europe than we are accustomed to think. To simplify a complex argument, Jones suggests that the United States and its hemispheric neighbors to the south share a number of historical experiences that give their societies certain common features and set them to some extent apart from Western Europe. These include the legacy of conquest and of slavery (both of which have contributed to race and racism as salient traits), marked religiosity, and relatively high rates of violence. We may add a rapacious attitude to natural resources, born of the abundance that confronted settlers.

Frederick Jackson Turner and the Turnerians undoubtedly wrote their history too much from the standpoint of "progress"—the impact of white settlers with apparently innocent motives. It is a valuable corrective to See the process from multiple points of view, and Limerick portrays the West as not so much an advancing line of settlement along which "civilization" overcame "savagery," but rather as a borderland where there was continuing cultural contact and assimilation between English-speaking Americans, the Indians, and Hispanic elements. The latter, a strong element in the history of the southwest, were especially invisible in Turner's original essay. Limerick went too far, however, for she rejected Turner's entire notion of the frontier *process*, seemingly because she believed that it—or indeed, any notion of developmental process—was inseparable from outdated notions of progress and of civilization versus savagery. That is to throw the baby out with the bathwater. From an Eliasian point of view one of the great virtues of Turner's thesis—whatever its defects—was that it was very much cast in processual terms. Limerick has been criticized for portraying an almost static image of an unchanging West of timeless borderlands (Adelman and Aron 1999). That is paradoxical, for the title of her book was *The Legacy of Conquest*, and conquest itself is a social process. Limerick, as she herself admits, took her clues from the present, just as Turner did from his own time (1987: 31). The problem with writing history from the standpoint of whatever happen to be the dominant values of the day is that it leads to moralizing, and moralizing reduces the shelf life of the product (Elias 2006: 33-34). Conquest—the acquisition of territory by force—is morally less palatable to people in the early twenty-first century than it was a century or two earlier, let alone in the Middle Ages. But understanding conquest as a structured social process that has occurred constantly, at least since the beginnings of agriculture about twelve thousand years ago—to the accompaniment of bloodletting that is typically repulsive to Western people nowadays (Goudsblom 1996) — is not assisted by viewing it through the lens of moral judgments that have emerged relatively recently.

Whatever happened through the mingling of cultures, what certainly did advance was a line of effective American conquest. The frontier process was a process of continuing state formation, using the term in its Weberian and Eliasian sense rather than in the constitutional sense of the admission of new states to the Union. Much of what is glimpsed through a silver screen darkly is in effect a folk memory of a process of internal pacification that was unfolding in the West in the decades after the Civil War. Richard Maxwell Brown (1991: 41) sets the cowboy era of the postbellum Wild West in context as a "Western Civil War of Incorporation." From the Hollywood image, it would be difficult to see that anything more was involved than many local quarrels between gunslingers. Brown, however, argues that America was a strongly politicized nation after 1860, and the political and ideological allegiances of the gunmen were important. Many of them strongly identified with the Union or the Confederacy, with the Republicans or the Democrats. Brown distinguishes between "incorporation" and "resister" gunfighters. Examples of the former are Wild Bill Hickok and Wyatt Earp, and among the latter was John Wesley Hardin. The process of incorporation "resulted in what should at last be recognized as a civil war across the entire expanse of the West — one fought in many places and on many fronts in almost all Western territories and states from the 1860s and beyond 1900 into the 1910s" (Brown 1991: 44).

The Western Civil War of Incorporation comprised several different kinds of conflict besides this echo of the Civil War in the more familiar sense. Apart from the insurgent Indians gradually forced by military pressure and economic encroachment into reservations, the process impinged on the traditional ways of life and livelihood of the Hispanos of the Southwest, who hit back through the activities of *bandidos*. Moreover, in the mines, mills, and logging camps on what Brown calls the "wageworkers" frontier of the West, conflicts between corporate industrialists and workers often resulted in strikes that culminated in violence between trade unionists and paramilitary and military forces. Government usually brought its growing strength to bear on the side of capitalism.

What, then, remains of Turner's celebrated frontier thesis? Even his "sharpest critics have rarely failed to concede the core of merit to his thesis," said Richard Hofstadter (1969: 119), and that has remained so in the most recent phase of the debate. And whatever its merits in the detailed academic historiography of expansion from the Appalachians to the Rockies and the Pacific, the frontier has, for better of worse, played a far from negligible role as a key *myth* of American life.

The Western Myth as a Form of Romanticism

The long-lasting appeal of the frontier (Slotkin 1973, 1985, 1992), and its apparently greater significance for those who came later than for those who lived through it, may make sense if it is seen as one instance of a romanticism associated with the tightening of social constraints. Elias wrote at length (2006: 230-85) about "aristocratic romanticism" in sixteenth- to eighteenth-century France. Why did poetry evoking a past rural idyll, tales of wandering knights, and novels about nymphs and shepherds appeal strongly to members of a court society? The feeling of estrangement from the land, of being torn from their native soil, and of longing for a vanished world resonated with their actual experience: the growing and more effective power of the central royal government stripped all the nobility of their former territorial autonomy, and for the upper ranks their existence now centered on life at court, with its intense constraints. They had been deracinated and deprived of their former social functions. Another example is the German bourgeois romanticism of the nineteenth century, reaching its pinnacle in the Wagner's music dramas. In *Lohengrin*, *Tannhäuser*, *Tristan*, and *Parsifal* there is again the glorification of medieval knighthood, and in *Die Meistersinger* of the free, autonomous medieval guilds. Again, this phase of romanticism arose

> precisely when the German bourgeoisie's hopes of a greater share of power had been broken and the pressures of state integration in conjunction with those of industrialization were increasing. It is, in other words, one of the central symptoms of romantic attitudes and ideals that their representatives see the present only as a decline from the past, and the future—as far as they see the future at all—only as the restoration of a better, purer, idealized past. (Elias 2006: 238)

It is no accident that, on a lower plane of cultural creation than Wagner, the Wild West novels of Karl May were immensely popular in late nineteenth-century Germany (Ridley 1983: 30-41). In America itself, the beginnings of romanticism can be seen in Jefferson's hatred of the cities and dream of an agrarian republic (White and White 1962). But, if Elias's interpretation of romanticism is valid, the social basis of the appeal of the myth of the frontier may better be sought—as well as in the more pacified and administered West *after* the closing of the frontier—in the vast migration into the fast-growing cities and in the imposition of industrial and bureaucratic discipline.

Conclusion

I have tentatively suggested that the long-discussed story of the American western frontier can in certain respects be viewed as a complex phase of liminality. The whole point of such episodes, however, is that they change things. People do not emerge from them unchanged. Liminality has lasting consequences, and the experience of the frontier is no exception.

One major consequence of the frontier—and of its associated myths— was the American empire. It was not an accident that the "closing" of the internal frontier was followed smoothly and immediately by the acquisition of the first U.S. empire in 1899 (Zimmerman 2002), from the war with Spain and with the annexation of Hawaii (among other territories) seen as essential for the security of American trade routes, and as part of the wider struggles among the world powers of the time. The United States invaded the Philippines, with British support—the American fleet sailed from Hong Kong—because both powers feared that either Germany or Japan would do so if the United States did not. About the acquisition of the second and larger United States Empire after World War II it is not necessary to say very much. But one point is important: Americans' mythic belief in their essential character as a force for good in the world, with the myth of Western "civilization" triumphing over barbarism, has continued to play an essential part.

The myth is sustained by the central historical experience of Americans, and experience that has left its mark upon the national habitus more than many other factors that are more often discussed: the experience that from the very earliest European settlements until the present era, the United States has steadily become more powerful vis-à-vis its neighbors. The most dramatic recent phase of this process was the end of the Cold War and collapse of the Soviet Union in 1989-91. It has been argued that, as long as the Cold War continued, mutually assured destruction (MAD) served as a functional alternative to a world state, providing a highly stable equivalent to a world monopoly of violence (van Benthem van den Bergh, 1992, 2008). When that source of external constraint upon the United States diminished, there was at first only intellectual triumphalism, such as Fukuyama's infamous "end of history" thesis (1992). I would argue that the (urban) myth of the frontier played, at a deep and unconscious level, a part in sustaining that sense of triumph and of national mission. It also buttresses the pernicious assumption that "America" is axiomatically a force for good in the world, and therefore whatever it does represents the same "manifest destiny" as westward expansion once did.

In the course of the 1990s and the early 2000s, the United States might be said to have entered another liminal phase. American governments—rather like individual people from early childhood onward—began to explore the limits of what they could get away with, and the result was the invasion of Iraq in 2003. The result of that, and of the financial collapse that began in 2008, is that the United States—virtually for the first time in its history—is entering a phase when power ratios between it and other major players in world affairs are becoming more equal, not less. It will be interesting to see—probably over many decades—what effect that will have on the myth of the frontier and associated elements in the national self-image.

References

Adelman, J., and S. Aron. 1999. "From Borderlands to Borders: Empires, Nation-States, and the Peoples in Between in North American History." *American Historical Review* 104 (3): 814–41.

Bergh, G. van Benthem van den. 1992. *The Nuclear Revolution and the End of the Cold War: Forced Restraint*. London: Macmillan.

———. 2008. *Naar een nucleaire wereldord*. Amsterdam: Mets & Schilt.

Billington, R. A. 1967. *Westward Expansion: A History of the American Frontier*. New York: Macmillan.

———. 1977. *America's Frontier Culture: Three Essays*. College Station: Texas A& M University Press.

Bolton, H. E. 1921. *The Spanish Borderlands*. New Haven, CT: Yale University Press.

Brown, R. M. 1991. *No Duty to Retreat: Violence and Values in American History and Society*. New York: Oxford University Press.

Elias, N. 2006. *Collected Works*, vol. 2, *The Court Society*. Dublin: UCD Press.

———. 2012. *Collected Works*, vol. 3, *On the Process of Civilisation: Sociogenetic and Psychogenetic Investigations*. Dublin: UCD Press.

Fukuyama, F. 1992. *The End of History and the Last Man*. London: Hamish Hamilton.

Goudsblom, J. 1996. "The Formation of Military-Agrarian Regimes." In J. Goudsblom, E. Jones, and S. Mennell, *The Course of Human History: Economic Growth, Social Process, and Civilization*. Armonk, NY: M. E. Sharpe.

Hofstadter, R. 1969. *The Progressive Historians: Turner, Beard, Parrington*. London: Jonathan Cape.

Jefferson, T. 1907. *The Writings of Thomas Jefferson*. Washington, DC: Thomas Jefferson Memorial Association.

Jones, C. A. 2007. *American Civilization*. London: Institute for the Study of the Americas.

Limerick, P. N. 1987. *The Legacy of Conquest: The Unbroken Past of the American West*. New York: W.W. Norton.

Mennell, S. 2007. *The American Civilizing Process*. Cambridge: Polity.

Mumford, L. (1926) 1957. *The Golden Day: A Study in American Literature and Culture*. New York: Dover.

O'Sullivan, J. 1845 "Annexation," *United States Magazine and Democratic Review* 17, no.1 (July–August 1845): 5–10.

Ridley, H. 1983. *Images of Imperial Rule*. London: Croom Helm.

Slotkin, R. 1973. *Regeneration through Violence: The Mythology of the American Frontier, 1600-1860*. New York: Atheneum.

———. 1985. *The Fatal Environment: The Myth of the Frontier in the Age of Industrialization*. New York: Atheneum.

———. 1992. *Gunfighter Nation: The Myth of the Frontier in Twentieth-Century America*. New York: Atheneum.

Szakolczai, A. 2009."Liminality and Experience: Structuring transitory situations and transformative events," in *International Political Anthropology* 2 (1): 141–72.

Turner, F. J. (1920) 1947. *The Frontier in American History*. New York: Holt, Rinehart & Winston.

Turner, V. 1967. *The Forest of Symbols*. Ithaca, NY: Cornell University Press.

White, M., and L. White. 1962. *The Intellectual Versus the City: From Thomas Jefferson to Frank Lloyd Wright*. Cambridge, MA: Harvard University Press.

Zimmerman, W. 2002. *First Great Triumph: How Five Great Americans Made Their Country a World Power*. New York: Farrar, Straus & Giroux.

Chapter 7

On the Margins of the Public and the Private

Louis XIV at Versailles

Peter Burke

In 1673, a young Italian nobleman, Primi Visconti, arrived in Paris and, as one might have expected, he visited the court of Louis XIV. He observed the king's behavior on a number of occasions, and when he later wrote his memoirs, he had this to say about Louis, who was in his mid-thirties at the time of observation (Visconti, 1988: 28):[1]

> In public, he is full of gravity and very different from his manner in private [*particolare*]. Finding myself in his chamber together with other courtiers, I have observed on a number of occasions that if the door is accidentally opened, or if he goes out, he immediately composes his posture and changes his facial expression, as if he was going to appear on stage.

We might speak of Louis as crossing not only a literal threshold but also a frontier of identity, caught by Visconti at the moment of switching between his public and private selves, a process something like the code-switching studied by sociolinguists.

Jumping over a gap of nearly three centuries, it may be instructive to compare this description of the king with one of Senator Joseph McCarthy who, so we learn from a reporter who observed him at first hand, "was capable of going into a tantrum before the television cameras" and then walking away to "a corner of the room outside the sweep of the television

---

Notes for this chapter begin on page 136.

cameras, there to observe calmly and be amused by the commotion he had caused," moving from normal to paranoid, and back, in moments (Rovere, 1959: 54-5, 58). Conversely, it is worth noting the occasions when political actors believe that the microphone is switched off, as in the case of George W. Bush talking to Tony Blair at a Group of Eight meeting in St Petersburg in 2006, believing, wrongly as it turned out, that he had already crossed the frontier into the private sphere (BBC News 2006).

Like the editors of this volume, I believe in the potential of an anthropological approach to politics, including fieldwork in parliaments and, if possible, committees and corridors of power. Such an approach should surely include a historical anthropology. The idea of an anthropologist at the court of Louis XIV may seem almost as odd as that of a Yankee at the court of King Arthur. All the same, there is not infrequently a close fit between anthropological observations and observations made in the seventeenth century itself, not only by foreigners but by natives as well.

The writer Jean La Bruyère, for instance, observed (1688: 213) that in a country "more than eleven hundred leagues by sea from the Iroquois and the Hurons," there was a chapel (meaning the chapel of Versailles) where "the people seem to adore their prince, and their prince appears to worship God." Again, in his study of the court system, the French historian Emmanuel Le Roy Ladurie presents the Duc de Saint-Simon as a kind of anthropologist *avant la lettre*, comparing his interest in hierarchy to that of Louis Dumont.

Within this anthropological approach, there seems a place for the study of borders. Returning to the passage of Visconti's memoirs, quoted above: if it had not been the subject of comment by earlier historians of Louis XIV but impressed me when I first came across it, this was probably because I had already read Erving Goffman (1959), a sociologist who behaved like an anthropologist. In his famous essay on "The Presentation of Self in Everyday Life," Goffman (1959) distinguishes between what he calls "front regions," where performances take place, and "back regions." To illustrate the distinction he quotes (1959: 121-2) a marvelous passage from George Orwell, writing—in 1933—about waiters:

> It is an instructive sight to see a waiter going into a hotel dining-room. As he passes the door a sudden change comes over him. The set of his shoulders alters; all the dirt and hurry and irritation have dropped off in an instant. He glides over the carpet with a solemn priest-like air.

That is one kind of frontier: a line that is crossed in an instant. Another kind, more like a zone that takes some time to traverse, is discussed by Victor Turner in his famous studies of rites of passage, such as initiations, and of liminality in general. As one commentator has remarked, in 1969, with his *Ritual Process*, Turner himself "crossed the threshold" from a more precise to a broader use of the concept (Babcock, 2001). He was sometimes criticized for making everything seem liminal, and in response he came to distinguish (1974: 640) between the narrower term "liminal" and the wider "liminoid," resembling the liminal but not identical with it.

It is possible to view Louis XIV from Turner's perspective. The king was no stranger to rites of passage. His baptism had turned him into a Christian; his coronation, or *sacre*, turned him into a king; his marriage turned him into a husband; while his funeral explored the liminal region between life and death, and between the king's reign and that of his successor. Turner (1974) also argued that we learn from disorder (or "anti-structure" as he called it) and that it may thus be regarded as the precursor of a new structure: in this case it is worth noting that Louis learned from his unhappy experience of the Fronde, the mainly aristocratic rebellion that took place in his youth, when a crowd invaded the Louvre, and that this memory of disorder underlay his efforts to create what historians describe as his "absolute monarchy."

All the same, it is not Turner, or the rites of passage that interested him so much, that will be discussed here. In what follows, the emphasis will fall not on the making or cultural construction of the king, but on his reconstruction, in other words the maintenance of his position through everyday performances, the daily metamorphosis of a rather small man into "Louis le Grand" (his official title), thanks to rituals and other props to identity, such as clothes—as the novelist William Thackeray brilliantly demonstrated in a satirical drawing (Burke, 1992: figure 27). The following anthropological view of Versailles will view the palace through Goffman's spectacles. Its focus will be on relatively rapid passages from one royal role, identity, or style of performance to another.

It is important to avoid identifying formality with the artificial, or informality with the real and the sincere. Louis, talking to a few select courtiers before going through the door, was also in a sense performing, following not a script but the promptings of the royal habitus that he had learned very early in life (he became king when he was five years old, following his father's death in 1643). All the same, there were differences between his formal and informal styles of performance, even if we know all too little about the informal style. For example, did the king take off his wig in his cabinet; in front of the courtiers; in front of Madame de Maintenon? We do not know.

The problem of the frontier between performance and reality was a general preoccupation in the seventeenth century, at least among the upper classes. The language commonly used to discuss the problem was the contrast between *être* and *paraître*, *Sein* and *Schein*, *ser* and *parecer*, and the need for unmasking, what the Spaniards called *desengaño*. One might link this preoccupation, or at least the language used to discuss it, to the rise of theatres and scenery and their consequent "reality effects." It may be instructive to make comparisons with our own time, with the rise of virtual reality and of performance art, "liminal acts" that cross the threshold between performance and audience (Broadhurst, 1999).

Plays within plays were not uncommon in the age of the Baroque (Forestier, 1981): among them were the *Comédie des comédiens* (1631) of Gougenot, the play of the same title by Georges de Scudéry (1634) and *L'illusion comique* (1635) by Pierre Corneille. The legend of St Genesius had considerable appeal at this time. According to the legend, Genesius was an actor at the time of the emperor Diocletian, who was converted to Christianity in the act of playing a Christian martyr, and then martyred himself. The story inspired the Spanish dramatist Lope de Vega Carpio's *Fingido verdadero* (1620), *L'illustre comédien* (1644) by Nicolas Desfontaines and, most famously, *St Genest* (c.1645) by Jean Rotrou (Buffum, 1957: 212-39). These plays illustrate another major baroque theme, metamorphosis (Rousset, 1953). The concern with change raises the problem of liminality once again: in the famous sculpture by Bernini, illustrating Ovid's *Metamorphoses*, where does Daphne end and the laurel tree begin?

This discussion of theater may seem a digression from politics, but it is not. "We princes I tell you are set as it were upon stages in the sight and view of the world," Queen Elizabeth is supposed to have remarked in the age of Shakespeare and the Globe (Levin 2003). The court may be seen as a stage, the scene of the dramatization or ritualization of the everyday activities of the ruler—for instance, his *lever* and *coucher* at the thresholds of night and day (Gunn and Janse 2006: 2).

Contemporaries were well aware of the theatrical aspects of courts. The language of Visconti, already quoted, is one example; another is the famous memoirs of the Duc de Saint-Simon (1983–88), who often uses the word *scène*, for instance (vol. 1: 714, 857; vol. 3: 86, 92, 105, 109), when writing about Versailles. He also refers to *comédie*, or *théâtre* (vol. 1: 781, 811; vol. 3: 233, 579, 733, 774, 957).

To illustrate the theatre of the court one might take the example of the so-called *appartements*. Following his permanent move to Versailles in 1682, Louis opened some of the more private rooms in the palace to his courtiers three times a week for them to play billiards or cards, engage in conversation, and take refreshments. It is stretching the term a little, but not too much, to describe these semi-formal occasions as "rituals," or at the very least as "ritualized," since they were devised to communicate a message, to display the king's accessibility to his subjects. In practice, Louis soon failed to make an appearance on these occasions, but the theatre of accessibility continued to run for a long time.

Within the theatre of the court, as in other theatres, the distinction between front and back, on-stage and off-stage, was an important one. The English already spoke at this time of what went on "behind the scenes" (the playwright Addison did so in 1711), while Saint-Simon (vol. 3: 888, 312, 458, etc.) wrote about *les derrières*. What Italian students of politics call *dietrologia* is not so new, after all.

Palace architecture both reflected and encouraged this distinction between front and back. As we have seen, Visconti already mentioned the royal *chambre* in the period before the king moved into Versailles. After he did so, the old public rooms were converted into private rooms for the king, called *cabinets*, into which a few favored courtiers were admitted (Saint-Simon was not included). These rooms included the *cabinet des médailles* and the *cabinet du conseil* (though they were used for other purposes as well), while the old *antichambre* became a room for Louis to play billiards and feed his dogs (Newton, 2000: 125).

The rooms were not exactly private—the binary opposition between public and private is not a useful one in this context. In any case, essentializing is particularly inappropriate when dealing with liminality. At the Versailles of Louis XIV, it is more illuminating to work with the idea of degrees of privacy and a liminal zone or zones of transition. There appears to have been not one "back region," but a succession of regions, a kind of *enfilade*.

There were major changes in the spatial arrangements during the king's long reign—more than half a century of effective rule. They become apparent if one compares the first Versailles (a hunting lodge used by the king's father, Louis XIII) with the *château* of Marly, a relatively small palace near Versailles where the king began to spend his leisure hours, together with select courtiers, in the later 1680s. Both palaces were originally constructed to allow the ruler to escape at least some of the everyday formality of the court, and both of them gradually became formalized in their turn. There were other frontiers between public and private in the milieu of Louis XIV, even if they were less sheer than they would be in later centuries—or less visible, or drawn in different places than they would later be the case—frontiers between what was known and what might be said, for instance, or between what was written and what might be printed. Two famous anecdotes cast a little light on these thresholds. Whether the stories were true or not, they were certainly current in the period, and so they have something to tell us about seventeenth-century attitudes.

The first story concerns the courtier Roger de Rabutin, Comte de Bussy and his *Histoire Amoureuse des Gaules*, an allegorical novel written in 1665 about sexual intrigues at court, including those of the king himself. Louis enjoyed reading something that Bussy had written, and as long as the "amorous history" circulated (in manuscript) among the right people, the author experienced no problems. When it began to be circulated more widely, however (and even printed, in 1665), the king was offended, and Bussy was imprisoned in the Bastille (Duchêne, 1992: 155, 163-7, 175-85).

The second anecdote, told by Saint-Simon (vol.1: 610), concerns a gaffe committed by the playwright Jean Racine, who was at one time in suffi-cient favor to be invited into the more private rooms of Versailles because Louis enjoyed his conversation. One day, Racine accidentally referred to the writer Paul Scarron, in the presence of the king. The problem was that Scarron was the first husband of Madame de Maintenon, while her second husband was the king himself. The marriage was a secret one but it was known abroad, in England for instance. It must have been known at home as well, but the topic was taboo. Everyone knew, but this was something that the king should never know.

For us, observing early modern courts from our position in the twenty-first century, the frontier between public and private is often difficult to discern. It was a vague zone rather than a precise line. Officials often treated state papers as their private property, for instance, and left them to their heirs. Rulers gave audience to ministers or supplicants, received information and took decisions while they were hunting, being shaved, or even while they were relieving themselves.

From the late-fifteenth to the late-seventeenth century, for instance, the Privy—in other words, private—Chamber formed a central part of the court. The Privy Chamber was a group of about fifteen people headed by the "Groom of the Stool," who attended the king everywhere. The Groom was in charge of the maintenance and transport of the royal close-stools, hence his title, but they gave him a position of power, since he was able to control access to the king, to allow or forbid individuals to catch the royal eye or whisper in the royal ear. The groom was a liminal person, a gatekeeper (Starkey, 1977).

Following this tradition, Louis XIV gave private audiences while sitting on his portable *chaise perceé* (Newton, 2006: 75). Even the king's sex life was semi-public. Although there appears to be no evidence in the archives concerning this part of his life, every time Louis made love to one of his mistresses there must have been at least two observers present, a valet and a bodyguard, one of the *huissiers de la chambre* who guarded the entrance to the room where the king happened to be (Newton, 2006: 68). One might describe these servants as liminal people in the sense that they were both there and not there at the same time.

Again, at the time of his operation for the fistula, Louis' private parts were the subject of public commentary in a way that one might have thought inconceivable today—at least, until the Clinton-Lewinsky affair. This relatively recent example prompts a final question: whether, thanks to intrusive media, such as photojournalism and especially television, the world is returning to the seventeenth-century situation. In principle, what many citizens want is transparency in government. In practice, they are offered another kind of transparency: what the butler saw, a view through the keyhole of the presidential bedroom.

Notes

1. Written in Italian, this text was first published in French by Jean Lemoine in 1908. Its first Italian edition, published in 1945, was translated from the French. My thanks to Francesco Boldizzoni for clearing up this problem.

References

Babcock, B. A. 2001. "Liminality." In vol. 13 of *International Encyclopedia of the Social & Behavioral Sciences*, 26 vols., edited by N. J. Smelser and P. J. Baltes. Amsterdam and Oxford: Elsevier.

BBC News. 2006. "Bush lunch is caught on tape," 17 July. http://news.bbc.co.uk/2/hi/business/5187276.stm.

Broadhurst, S. 1999. *Liminal Acts: A Critical Overview of Contemporary Performance Theory*. London: Cassell.

Buffum, I. 1957. *Studies in the Baroque from Montaigne to Rotrou*. New Haven, CT: Yale University Press.

Burke, P. 1992. *The Fabrication of Louis XIV*. New Haven, CT: Yale University Press.

Duchêne, J. 1992. *Bussy-Rabutin*. Paris: Fayard.

Forestier, G. 1981. *Le Théâtre dans le théâtre sur la scène française du XVIIe siècle*. Geneva: Droz.

Goffman, E. 1959. *The Presentation of Self in Everyday Life*. New York: Doubleday.

Gunn, S., and A. Janse, eds. 2006. *The Court as a Stage*. Leiden: Brill.

La Bruyère, J. 1688. *Les Caractères ou les Mœurs de ce siècle*. Translated by H. Van Laun. London: Nimmo.

Le Roy Ladurie, E. 1997. *Saint-Simon ou le système de la cour*. Paris: Fayard.

Levin, C. 2003. "'We Princes, I Tell You, Are Set on Stages': Elizabeth I and Dramatic Self-Representation." In *Readings in Renaissance Women's Drama*, edited by S. Cerasano and M. Wynne-Davies. London: Taylor and Francis.

Newton, W. R. 2000. *L'espace du roi: la cour de France au château de Versailles, 1682-1789*. Paris: Fayard.

———. 2006. *La petite cour: services et serviteurs à la cour de Versailles au 18ème siècle*. Paris: Fayard.

Rousset, J. 1953. *La littérature de l'âge baroque en France: Circé et le Paon*. Paris: Conti.

Rovere, R. H. (1959) 1996. *Senator Joe McCarthy*. Berkeley: University of California Press.

Saint-Simon, Duc de. 1983–88. *Mémoires*. Edited by Y. Coirault. 8 vols. Paris: Gallimard.

Starkey, D. 1977. "Representation through Intimacy." In *Symbols and Sentiments: Cross-Cultural Studies in Symbolism*, edited by I. M. Lewis. New York: Academic Press.

Turner, V. W. 1974. "Liminal to Liminoid in Play, Flow and Ritual: An Essay in Comparative Symbolology." *Rice University Studies* 60: 53–92.

Visconti, P. G. B. 1988. *Memoires sur la cour de Louis XIV, 1673–1681*. Edited by J.-F. Solnon. Paris: Perrin.

Part III

Liminality and the Political

Liminality, the Execution of Louis XVI, and the Rise of Terror during the French Revolution

Camil Francisc Roman

Thirty years after being an eyewitness to the battle at Valmy, Goethe wrote of it that "from this place and from this day forth commences a new era in the world's history, and you can all say that you were present at its birth" (Goethe 1849: 81). Back in Paris the National Convention proclaimed the republic on 22 September 1792, and less than two months later, the revolutionaries began the trial of Louis XVI. The revolutionary armies' first victory, in a battle that was nothing more than a daylong exchange of artillery fire,[1] gave the revolution inside France the time and confidence to continue its course. In this context, among the many events that made up the life substance of the French revolution, the trial and execution of "Louis the Last," as the king was "celebrated" by many of the regicides, stand out as key moments. These occurrences marked the apex of two congruent social processes that were unfolding at the time: the regress of royal power and charisma, and the consolidation of a new democratic community of experience.

The historical centrality of the king's death was maybe best recognized and brilliantly hyperbolized in Albert Camus' *The Rebel*, where the philosopher asserted that "the condemnation of the king is at the crux of our contemporary history. It symbolizes the secularization of our history and the dematerialization of the Christian God." For him, the person who died on the scaffold was not Louis Capet, the ordinary man whom Saint-Just

---

tried to exclude from the social contract, but "Louis appointed by divine right," the consequence being that "with him, in a certain manner, died temporal Christianity" as well (Camus 2000: 90, 91). Camus' philosophical reflections open the floor to the essential problems of the advancing revolutionary drama: the role of the royal trial and death in the demise of an ancient political theology that wrapped the worldly French prince in a Christian transcendental cosmology (Kantorowicz 1957), and the bearing Louis XVI's execution had on the subsequent revolutionary trajectory.

Although the French revolution really did concern the social overcoming of the ancient French monarchy of divine right, it often almost seems this drama played out without its central piece, as it were—without the leading actor on the stage. As Michael Walzer (1992: 89) has observed, the king's trial remains on the margins of most histories of the revolution and also has a low profile in the normative debates on the value of revolutionary politics. Ferenc Feher (1987: 97) concludes on the same topic that left and right, liberals and radicals alike seem to agree on at least one aspect: "whether the trial and the execution was a crime or a beneficial deed, the King's person and personal fate was just an ephemeral factor in the great drama." This myopia about the problematic of the king's person, trial, and execution, and the minimization of these elements' relation to the revolution as a whole, are puzzling to say the least.[2]

Using theoretical insights provided by the anthropological theory of liminality, this chapter attempts to reverse this tendency by bringing Louis' trial and death to the attention of any theoretical analysis of the French Revolution. To accomplish this task, in the following I will first expose the paradigmatic positions of three great scholars—the liberal philosopher Michael Walzer (1992), the critical Marxist philosopher Ferenc Feher (1987), and the revisionist historian Francois Furet (1997)—on the way the trial and execution of Louis XVI links to the succeeding open civil war and rise of revolutionary terror. After summing up some of their shortcomings and contradictions, I will take a liminality approach to the king's trial and execution, showing the need to connect these events to the broader dynamic of the revolution, thus clarifying the theoretical advantages of using the proposed framework of analysis to deal with moments of radical social discontinuity.

Michael Walzer and the Illusionism of the Sacred

For Walzer, a liberal philosopher bent on defending the republican regicide, the trial and execution of Louis XVI were crucial episodes in the emergence of a republican democratic consciousness inside France. By building on classic works of such authors as Kantorowicz (1957), Kern (1948), Schramm (1937), Bloch (1973), or Kant (1887), Walzer sets out a twofold demonstration. First he explains the political theology of the royal office in Western Europe and fleshes out the person of the king as the inviolable symbol and embodiment of the polity. God's anointed on earth should be understood as not simply sovereign but also "mysterious and sacred," his inviolability being "a matter of personal right" (Walzer 1992: 42). As the incarnation of the body politic and solely unifying principle of his subjects, the royal person was therefore the only public person of the realm, and politics was essentially court politics (ibid.: 28).

Starting from these premises, Walzer then defends the choice of the majority of deputies in the National Convention to propose a trial with a possible execution (as opposed to the Jacobin solution of assassinating the king) because these measures displayed a more profound understanding of how to overcome the monarchy of divine right. For Walzer, given all the mentioned characteristics of the royal office, the king could die as both a natural body and an embodiment of the realm; that is, he could die as a symbol, but only if he died in public. To this end, a ceremony had to play out, not just in front of the nation "but in ways that involve and implicate the nation" because "the former subjects of the king must witness the destruction of kingship; they must somehow share in the renunciation of their own servitude" (ibid.: 13, 88, 89).

By choosing to look at the political theology of the monarchy of divine right and hence to analyze Louis XVI's trial and execution from a symbolic-phenomenological perspective, Walzer comes to recognize the important role these moments played in the revolution. However, after emphasizing the crucial weight these events should take in any analysis of the consolidation of democratic consciousness during the French revolution, Walzer strives to separate the rise of revolutionary terror after the king's death from the legal proceedings at the trial. To accomplish this he resorts to a political and legal reasoning that essentially argues that, given the specifics of the monarchic mystery and the revolutionary circumstances, a trial that attempted to approximate the conditions of normalized law and to judge specific crimes was not juridically a crime. Therefore, the trial was fundamentally disconnected from the principles of terror: it was a punishment deeply focused on the past, not an act of terrorism (ibid.: 7, 47–89).

In this way, Walzer switches from a symbolic inquiry of the social aimed at highlighting the impact these events had on the rise of democratic consciousness in France, to a narrowly legalistic argument designed to disconnect the death of the king from the further event sequence of the revolution. However, in doing so, the author fails to reflect on the circumstantial effects the newly born democratic consciousness had on the revolutionary course. He thus ends up impoverishing his analysis and contradicting his own very symbolic and phenomenological assumptions, constructed for the study. In consequence, he artificially introduces a radical hiatus between the death of Louis XVI and the aftermath of revolutionary politics, in one stroke downplaying the relevance of this event and thereby contributing to the same scholarly belittling of it that he deplores. Ultimately, Walzer's analysis of the royal death appears to be sacrificed to the superior normative goal of defending the republican regicide.

Ferenc Feher and the Negation of the Sacred

Feher's position on the subject matter looks more coherent at first sight. Like Walzer, he sees the symbolic dimension of the trial as quintessential. Yet the point he is resolved to make is not that the trial and execution of Louis XVI were propitious milestones in the emergence of democratic consciousness, or at least key rituals in the demise of the magical figure of the king. Quite the contrary: for Feher the trial was a politically irrelevant act in actual history, as the monarchic principle did not die on the scaffold, Louis did not become a political martyr, and the execution sparked no civil war (Feher 1987: 100–101).

What Feher aims to show, then, is that the symbolic dimension of the legal proceedings made the trial the founding act of a republic bound to drown in revolutionary terror. By trying not only an actual personal subject but also, and mainly, a fictitious-symbolic person who stood guilty of incorporating "the symbol of a metaphysical idea which had reigned supreme for centuries" (ibid.: 102), the proceedings at the National Convention had nothing to do with justice in any legal sense and were simply a political act. Recognizing the symbolism of the trial—"the personal decapitation of an institution can only be crucial for those who intend to crush a tradition by symbolic acts" and "substitute a new mythology for an old one" (ibid.: 101)—Feher shows how the king's execution was facilitated by two modes of thinking that would lay the foundation of the revolutionary terror led by the Jacobin dictatorship. These are Robespierre's theory of exceptional measures in a state of insurrection; and Saint-Just's radical philosophy of natural law, which came to anathematize whole social categories (ibid., p.109).

This theoretical construction indicates that in Feher's symbolic analysis, the trial of Louis XVI occurred only in the realm of legal and moral philosophy, which becomes the driving force behind the further political unfolding of the revolution. In important ways, his legalistic hermeneutics seems to drift above a field emptied entirely of the social. The symbolism of the king's execution was an important episode in the revolution only insofar as it expressed and catalyzed a radicalizing trend in the revolutionary justice of terror; otherwise it appears to have been essentially marginal to the social processes that sustained that terror. As such, Feher's account reads like Walzer's, only in reverse: whereas Walzer starts his analysis by emphasizing the social role of a unique ritual of power and ends by unwarrantedly magnifying a legal perspective of this ritual, Feher highlights symbolic politics by inflating a legalistic analysis of the royal trial and death and completely marginalizing the social grounding of the considered events. The result is that both misconstrue important elements in the historical outcome. Feher's historical judgment is particularly prone to blatant error when he denies that the king's trial and personal fate were at all relevant to the unfolding revolution. Contrary to his assertion, the monarchic principle of divine right did in fact die on the scaffold, as the French monarchy was never the same again, the person of Louis XVI as martyr actually occupied much of the French political-literary imaginary throughout the nineteenth and twentieth centuries (Dunn 1994), and civil war did indeed come very shortly after the execution of the king. A disenchanted observer, Feher denies the sacred dimension implied in his symbolic analysis and overlooks its bearing on immanent reality.

François Furet and the Absence of the Sacred

François Furet was the last French historian to produce a new great narrative of the French Revolution. In his history of the revolution, Furet remains in effect silent on the meaning of the king's trial and execution in the French political imaginary.[3] But as will become clear, Furet is important to the present analysis for this very reason. For Furet, a revisionist historian trying to dislodge a hegemonic neo-Jacobin/Marxist scholarship inside France, the person of the king is a negligible quantity in the revolutionary drama and in this regard is, as one of Louis' biographers already observed, in agreement with leftist predecessors like Matthiez, Lefebvre, or Soboul (Hardman 2000: ix). This should come as no surprise, considering his theoretical outlook on the revolution and the way it encrypts the two most important aspects of the period following the king's execution: raging open civil war and the rule of terror.

Borrowing the concept of political sociability from Cochin, Furet starts by positing the existence of a democratic political sociability that in 1789 could neither inevitably take over nor for that matter fully crystallize. The electoral battles for the Estates General in spring 1789 changed this situation by creating revolutionary consciousness and actors, or in other words the French Revolution (Furet 1997: 40, 43, 45). As such, for Furet (ibid.: 46), the revolution is conceptually the gap "that opened up between the language of the *Cahiers* and that of the *Ami du pœple* in the space of only a few months."[4] This period holds all the essential elements of the coming revolution: the discourses of democratic politics, the future range of conflicts, and the outbursts of a Terror that would reach its purest form in the Jacobin dictatorship.

Following this lead, Furet begins to push his theoretical model to its logical extremes: for him, the most striking attribute of the period from May–June 1789 to the fall of Robespierre in July 1794

> was not the conflict between Revolution and counter-revolution, but the struggle between the representatives of the successive Assemblies and the club militants for the dominant symbolic position, the people's will. For the conflict between Revolution and counter-revolution extended . . . far beyond 9 Thermidor, while the fall of Robespierre marked the end of a political-ideological system . . . (Furet 1997: 50–51).

Therefore, Furet conceptualizes the first period of the revolution up to 1794 as an ascending spiral in which competing factions for the embodiment of the people's will provoke a growing overlap between an ever more radical revolutionary ideology and the government. This in turn unleashes the intensified terror and the total loss of society's autonomy in relation to the revolutionary government (ibid.: 51–60).

In Furet's understanding, the trial and execution of Louis XVI were, as is now clear, peripheral to the development of the revolution. If terror was an integral part of revolutionary ideology and discourse (ibid.: 61–62), if civil war aptly describes the evolving dynamic among groups trying to appropriate the people's will and hence to embody the nation, and if both of these are present from the revolution's outset, then the person of Louis XVI, the sacred priest-king, becomes a muted figure completely absent from the unfolding social drama. However, Furet's account reduces the value of lived-through experiences to an appendix of freely floating initial discourses that gain ontological explanatory prevalence over the very revolutionary eventfulness he so well defends.[5] Ironically, this preference for a discursive phenomenological analysis seems to blind him to the way historical events symbolically encode the social, thus rendering him analytically insensitive to the sacred dimension tangled in the symbols and actions of collective representation.

All this means that his analytical model could explain revolutionary terror as almost congruent with initial spontaneous mob violence, and open civil war as proclaimed where initially there were only sporadic outbursts of violent social and political conflict. Focusing the attention on discourses, Furet loses sight of the difference between the killings around the Bastille in 1789 and the human sacrifices legally endorsed after the king's death and publicly exposed on the altar of the nation and in the name of a republic of virtue. Equally so in this view, the peasant revolution of 1789 looks much like peasant mutinies throughout the history of the French monarchy, and thus hardly a conflict that needs to be conceptualized from the start as a civil war specific to the revolution. Further, a clear symbolic and existential difference sets these uprisings apart from the civil wars of the Vendee in 1793–94 and other counterrevolutionary areas. In the latter cases, the people fought against the revolution and its missionary zeal; the revolutionary generals and soldiers, for their part, conducted public ceremonies of mass drownings and executions targeting the political adversaries of a newly enacted god, the republic.[6] Of course this does not mean that the initial eruptions of violence were disconnected from the revolution understood as a social process of overcoming the monarchy of divine right—quite the contrary.[7] Rather, it argues that before the execution of Louis XVI, they were existential manifestations of a different degree and their terrifying appearance should not be mistaken for Terror. As long as the king was still the sole legitimate heir of the French nation, a sacred person embodying the symbol of national unity, there was no revolutionary terror as a principle of government applied in the service of a new political religion.[8] A possibly helpful way of understanding this existential distinctiveness may lie in one of René Girard's (1986, p.12) conceptual differentiations between *collective persecutions* as occurrences of mob violence against a target, and *collective resonances of persecutions*, in which acts of crowd violence against a victim are pursued under legal protection. Although Girard himself does not belabor this distinction in his endeavor to pinpoint the scapegoating mechanism, it is nevertheless significant for us, as these concepts could denote two different stages in the ongoing social crisis of the French Revolution. That is, whereas in the first instance the phenomenon of violence could be seen as an expression of a developing sacrificial and cultural crisis seeking a conclusion; in the second, it is already recollecting the initial results of that crisis. In this later stage, the terror is manifested in attempts to enforce the existential "solution" that has emerged from the crisis, in this case the French republic. The point here is that the closer one gets to the "resolution" of the crisis, the more violence intensifies and becomes widespread, resembling a state of civil war. In this context, given the experience of generalized violence, a social threshold to cross toward order and harmony becomes indispensable and is feverishly sought after. The execution of Louis XVI needs to be grasped as precisely that threshold, as this chapter's analysis will further clarify.

The Liminal Context of the French Revolution: The Meaning and Place of the Trial and Execution of Louis XVI in the Revolutionary Crisis

By summing up the arguments of authors like Walzer, Feher, and Furet, I presented three paradigmatic positions on the trial and death of the king that seemed analytically sympathetic toward either political symbolism (Walzer, Feher) or an explicitly phenomenological understanding of the revolution (Furet). The underlying assumption was that such positions are likely to clarify these events' significance for the French political imaginary and their bearing upon the revolutionary dynamic. In the following I will analyze the trial and beheading of the king in the context of liminality to further elucidate the critiques of the mentioned authors.

Starting as a concept of cultural anthropology at the turn of the twentieth century (van Gennep 1960), liminality describes the part of the rites of passage in which entire small-scale communities, or some members of them, experience transformative moments that undo the previous social structure before being eventually reconfigured along reinforcing lines of incorporation. After going through a process of revival thanks to Turner's (1969, 1985) works on the anthropology of experience, liminality has more recently come to be explored as a tool of analysis applied to moments of crisis in large-scale societies, or even across whole epochs and geographical spaces (Wydra 2000, 2007; Mälksoo 2010; Eisenstadt 1995; Szakolczai 2000, 2003, 2008; Thomassen 2009, 2012; Norton 1988). As the present volume plainly shows, the liminality approach presents a possible paradigmatic challenge to current structural, systemic, or normative narratives of social and political transformations. In this context revolutions, with their situations of social boundlessness, are particularly suited to being studied through the prism of liminality. Describing places where political imaginaries are marked by radical processes of dissolution and reconstruction, and where guiding symbols and previous markers of certainty are crushed and reconstituted, revolutions neatly approximate the liminal situations of small-scale societies.[9]

By the time Louis XVI—by the grace of God, King of France and Navarre; and by the gift of the Pope, Rex Christianissimus, the most Christian king[10]—was first brought before the bar of the National Convention as the humbled Louis Capet in December 1792, the revolution inside France had advanced enormously in just a few years. The political crisis at the society's core had opened a rift, exposing the parts of the French that were disenchanted with the monarchy of divine right. In the social space of liminality, revolutionary events formed the social fluidity through which people from all walks of life were put together, shrinking the social distance and symbolic space that separated them in times of stability and calm. This contraction of the social eroded the ritual order and the compartmentalization of society that supported this order. The revolutionary events should therefore be apprehended as developments of social undifferentiation that intensified the sacrificial and ritual crisis at the heart of a decaying cultural order. The resulting escalation of violence in turn reinforced the initial political crisis. Without a deus ex machina to control, give meaning, and guide a very troubling social experience, crowds affected by the between and betwixt of liminality tried to make sense of their lives and find a way out of their existential disorientation. Spontaneous mob violence, symbolic representations, the performance of power rituals, and desecrations of "holy" objects were essential means by which these crowds attempted to regain cosmologic certainty, expel the maleficent sacred, and restore social harmony. Along with mimetic processes of desire engulfing large spans of society, these evolutions set in motion dramatic outbursts of social contagion related to newly discovered and adored images of power.[11]

On this basis, a new democratic community of experience emerged within the bounds of the French revolution. Transcending so-called class lines, it helped to reconfigure a shattered political imaginary along the lines of "the people" as a new category of existential representation.[12] In this sense, the French Revolution is a fascinating example of how, in liminal social conditions, revolutionary events were symbolic breaks with the past, socially disincorporating an old political theology of the state—in this case the monarchy of divine right—and reincorporating it within new political boundaries. Like the previous categories of collective representation, the new images of power shaped in those moments were sacralized references endowed with charisma and redeeming powers against the evils experienced by society.

In the flow of revolutionary events, therefore, the trial and execution of Louis XVI should be seen as the most out-of-the-ordinary expression of crisis—the apex heralding the advent of the people as the new sovereign. Walzer (1992: 88) captures this very well, remarking that "the symbolic disenchantment of the realm as well as the establishment of a secular republic" is a very special aspect of this affair, and that its place in the revolution stands out because in 1792, "kings were still magical figures for large numbers of their subjects and royalism was still a popular ideology," so the disincorporation of royal power was far from an accomplished social fact. Thus we should remain wary of the philosophical undertones that often run through scholarly accounts, especially those of positivist and rationalist inspiration, implying a linear, inevitable historical development pointing in one direction.[13] The experience of liminality in revolutionary crises has no master of ceremonies to guide the process along economic interests, class lines, or other analytical categories constructed ex post facto by scholars attempting to rationalize history. For this reason, a liminality understanding of a revolution defies the "illusion of historical consciousness" that projects only one possible future onto the past (Furet 1997: 19), and instead emphasizes the radical open-endedness of such moments.

In relation to the French Revolution, maybe no historian has comprehended this better than Furet himself, who argued skillfully that the language of causality is misplaced, as the revolutionary event produced "a new mode of historical action that was not intrinsically a part of that situation" or, put another way, that "the debate about the causes of the Revolution does not cover the problem of the revolutionary phenomenon" (ibid.: 22). Yet surprisingly, despite Furet's argument for a phenomenologically grounded analysis, he not only ignores the trial and execution of the king as important events of the revolutionary dynamic, as we have seen, but also sees the absolute monarchy as having died "in theory and in practice" in 1787, when the intendants shared power with elected assemblies (ibid.: 44). Further, the sacred person of the monarch was overcome after Varennes, when "his route by the silent rows of his erstwhile subjects, was . . . a coronation in reverse, the final undoing of what had been done at Reims" (ibid.: 64). Likewise, Walzer (1992: 88) had observed that Geertz considered the principle of kingly authority destroyed long before the trial and execution of the king, thereby underestimating the symbolic impact these events had on the disincorporation of royal power itself.[14] An anthropologically driven theory like liminality can overcome such analytical inconsistencies by emphasizing the power of lived-through experiences in shaping social situations and stamping historical dynamics.

From this it follows that bringing to justice a monarch of divine right whose very bodily existence symbolized the unity of the realm,[15] and whose death provoked "hysterical scenes of suicide and madness" (Camus 2000: 90) was not simply a profane act devoid of any historical significance or an event driven mechanically by history's inexorable logic toward the fruition of an inescapable *telos*. Rather, the trial and death of Louis XVI need to be placed in the sequence of symbolically highly charged revolutionary events through which a new political imaginary was created concomitantly with the demise of an old one. As such, the king's execution was an expression of the existential crisis at the heart of French society, a critical juncture that provided a powerful legitimization weapon in the drift toward a different political community, and a ritual of transgression sustaining the energy the new sovereign could feed on in the unfolding revolution, and on which it could hope to reconstitute its broken cosmos.

By the time his trial began, Louis XVI had been imprisoned for several months. Stripped of his power and deprived of contact with his family and the outside world, the pious king intensely read *Imitatio Christi*, thus paying a final tribute to the political theology of the royal office. Before death, and perhaps more than at any other point in his life, the image of the priestly king took over in his dealings with his former subjects (Fay 1968). It almost seems that by a strange working of chance and destiny, the French monarchy was peeled of its cultural layers at the moment of its greatest peril, only to reveal more clearly, in the person of the ultra-devout Catholic Louis XVI, its trans-historic cosmologic core: the Christ-imitating ritual that had founded and oriented its subjects' lifeworld for a millennium and would soon be performed one last time.

Back in the National Convention, the legal proceedings of the trial brought the revolutionary drama to the surface in the most eloquent of terms as the ancient monarchy of divine right faced the implacable voices of Quinet's people-God. Unlike the political process of convoking the General Estates in 1789, which had involved virtually the entire nation, the first universal vote in history took place in an atmosphere of fear combined with disinterest, and no more than 10 percent of French electors participated in the poll (Allen 1999: 175–76). In practice this meant that the parliamentary assembly was purged of all royalist elements: not a single deputy of the Convention ran as a royalist in the elections, and when the vote on the trial came, 693 out of 719 present deputies judged the king guilty of treason, 26 deputies added some conditions to their incriminating vote, and none of them found the king innocent (Jordan 1979: 46, 172).

In this context, this trial reveals the extraordinary aspect of the power and fascination the royal symbol still exerted over the minds and hearts of the present deputies, even as they affirmed the unlimited claims of the people's legitimacy. As Susan Dunn shows, far from being a mere royal shadow or, in the poetic words of Michelet, "a wooden head, meaningless and hollow, a vacant thing" (Dunn 1994: 72), Louis was indeed very much alive as a king of divine right, maybe mostly so for the Jacobins and all his regicidal enemies. In the debates at Louis' trial, the *convention-nels* hyperbolized the king's role in the course of the French Revolution, depleting him of any human attributes and blaming him for all the evils of the French or even of all humanity. To give a few examples, Carra described the king as "the source of corruption and servitude," a "fatal talisman of all our ills" and "a monster covered with all species of crime." For the Abbé Gregoire, "dynasties have never been anything but voracious breeds living of human flesh" and a "talisman whose magic power may still stupefy many more people." In Bertucat's eyes, the people's salvation lay in "cutting off the head of a monster so as to paralyze his whole race with fear," whereas for Lakanal, Louis was a "monster made out of blood and mud." Not least, Joseph Serre saw the French king as "a monster soiled by crime," and Louchet called him "a monster dripping with the blood of the French" (Dunn 1994: 15–18). Just as Oedipus the King had faced a decaying cultural order, escalating reciprocated violence, and a spiraling sacrificial crisis (Girard 1979: 68–88), the intensification of the French drama confronted Louis XVI with the specter of unanimous violence targeting the community's most powerful but also most vulnerable person: a king who was both the source of political meaning and the main transgressor of the promised social order and public happiness. In other words, the drama converged against the symbol most likely to be stigmatized and marked for a ritual sacrifice.

In the liminal conditions of the revolution, fear of the unknown invaded social spheres, upending previous categories of beneficent sacredness and transforming them into manifestations of a sacred evil. As Dunn (1994: 15) observes, the people experiencing this saw Louis XVI as a supernatural being, a healer with magical powers whose death by a ritual of human sacrifice would solve France's social problems and purify its relation to the past. For the newspaper *Revolutions de Paris*,

> the blood of Louis Capet, shed by the blade of the law . . . cleanses us of a stigma of 1300 years . . . Liberty resembles the divinity of the Ancients which one cannot make auspicious and favourable except by offering to it in sacrifice the life of a great culprit (ibid.: 19).

For Marat, a member of the National Convention and one of the most fanatic "priests" of the revolution, there would be "no freedom, no security, no peace, no tranquillity, no happiness for the French, no hope for the other peoples of breaking their chains, if the tyrant's head does not fall" (ibid.: 18).

The legal procedures through which the fate of Louis XVI was decided were undoubtedly fallible. The trial was public, but otherwise the provisions of the Criminal Code of 1791 were all violated (Jordan 1979: 101–16).[16] The "sacred" character of the king's person, declared in the constitution of 1791, meant that although he was impeachable under certain circumstances, he was legally accountable only for acts made after he was deposed (Feher 1987: 104). In the face of these facts, Louis XVI's trial and execution clearly were social acts occurring outside the sphere of formal law—a collective ritual of desecration through which a minority, congregated under the cupola of the nation, tried to strip the king of his magical mystery and institute a new cosmological order. As such, they were an expression of symbolic politics in its purest form, a key anthropological manifestation of the "people" as a sacred symbol, an entity endowed with the supernatural capacity to orient action through the nemesis and potential catharsis of existential chaos.

In that respect, nothing evokes the awe-inspiring experience of the nation who replaces the old sovereign more than certain widely popularized sentences of the two most important regicides in the Convention: Saint-Just and Robespierre. For the former, "a king should be accused, not for the crimes of his administration, but for the crime of having been king," "the revolution begins when the tyrant ends," "this man must reign or die," and "all evil men are of the king's party" (Saint-Just 1992a: 123, 124; 1992b: 175, 176). The latter asserted that "Louis must die because the nation must live," "we invoke forms because we lack principles," "Louis cannot be judged; he has already been condemned, else the Republic is not cleared of guilt," and "you ask for an exception to the death penalty for the only man who could make that penalty legitimate" (Robespierre 1992a: 131, 133, 138).

The socialist historian Jean Jaurès, having studied the arguments at the trial and found that the radicals' perorations and accusations magnified the image of Louis as history-moving myth and symbol, suspected they had unwittingly worked to re-legitimize the monarchy (Hardman 2000: 166).[17] However, the point here is not to trivialize dramatic historical moments by singling out the sheer irrationality of the Jacobins or of the royalists on the basis of contemporary discourses on human nature, as Walzer (1992), Dunn (1994), and many other commentators tend to do. This would amount to superimposing a present worldview based on a normative clarification that was not a part of but mainly a result of the social situation that is supposed to make sense of. To avoid this, what is needed is methodological "normalization" and incorporation of these expressions of emotions and will into the analytical framework. From this emerges the understanding that in situations of liminal crises, there will always be "Jacobins" or radicals of some sort who will epitomize the experience of a new sacralized symbol of political community and try to transpose it into immanent reality. And the highly emotional rejection of the "anti-symbol"[18] — of everything that reflects different political-historical boundaries for personal and collective deliverance — is integral to the rise of a new category of collective political representation aimed at restoring order and dispelling the previous social chaos.

Beyond the Jacobins' and their acolytes' radical speeches demanding immediate death without trial for the king, it is important to recall that the ritual of symbolic law performed through the trial and execution of Louis XVI was the royal *punctus terminus*, brought about by *all* national deputies, though with varying degrees of responsibility. Virtually the entire assembly of deputies found the king guilty of treason (Furet 1996: 118; Jordan 1979: 233), so the only relevant question was how to best get rid of the person of the king so as to save the republic — not, as often unintentionally leaks from many historical texts, how to save the king. In the shifting political dynamics of the National Convention, the trial was pushed forward by the Girondins and a large majority of the Plain, and the unappeasable Jacobin logic demanding the royal beheading made the execution unavoidable; hence the deputies of the Convention came together to stage and enforce the most powerful symbolic act of the revolution. At the sharp end of the guillotine, this was a regicide Convention aiming to end a sacrificial crisis. The trial and death of Louis XVI became a ritual on the altar of the republic performed by all the deputies in concert, irrespective of their intentions or actual final votes on the sentence. The enduring tribulations in which they found themselves — the exhausting and despairing discussions on the fate of the king that brought so many Jacobins to sheer desolation, the 36-hour final vote on Louis' death, the repetition of this vote, the tragicomic personages painstakingly changing their minds from debate to debate and sometimes from day to day[19] — dramatically attest to the shaken consciousness of a congregation aware of the sacrificial and symbolic dimension involved in their dealings with the royal person.

To conclude on this point, the execution of Louis XVI was indeed an extralegal ritual act of republican justice and foundation, and all the deputies at the Convention inescapably shared symbolic and real responsibility for it. And in it lies one of the keys to this act's symbolic effectiveness and endurance in the political imaginary of the radical revolutionaries and, by extension, many French. Involving the nation in a "ritual act of sacrifice," as Walzer refers to the event, meant among other things being part of an awe-inspiring brotherhood of crime that could be overcome (or lived with) only as long as the newly revealed existential truth was continuously confessed. In this way, the bridges to the past were indeed burned as the Jacobins had hoped, and the revolution carried on for better or worse, blown by the winds of the past revolutionary events. The royal blood added a sinister energy and impetus to the coming revolutionary terror and civil war.

When the royal cortege left the Temple prison at 7:00 a.m. on 21 January 1793, some eighty thousand citizen-soldiers participated in one capacity or another in the security measures around the execution of Louis XVI at the Place de la Revolution.[20] The king's two dignified, serene, courageous appearances at his trial had made a huge impression, not only on the Convention but also on Parisian public opinion and contemporaries across France (Jordan 1979: 112, 141, 153–54, 214), so no one wanted to take chances. Louis' guard alone was composed of 1,400 fully armed soldiers paced by 60 drummers, and the entire road to the guillotine was protected by rows of soldiers and trustworthy onlookers keen to witness these most extraordinary moments in French royal history. After two hours, the kingly Via Dolorosa ended amidst deathly alluring drumbeats, biblical readings, and prayers—not without incident, as royal sympathizers were killed, or nearly so, for various desperate, senseless acts of bravery. When the king arrived at the Place de la Revolution, about 20,000 people were packed in the square and its surroundings, melting into a veritable republican community of experience (Jordan 1979: 213–19).

As soon as Louis' head fell into the basket, the delivered crowd started chanting republican songs. Civilians and soldiers alike waved their hats and arms in the air, cherishing the longed-for moment. Some formed a chain around the scaffold and danced and sang the Marseillaise. Mobs stormed around the executioner seeking souvenirs—pieces of the king's clothes and hair—and soaking one's handkerchief in the king's blood was a priceless privilege ardently fought for (Jordan 1979: 220). That day, the human sacrifice of the most holy subject of the monarchy of divine right concluded a lengthy mechanism of persecution by which a community immolated a surrogate victim assumed to be the source of the communities' crisis (Girard 1979). Just as small-scale communities pass through phases of transition and experience an unsettling undifferentiation between the pure and the impure, the sacred and the profane (van Gennep 1960), the lifeworld opened up by the liminal period of the revolution was characterized by a sense of blurred reality in need of strict lines of differentiation between the maleficent and the benevolent sacred. The attempt to rally popular unanimity around the royal execution served as a ritual of incorporation into a new cultural order with new gods and a new sense of good and evil. The nation as sovereign hereby performed at once a rite of consecration of the self-aggrandizement of the people, and one of expiation that de-sacralized the royal mystery.[21] According to Hubert and Mauss (1964: 50–60), these overlapping categories of rites generate a state of sanctity and dispel one of sin, and this is the key to decoding the frenzied scenes of joy playing out at the Place de la Revolution. Ideas of redemption—implicated in any human sacrifice (ibid.: 98–99)—and expectations of reconciliation and the return of order (Girard 1986: 42) were integral parts of the royal execution.[22]

To conclude, with the death of Louis XVI, the democratic community grown out of the experience of liminality enforced its newly found existential truth in immanent reality. Messianic expectations and missionary acts were key elements of this resurgence. The political religion born of the revolution proclaimed to the whole world that there could be no justice common to humanity and kings (Saint-Just 1992a: 121–27), and that "the minority retains an inalienable right to make heard the voice of truth, or what it regards as such. Virtue is always in the minority on this earth" (Robespierre 1992b: 192). It also declared that "the revolutionary government owes to good citizens all the protection of the nation" but "owes the enemies of the people only death"[23], and that "we must govern with steel those who cannot be governed with justice."[24] These statements, made by Saint-Just and Robespierre at various points of the revolution, illustrate the state of mind that led to the rule of terror and to civil war. The awesome experience of the people as a fundamentally sacral entity prompted its apostles[25] to perform acts of human sacrifice on the newly erected political altars of the republic. Geertz (1964: 63–64) notes in this regard that the French Revolution was the greatest breeder of extremist ideologies—not because of exacerbated social antagonisms, but because the central organizing principle of political life was destroyed, whereupon autonomous politics and all-encompassing ideologies emerged to fill the void of meaning and make the social situation comprehensible.[26] In other words, the killing of the mystical incarnation of the body politic, expression of French unity and reconciliation, and political mediator between heaven and earth left behind an entirely shattered moral universe, a traumatized society in which ancient social and political practices were crushed and society was far from any enduring recomposition.

However, there is more to this than Geertz lets us believe. Once again, the decisive insight might come from Girard, who argued that the use of a ritual victim in "primitive" societies has to be understood as a way of assuring the perpetuation of a given cultural order by ritually repeating the successful resolution of an initial sacrificial crisis. As this crisis was ended by the death of a surrogate victim, the ritual victim—which, over time, does not necessarily remain human—takes its place (Girard 1979: 101–2). Putting this in perspective, it is hard to ignore that the great Jacobin terror unleashed after the death of Louis XVI was a genuine expression of a regime whose multiplying ritual victims dovetailed with the original model of the royal execution. As soon as the king's head fell under the blade of the guillotine, a web of countless other "national razors" or "mills of silence"[27] spread across the territory of France, all with the specific mission of replicating the original founding act of the new cosmos. For over a year, one head after another fell more or less randomly, outside the protection of any kind of considerations for formal law, justified by rather metaphysical incriminations referring to what the victims were thought to represent.

This enduring festival of republican political order and the sheer violence and brutality emanating from it had a major impact. Contrary to the common assumption that the terror exhausted the revolution, this violence replicated the unbridled social ecstasy at the king's execution, so the beheadings long served as occasions of genuine public celebration in the most literal sense. By reenacting the republican unanimity unleashed by the execution of the king, the public killings of innumerable "miniature kings" during the subsequent reign of terror became both frightening human sacrifices and rites of incorporation into a new political community that strengthened the republican credo and the belief in a redeeming new world. The exorcism of the monarchic idea through the physical elimination of presumed opponents dramatically altered the social imaginary and shifted prevailing understandings of political community toward the republican sacred.

Still, at this point one might ask why, despite the ritual reenactment of republican solidarity through such a formidably ruthless weapon as the rule of terror, the revolutionaries never managed to achieve the hoped-for unanimity and return of order and social harmony. Why did crossing the social threshold of the royal execution fail to produce the expected results? Aside from the problem of real conflicts of interest underlying French society, the crucial aspect here concerns the nature of the democratic political theology in whose name the regime's actions were undertaken. The sacralization of the victim, common to all rituals of sacrifice (Girard 2010: 22), meant that as soon as the king was dead, the French political imaginary was haunted by, and longing for, the one personification that could halt the social chaos and give meaning to the nation. Against this backdrop, the rising democratic political theology—characterized by what Lefort (2006: 159) captured so well as the "symbolic empty space of power"—aggravated the situation, inasmuch as the impossibility of embodying the people in any lasting, meaningful way led straight to schismogenic conflict (Bateson 1958), terror, civil war, and, quite "naturally," various forms of modern dictatorships, from the rule of the Committee of Public Safety to the empire later incorporated by Napoleon. As the king had once touched the scrofulous and healed all the faithful children of God with divine grace (Bloch 1973), the nation and its ephemeral representatives desperately tried to touch factions and eliminate all opposition to its mission to redeem humanity and bring about the happiness of a new age.

The totalitarian democracy, open civil war, and governmental terror in the aftermath of the king's execution therefore arose at the crossroads between the destruction of an ancient unifying principle of the body politic that still dominated the political imaginary of the French, and the emergence of a symbol of political representation whose very anthropological fundaments are necessarily based on expressions of temporary charisma. Here Furet is right when he argues that the flux of terror was independent of political externalities.[28] As he correctly points out, not every situation of extreme national danger causes revolutionary terror; indeed, the military situation had already improved when the Great Terror of spring 1794 surfaced (Furet 1997: 62).

Final Remarks

In this chapter I argued that the French Revolution was a liminal social space marked by existential insecurity and the dissolution of markers of certainty, in which transformative experiences and authoritative symbolic acts accomplished the destruction and reconfiguration of the political sacred. Though recent debates about the French Revolution usually neglect the trial and execution of Louis XVI, I showed how the anthropological theory of liminality shifts the perspective on these moments to highlight them as key elements in any analysis of the unfolding French social political crisis. As important rituals of transgression, through which the monarchy of divine right was partially overcome and the political power symbolically reincorporated in the form of the people, these events contributed substantially to the rise of a democratic consciousness and community of experience. However, a liminality approach in which the symbolic dimensions of actions of collective representation are built into the analytical framework also draws our attention to the very dangerous aspects of radical social discontinuities, and finds purely celebratory accounts of such situations overly facile and problematic. After the death of the king and the loss of the unifying symbol of the French nation, the new democratic cosmos with its enduring empty space of power translated into immanent reality as the politics of ultimate ends (Pizzorno 1987), confronting French society with open civil war and revolutionary terror. The symbolic-phenomenological study by Walzer, the legal-symbolic philosophical perspective of Feher, and the discursive phenomenological analysis of Furet failed or refused to recognize this connection, even though their various theoretical premises might have led them to do so. A detailed phenomenology of the terror and open civil war that followed the death of Louis XVI would need to further clarify conceptually the relation between the execution of a once solely legitimate embodiment of national unity and the dynamics of personified temporary charisma in the context of a rapidly spreading new democratic political religion.

Notes

1. The combat on 20 September 1792 was "tactically inconclusive but strategically decisive" (Hardman 2000, p.158). With the retreat of the Prussian forces, the rather dull fighting ended with fewer than 400 victims in total (Saine 1988: 143). For very good coverage of the 1792 allied campaign in France, see Saine's *Black Bread–White Bread: German Intellectuals and the French Revolution* (1988: 93–150).
2. Robespierre himself thought of the king's trial as the "most dangerous crisis of our entire revolution" (Jordan 1979: 231), but the magnitude of the event does not seem to have resonated much among twentieth-century scholars. This certainly contrasts with nineteenth-century France, when the trial and death of the king haunted the imaginary across the political and literary landscape (Dunn 1994).
3. When his history comes to the phase of Louis XVI's trial and death, only two paragraphs deal with the question of meaning (Furet 1996: 122).
4. The "cahiers" were reports drafted by communities of France representing the various French estates. Addressed to the king and to the coming assembly of the Estates General, these reports were the monarchy's way of consulting the population at large regarding its grievances. Furet did not find in them any noteworthy semantic evidence indicating the potential outbreak of a revolution, so the period Furet refers to lasted from spring to September in 1789.
5. As we shall shortly see, Furet is one of the main theorizers of the French Revolution as an event or sequence of events.
6. For testimonies of mind-blowing atrocities, see Secher's (2003: esp. 98–145) work on the war in the Vendée.
7. The historian Georges Lefebvre, who is still a leading authority on the rural world of the revolution, asserted for example that the generalized peasant uprisings in 1789 were

deeply connected to the convocation of the Estates General and the fall of the Bastille. In other words, they were linked to two of the most far-reaching *events* of the revolution. Still, as their mutinies targeted mainly the aristocracy, the peasants curiously thought of them as following the king's will (Lefebvre 1967: 143–47). The revolts spreading through the countryside in the context of the "great terror" then dealt a massive blow to what was left of the feudal social system on the night of 4 August 1789, when the deputies were induced to outlaw many of its ancient prerogatives.

8. On the concept of political religion, see, e.g., Eric Voegelin's (1986) classic discussion of fascism and communism. For a general problematization and application of the concept, see, e.g., Griffin, Mallet, and Tortorice's (2008) *The Sacred in Twentieth-Century Politics*.

9. For a detailed review and contextualization of the concept of liminality, please refer to the introduction and first two chapters of the present volume.

10. For all the titles and names Louis XVI was known by throughout his life—names symbolizing as many rituals of incorporation into the royal cosmos—see his biography by Hardman (2000: xiii).

11. For an elaboration of the relation between a decaying cultural order, social crises, and the undifferentiation of the social, and for how these comprise processes marked by the mimetics of desire and mimetic violence, see René Girard's (1979) *Violence and the Sacred*.

12. Existential representation is used here in the understanding of Eric Voegelin (1987: 27–51), that is, as the principle according to which existence in society is articulated and represented institutionally through the acts of giving meaning to common life.

13. A classic example in relation to the French Revolution is Skocpol's (1979) *States and Social Revolutions: A Comparative Analysis of France, Russia and China*. An even more "grandiose" example of an overly deterministic theoretical structure is Wallerstein's (1974) *The Modern World-System: Capitalist Agriculture and the Origins of the European World-Economy in the Sixteenth Century*. For very pertinent critiques of these theoretical models from a phenomenological perspective, see Sewell's (2005) essay "Three Temporalities: Toward an Eventful Sociology."

14. See Geertz's explicit position on this aspect in his essay "Centers, Kings and Charisma: Reflections on the Symbols of Power" (1985: 38n43).

15. On the double nature of the king's body, see Kantorowicz (1957).

16. To give some major examples, the members of the Convention were at once judges, jury, and attorneys for the prosecution, whereas the king was not informed about the charges against him until he appeared before the bar and was provided with a lawyer only after his first interrogation (Jordan 1979: 102).

17. Jaurès conceived of the following as part of the imagined defense Louis should have articulated at his trial: "Prenez garde, vous qui vous croyez républicains! penser ainsi, c'est être encore monarchist, car s'il est vrai qu'un seul home determine, en bien ou en mal, la marche de l'histoire, le droit de la royauté est fondé," and therefore "vous cédez, plus qu'il n'est raisonnable, au prestige séculaire de la royauté" (Jaurès n.d.: 883).

18. The essential anti-symbol from the revolutionaries' standpoint was obviously the king.

19. For a fascinating account of the deputies' highly emotionally charged behavior, see Jordan (1979: 101–207).

20. For an idea of how extravagant these security measures were, note that in 1793 the population of Paris could not have exceeded a gross maximum of 640,000 people, whereas on the eve of the revolution Paris held between 525,000 and 550,000 people. Thus the inhabitants of Paris at the time of the execution probably numbered between 550 and 640 thousand (Chevalier 1973: 175–85).

21. Geertz overlooked this last, usually forgotten dimension of the king's execution.

22. My analysis is partially indebted to Susan Dunn (1994), who depicts the specific scene of the execution of Louis XVI in similar anthropological terms, using some of Girard's and Mauss and Hubert's insights. However, her overall goal of illuminating the Jacobin political imaginary takes the form of literary exegesis rather than making social theoretical arguments about the processes of these events and their impact on the revolutionary dynamic. She therefore misses several points, including that the trial and execution of the king were mainly about a *collective* attempt to finish a sacrificial crisis, rather than a debate and conflict between "good" and "bad" Girondins and Jacobins.
23. These phrases of Robespierre's were formulated in 1793 (Secher 2003: 2).
24. This sentence by Saint-Just was formulated during the Reign of Terror (Secher 2003: 3).
25. After the fall of the Bastille, the stones of that erstwhile symbol of despotism were carried to all cardinal points of France by "apostles of Liberty" (Godechot 1970: 265).
26. Geertz's argument was noticed and emphasized also by Dunn (1994: 25–26).
27. Carrier gave the guillotine these nicknames (Secher 2003: 111).
28. "There were no revolutionary circumstances; there was a Revolution that fed on circumstances" (Furet 1997: 62).

References

Allen, R. 1999. *Threshold of Terror: The Last Hours of the Monarchy in the French Revolution.* Stroud: Sutton.

Bateson, G. 1958. *Naven: A Survey of the Problems Suggested by a Composite Picture of the Culture of a New Guinea Tribe Drawn from Three Points of View.* Stanford, CA: Stanford University Press.

Bloch, M. 1973. *The Royal Touch: Sacred Monarchy and Scrofula in England and France.* London: Routledge & Kegan Paul.

Camus, A. 2000. *The Rebel.* London: Penguin Books (in association with Hamish Hamilton).

Chevalier, L. 1973. *Labouring Classes and Dangerous Classes in Paris During the First Half of the Nineteenth Century.* London: Routledge & Kegan Paul.

Dunn, S. 1994. *The Deaths of Louis XVI: Regicide and the French Political Imagination.* Chichester: Princeton University Press.

Eisenstadt, S. N. 1995. "The Order-Maintaining and Order-transforming Dimensions of Culture." In *Power, Trust and Meaning: Essays in Sociological Theory and Analysis,* edited by S. N. Eisenstadt. Chicago: Chicago University Press.

Fay, B. 1968. *Louis XVI or the End of a World.* London: W. H. Allen.

Feher, F. 1987. *The Frozen Revolution: An Essay on Jacobinism.* Cambridge: Cambridge University Press.

Furet, F. 1996. *The French Revolution. 1770–1814.* Oxford: Blackwell.

———. 1997. *Interpreting the French Revolution.* Cambridge: Cambridge University Press.

Geertz, C. 1964. "Ideology as a Cultural System." In *Ideology and Discontent,* edited by D. E. Apter. London: Collier-Macmillan.

———. 1985. "Centers, Kings, and Charisma: Reflections on the Symbolics of Power." In *Rites of Power: Symbolism, Ritual, and Politics Since the Middle Ages,* edited by S. Wilentz. Philadelphia: University of Pennsylvania Press.

Gennep, A. van. 1960. *The Rites of Passage.* London: Routledge and Kegan Paul.

Girard, R. 1979. *Violence and the Sacred.* London: Johns Hopkins University Press.

———. 1986. *The Scapegoat.* Baltimore, MD: Johns Hopkins University Press.

———. 2010. *Battling to the End: Conversations with Benoit Chantre.* East Lansing: Michigan State University Press.

Godechot, J. 1970. *The Taking of the Bastille. July 14th 1789*. London: Faber and Faber.

Goethe, J. W. von. 1849. *Campaign in France in the Year 1792*. London: Chapman and Hall.

Griffin, R., R. Mallet, and J. Tortorice. 2008. *The Sacred in Twentieth-Century Politics: Essays in Honour of Professor Stanley G. Payne*. New York: Palgrave Macmillan.

Hardman, J. 2000. *Louis XVI: The Silent King*. London: Arnold.

Hubert, H., and M. Mauss. 1964. *Sacrifice: Its Nature and Function*. London: Cohen & West.

Jaurès, J. n.d. *Histoire Socialiste*, vol. 4, *La Convention*. Paris: Rouff.

Jordan, D. P. 1979. *The King's Trial: The French Revolution vs. Louis XVI*. London: University of California Press.

Kant, I. 1887. *The Philosophy of Law: An Exposition of the Fundamental Principles of Jurisprudence as the Science of Right*. Edinburgh: T. & T. Clark.

Kantorowicz, E. H. 1957. *The King's Two Bodies: A Study in Medieval Political Theology*. Princeton, NJ: Princeton University Press.

Kern, F. 1948. *Kingship and Law in the Middle Ages*. Oxford: Basil Blackwell.

Lefebvre, G. 1967. *The Coming of the French Revolution, 1789*. Princeton, NJ: Princeton University Press.

Lefort, C. 2006. "The Permanence of the Theologico-Political?" In *Political Theologies: Public Religions in a Post-Secular World*, edited by H. de Vries and E. L. Sullivan. New York: Fordham University Press.

Mälksoo, M. 2010. *The Politics of Becoming European: A Study of Polish and Baltic Post–Cold War Security Imaginaries*. Oxon: Routledge.

Norton, A. 1988. *Reflections on Political Identity*. Baltimore, MD: The Johns Hopkins University Press.

Pizzorno, A. 1987. "Politics Unbound." In *Changing Boundaries of the Political: Essays on the Evolving Balance Between the State and Society, Public and Private in Europe*, edited by C. S. Maier. Cambridge: Cambridge University Press.

Robespierre. 1992a. "Speech from 3 December 1792." In *Regicide and Revolution: Speeches at the Trial of Louis XVI*, edited by M. Walzer. New York: Columbia University Press.

———. 1992b. "Speech from 28 December 1792." In *Regicide and Revolution: Speeches at the Trial of Louis XVI*, edited by M. Walzer. New York: Columbia University Press.

Saine, T. P. 1988. *Black Bread–White Bread: German Intellectuals and the French Revolution*. Columbia: Camden House.

Saint-Just. 1992a. "Speech from 13 November 1792." In *Regicide and Revolution: Speeches at the Trial of Louis XVI*, edited by M. Walzer. New York: Columbia University Press.

———. 1992b. "Speech from 27 December 1792." In *Regicide and Revolution: Speeches at the Trial of Louis XVI*, edited by M. Walzer. New York: Columbia University Press.

Schramm, P. 1937. *A History of the English Coronation*. Oxford: The Clarendon Press.

Secher, R. 2003. *A French Genocide: The Vendeé*. Notre Dame, IN: University of Notre Dame Press.

Sewell, W. H. Jr. 2005. "Three Temporalities: Toward an Eventful Sociology." In *Logics of History: Social Theory and Social Transformation*, edited by W. H. Sewell Jr. Chicago: University of Chicago Press.

Skocpol, T. 1979. *States and Social Revolutions: A Comparative Analysis of France, Russia and China*. Cambridge: Cambridge University Press.

Szakolczai, A. 2000. *Reflexive Historical Sociology*. London: Routledge.

———. 2003. *The Genesis of Modernity*. London: Routledge.

———. 2008. *Sociology, Religion and Grace: A Quest for the Renaissance*. London: Routledge.

Thomassen, B. 2009. "The Uses and Meanings of Liminality." *International Political Anthropology* 2 (1): 5–27.

———. 2012. "Notes towards an Anthropology of Political Revolutions." *Comparative Studies in Society and History* 54 (3): 679–706.

Turner, V. 1969. *The Ritual Process: Structure and Anti-structure.* London: Routledge and Kegan Paul.

———. 1985. *On the Edge of the Bush: Anthropology as Experience.* Tucson: University of Arizona Press.

Voegelin, E. 1986. *Political Religions.* Lewiston, NY: Edwin Mellen Press.

———. 1987. *The New Science of Politics. An Introduction.* London: The University of Chicago Press.

Wallerstein, I. 1974. *The Modern World-System: Capitalist Agriculture and the Origins of the European World-Economy in the Sixteenth Century.* London: Academic Press.

Walzer, M. 1992. "Regicide and Revolution." In *Regicide and Revolution: Speeches at the Trial of Louis XVI,* edited by M. Walzer. New York: Columbia University Press.

Wydra, H. 2000. *Continuities in Poland's Permanent Transition.* Basingstoke: Macmillan.

———. 2007. *Communism and the Emergence of Democracy.* Cambridge: Cambridge University Press.

Chapter 9

In Search of Antistructure

The Meaning of Tahrir Square in Egypt's Ongoing Social Drama

Mark Allen Peterson

Introduction

Revolutions are usually sprawling, unpredictable, inchoate things whose structures become apparent only from a distance as they unfold over time. Certainly this is true of the Egyptian revolution. Beginning as a carefully orchestrated protest by experienced agitators against the police as agents of state oppression, held on the national holiday Police Day, it was dispersed, seemingly almost routinely, late at night by police cannons. But it reemerged as a heroic, disorganized march against the regime that then morphed into a long-term, well-documented seizure of public space. It endured attacks that created martyrs to the cause; spread into other cities, from Alexandria to Ismailia to Luxor; and ultimately achieved its core objective: the resignation of Hosni Mubarak, president for thirty years. It was, in other words, an improvised, even accidental revolution. Yet within days of the president's resignation, a coherent narrative of the eighteen-day revolution began to emerge, one in which "the Egyptian people" of all classes, sexes, sects, ages, and types, united by "the spirit of Tahrir" and organized by "the Facebook generation," expressed their just demands for change and ultimately, with bravery, persistence, and the blood of martyrs, received it.

Notes for this chapter begin on page 180.

Subsequent events similarly unfolded in a series of unexpected twists and turns as disorganized remnants of the Mubarak regime, military leaders, the Muslim Brotherhood, various secular democratic movements with visions ranging from revolutionary socialism to Nasserism to American-style libertarianism, the judiciary, newly emerged Salafi politicians, and labor unions old and new all sought to advance their agendas through means both legal and extralegal, even as the very understanding of what might or might not be legal, and who had the authority to declare it, was part of what was at stake. In this struggle, the eighteen-day protest in Tahrir Square from 25 January through 11 February became an influential symbol for all parties involved. Variously construed as "the eighteen days" (*yom tamantasher*), the "spirit of Tahrir" or simply "the Revolution" (understood by some as completed, by others as unfinished), Tahrir Square in post-Mubarak Egypt stood as a heterotopic and chronotopic sign infused with multiple meanings, which could be repositioned, narratively, to multiple political ends and effects.

This chapter is about the iterative and contingent relationship between the Egyptian revolution as a social process and the revolution as a congeries of contested narratives through which people assigned meaning to social events. I focus on one approach that takes seriously the relationship between the structure of unfolding events and the narrative structures through which people give them coherence: the processual analysis of Victor Turner. I argue that although the eighteen days in Tahrir Square neatly fit Victor Turner's notion of a social drama, in which liminality, *communitas*, and antistructure steer the unfolding of events, the revolution failed to exhibit the inexorable "decline and fall into structure and law" that Turner's model predicts (Turner 1969: 132). On the contrary, the following year saw dozens of attempts to reconstitute that experience of antistructure—the experience of possibility that exists when the old system ceases to operate but no new system has yet emerged to take its place. Moreover, each public iteration of "the revolution" was accompanied by contested metacommentaries evaluating the success or failure of each new gathering in Tahrir. These discourses constitute multiple versions of what the "real" uprising in Tahrir was about, and thus construct moments of meaning in the contingent, unfolding experience of the ongoing revolution.

My analysis is methodologically rooted in a kind of "anthropology at a distance" (Mead and Metraux 2000) derived from my technologically mediated experience of the revolution. This included round-the-clock viewing of Al Jazeera's live coverage (in shifts with my wife), supplemented by a continuous flow of e-mails, Facebook posts, and tweets from our networks of friends and colleagues in Egypt. "Anthropology at a distance" refers to the study of cultural systems not through direct participation and observation but through literature, news media, films, music, and other types of expressive culture understood as "stories we tell ourselves about ourselves" (Geertz 1973). Analysis of these stories is usually contextualized by interviews with travelers, migrants, or refugees from the place in question, or (as in my case) by the experience of extensive prior fieldwork. While always subject to criticism within anthropology (even by its practitioners), this approach has served anthropologists' work during periods like World War II, when most international field sites were closed off; in the contemporary global world system, where ethnography is difficult or impossible in places like Iraq (Robben 2009) and Afghanistan (Kucera 2012); or at times when events are temporally displaced from direct ethnographic participation (Lindholm 2002). Contemporary work of this type has been transformed by the temporal immediacy of electronic communication, which "has made the pursuit of fieldwork in new contexts of time-space (or here, simply a return of an intimate version of 'anthropology at a distance') possible" (Marcus and Mascarenhas 2005: xv). Moreover, even though my absence from the Tahrir Square protests clearly makes me a nonparticipant in the central events of the revolution, my wider, mediated participation in the Egyptian revolution differs little, in some aspects, from that of the many Egyptians who also experienced it partly, or even largely, through electronic and social mediation.

Taking Part in Tahrir

My argument centers on the historical "experience" of Tahrir Square as a place in which momentous events happened, a sequence of events and activities that took place in and around the square, and a set of narratives that arose to assign structure and meaning to that place, time, and action. Tahrir Square, and particularly the eighteen-day protest, came to stand for a hopeful process of revolutionary change, and participation in Tahrir Square became an important category through which people experienced themselves and others as participating in a revolutionary effort that expressed the collective power of the Egyptian people.

However, the meaning of "participating" in Tahrir Square, and by extension the revolution, was inchoate and needed to be given structure through narratives. The maidan was famously occupied around the clock by thousands living and sleeping there, but thousands more traveled there, joined the protest for hours or days, and then permanently or temporarily returned home. Others experienced Tahrir Square vicariously through the narratives of family, friends, and neighbors who participated. Still others experienced the maidan in various mediated forms, through television or social media of different kinds, each with its own ways of framing events.

Subjectivities are not limited to any one of these categories. An Egyptian friend who saw himself very much as a participant in the revolution told me a story that cuts across many of these experiential categories. Having seen the protests on television, he went to the maidan with two friends just in time to be caught and slightly injured in the incident known as the battle of the camels.[1] Returning home, he was taken to task by his mother and sisters for risking his life when he was the only adult male to head the family. He then took leadership of the neighborhood security committee, speaking frequently with friends who returned to Tahrir several times, followed events on Al Jazeera and Dream TV, argued with neighbors who followed the events on state television, followed the tweets of some of his college friends who were at the maidan, and watched the video clips to which the tweets referred him. His story captures well the complex nature of "participation" in postmodern protest.

Those who traveled to Tahrir Square daily or every few days often described the journeys, especially in the early days, in terms that reflect another liminal state, that of the spiritual pilgrimage (Fox 1987; Aguilar 1999). Participants described families' and neighbors' efforts to persuade them not to go, and the complications of reaching the maidan despite metro shutdowns, taxi drivers' refusals, and police blockades. Their narratives expressed the classic pattern of "separation from the community and/or ordinary world of reality, penetration of a previously unknown realm and initiation into the secrets of its power, and finally . . . return, bearing a 'boon' of special wisdom or potency to the community originally left behind" (Burns 1992). From their accounts, it appears that their participation in the Tahrir uprisings gives them a special status in their neighborhoods—"Literally and spiritually, individuals are distinguished by their journeys" (Fox 1987: 526)—although the nature of this new status was not uncontested. Such experience fits with Turner's own observations on the liminal nature of pilgrimage: he (with Edith Turner) argued that pilgrimage encouraged people to move both literally and symbolically out of their everyday lives (separation) and temporarily enter alternative social and spiritual worlds (liminality). While in this liminal state, one loses one's old identity, formed by normative social categories such as class, race, and gender; and freely and spontaneously encounters others (*communitas*). After such an experience, the person ultimately returns to the place from which he or she had come (reaggregation), often in a socially transformed way (Turner and Turner 1978).

The act of travel to and from Tahrir Square created a kind of double liminality. Participants were separated from their families and neighbors, traveled to Tahrir under frequently difficult, even dangerous circumstances, and were welcomed and integrated into the *communitas* of the maidan. Then, on their return, they were reintegrated into the home with new status as sources of news, recipients of praise and recrimination, and participants in something powerful that lay outside the community but nonetheless affected it significantly. Yet their travels also set them apart from those who camped out in Tahrir Square. They separated themselves from the *communitas* of the maidan; undertook the difficult journey into the residential parts of the city, which were increasingly impacted by events in Tahrir; and then returned to the Tahrir community, bearing news and able to describe the tensions between supporters and denouncers of the Tahrir occupation.

In addition, of course, hundreds of thousands of other Egyptians marched, protested, and demonstrated in Alexandria, Ismailia, Luxor, Aswan, and elsewhere. Many of them followed courses quite unlike the protests in Tahrir Square, being inflected by local social and political concerns. Ismailia, long a locus of labor protests and itself imbued with symbolic significance by the 1952 revolution, was the site of several violent anti-police skirmishes. Friends in Luxor described their march on the governor's palace as a battle against Cairo-based business interests' efforts to monopolize the tourist trade, with the clear connivance of the Mubarak regime. Tahrir Square synecdochically stands for all these places, and for their protestors and activities.

A particularly powerful symbol of participation in Tahrir was that of the martyrs—protesters, killed by police and *baltagiyya* (hired thugs), whose names and faces were widely circulated in various media after their deaths. The martyrs' deaths were not merely powerful symbols of the need for change. Protesting for political reform against an oppressive regime that tortured, imprisoned, and killed its opponents without respect for law, they were themselves killed by the regime. They were sacramental, in the semiotic sense proposed by the anthropologist Gregory Bateson: signs that become what they signify (Bateson 1972: 33–37). This put new steel into the will of many protesters who argued that going home—no matter how deeply entrenched and willing to ignore them the regime appeared to be—had become morally impossible. It was unthinkable that these men and women would have shed their blood for an uprising that failed.

Finally, it is useful to follow Turner's distinction between *liminal* and *liminoid* participation (Turner 1974, 1977b, 1982). Turner saw liminal phenomena as tied to direct and collective experiences of a crisis in the social process, even those ritually organized around recurring biological or seasonal changes (such as coming-of-age rites, life-crisis rituals, or rituals designed to ensure food supply). He used the term *liminoid* to refer to the quasi-liminal character of cultural performances in modern societies—theater, concerts, exhibitions, television, film—usually produced by specialized groups or industries and not deeply integrated into the collective core of social experience. Liminoid activities are thus less impactful, in that they are experienced individually or in small groups relatively isolated from the experiences of the community as a whole (though precisely because of this they may offer even more radical modes of social critique against the prevailing social order). Participation in the revolution via newspaper and television news coverage is clearly a form of liminoid activity. What is fascinating about the stories of those who participated variously in the protests is the activities' easy interweaving between the liminal and the liminoid.[2]

Invoking *Communitas*

One of the aspects that distinguishes the liminal from the liminoid, in Turner's work, is the experience of *communitas*. Again and again, participants in the Tahrir Square experience describe this element of it as an experience of intense social cohesion, creativity, camaraderie, and enthusiasm. One protester compared it to Brechtian theater: singing, poetry recitals, philosophical discussions of human rights and the dignity of (hu) man(kind), and political arguments about how best to move forward, all happening simultaneously, commenting on one another to create a meaningful cacophony. And myriad participants and commentators have expressed astonishment at the way the protesters pooled their skills and pitched in to organize food banks, clinics, waste management, and even the construction of a small catapult to chase a sniper from a nearby location. Those writing about events in Tahrir also emphasized the collapse of class, gender, and sectarian distinctions that have long troubled Egypt and fueled the regime's claim of standing between a stable society and social collapse. For the protesters and many of their watchers and supporters, Tahrir represents in miniature the free nation they aspire to. Without leaders, elected or otherwise, but with high energy, charismatic organizers stepped forward and offered their skills as needed.

These accounts of the community created in Tahrir Square perfectly fit Turner's notions of liminality, communitas, and antistructure. Turner employed the term "liminality" to refer to the state of being betwixt and between two states. For example, in a rite of passage in which people move from childhood to adulthood, they usually go through an in-between state of being neither child nor adult, during which they are perceived both as dangerous and at risk, and experience intense social bonding with others in a similar state. Turner claimed that many social processes, including revolutions and uprisings, have similar liminal stages in which the structures of everyday life of the immediate past have been disrupted or overturned, but new structures have not yet emerged to replace them, a situation he termed "antistructure." Antistructure refers not to a reversal or upending of the existing social structure but to situations in which many or most of the characteristics that defined the normal configuration of political, social, and economic life have ceased to function. This certainly described the situation in Tahrir, where youth replaced elders as organizers, protests multiplied in both location and number, the police and *mukhabarat* (security forces) were rendered powerless, and headless collectives emerged to manage civil society and domestic security.

Participants in the Tahrir protests described a diminishment of the class, sectarian, and gender distinctions that govern much of Egyptian society (Ghoneim 2011). Many participants in Tahrir Square protests reported experiencing a lessening of the practices of bodily separation that are typically a means of producing class and gender distinctions (Hafez 2012; Winegar 2012). According to eyewitness accounts, 20 to 50 percent of the Tahrir Square protesters were women. Multiple generations of Egyptians from many different backgrounds, some of whom were Leftist protesters in their own youths, responded to and participated in the current events (Winegar 2011a). Volunteer work crews cleaned up the square in a literal enactment of the people taking care of Cairo's center because they have reclaimed it—an act that must be understood in the context of decades of indifference to dirt, litter, and pollution. The cleanup also symbolized the growing sense that people were taking out the political trash that had polluted their country for so long, and caring for one another as fellow citizens in a national family (Winegar 2011b).

Sectarian unity was also emphasized (Agrama 2012; Hirschkind 2012). Christians famously formed a cordon around their praying Muslim colleagues on Friday, 5 February, and Muslim Brothers vowed to protect Christians during their Sunday worship services on 7 February. A Muslim cleric interviewed by *Al Jazeera* on 5 February said: "This is an Egyptian movement, with Christians and Muslims taking part. It does not have a religious goal. It is spontaneous, and is not driven by party-political aims. Our aims are to get rid of Mubarak and his regime." Salma Ismail (2011) argues that these activities reflected the emergence of new forms of civility and citizenship that were "disencumbered of the secular versus religious oppositional logic and its concomitant forms of political rationality" (Hirschkind 2012: 49). Agrama suggests that Tahrir Square represented an "asecular moment," a time and space in which people expressed visions of national solidarity that were largely indifferent to "the question of where to draw a line between religion and politics and the stakes of tolerance and religious freedom" (Agrama 2012: 26).

A concurrent explosion of creative arts has been understood as integral to the protest movement (Makar 2011; Demerdash 2012; Findlay 2012; Saad 2012). Elliott Colla won an award for his essay, published on the Middle East website *Jadaliyya*, celebrating the poetics of the slogans used at Tahrir and their resonance with past revolutionary events and traditional and literary genres of poetry (Colla 2011). A collection of several photo-essays explored the artistic expressions of the revolution through posters, graffiti, and murals (El Zein and Ortiz 2011; Khalil 2011). Rich musical protest art across multiple musical genres was also celebrated, and certain artists—from Ramy Essam to Mohamed Mounir, Azza Balba, Karim Rush, Arabian Knightz Eskenderella, Dina el Wadidi, and Ashraf el Samman—became iconically associated with the revolution. Much of this visual and audio work was digitally archived even as it was being created on websites.[3]

This creative energy and camaraderie experienced by the protesters in Tahrir Square is what Turner calls *communitas*. This intense feeling of community, social equality, solidarity, and togetherness is experienced by people living together at a site where normal social statuses and positions have broken down. Turner explains that in society, *communitas* often emerges from one of three directions: the liminal gaps and apertures of social structure; the marginal limits and borders of social structure; and the inferior bottom of the social structure. Participants describe Tahrir Square during the eighteen days as a place where all three sources of *communitas* were present, and where an open readiness to unplanned action and social relations (which Turner describes as the *negative capability* of *communitas*) created circumstances in which people of many different walks of life could participate in unity. *Communitas* thus liberated people from conformity to general norms.

In Turner's language, the protests shifted Tahrir Square from being part of the normative space of everyday life under the Mubarak regime into a *field*, an interstitial cultural domain where alternative paradigms for social interaction, values, and symbolic representations are formulated, shared, and exposed to conflict with existing social and symbolic structures. Fields are sites of antistructure, alternative forms of structure and symbolism that derive from and reconstruct the social structure of the cultural mainstream. In antistructure, then, the gender and sectarian distinctions present in mainstream society may be dramatically exacerbated—or dramatically minimized, as participants reported happening in Tahrir Square during the eighteen days. Antistructure opens up enormous potential for creativity and the imagining of alternative possibilities, as shown by those who saw Tahrir as a model for the egalitarian, populist Egypt they hoped to create in the aftermath of Mubarak's ouster. According to Turner, periods of antistructure cannot last. While they do exist, however, such situations hold enormous transformative potential. Indeed, that sense of possibility clearly drove the unprecedented popular struggles that continued in Egypt long after the dictator's resignation, elections, trials of regime leaders, and other events ushered in by the uprising had taken place.

In the case of the formal rituals Turner studied, antistructure gave way to a restoration of the preexisting social structure, while those who had undergone the ritual changed in status because of their experience. However, Turner argues, people involved in larger processes like uprisings and revolutions may pass into a situation and space he terms an *arena*, that is, the situation in which new symbolic structures and cultural configurations are established and organized into a new social order. As the name suggests, the arena is a site of struggle between groups promoting different models of sociocultural structure. This describes the situation in Egypt since Mubarak's resignation. And for the various actors in this arena who sought to sponsor and enact particular visions of the new Egypt, few symbols were as powerful as the ability to reclaim the creativity, communitas, and antistructure of the eighteen days and yoke it to their specific political and social project.

Participation as National Rite

The eighteen days in Tahrir Square was a process, a set of public political actions that led directly to the resignation of Hosni Mubarak. As the site of this process and many additional protests in a larger, ongoing process of political change, Tahrir Square has also become an extremely complex symbol with multiple meanings for those who participated in the maidan protests not only in person but in manifold mediated ways.

Once Mubarak had resigned, the need to control the meaning of Tahrir Square emerged almost immediately. Aided by the influential state media, the Supreme Council of the Armed Forces (SCAF), to whom Mubarak had passed the reins of power upon stepping down, moved quickly to contain the revolution by endorsing it but limiting the term to refer only to the eighteen days in Tahrir Square.[4] By restricting the 25 January revolution to the events at Tahrir that ended on 11 February, the SCAF succeeded in limiting the meaning of the revolution to the fall of Mubarak, rather than the larger national reform called for by many vocal participants in Tahrir Square. This restriction also allowed SCAF to portray all subsequent protest activity as either hooliganism or counterrevolutionary activity. The former vice-president and intelligence chief Omar Suleyman took this line in his abortive presidential candidacy.

For tens of thousands of protesters, bloggers, political actors, and intellectuals, the events in Tahrir Square were only the beginning of an "ongoing" revolution. "*Al-sha'b yurid isqat an-nizam*" (the people want the fall of the regime) was not the only major slogan chanted in Tahrir Square during the uprising. Equally prominent was "*aish, hurriya, adala igtima'iya*" (bread, freedom, social justice), a bare-bones outline of what the protesters wanted the post-regime government to deliver. The ongoing reoccupation of Tahrir Square, marches on government buildings, and clashes with police and other security forces represented a continued effort to demand that the shifting authorities—the military, the new parliament, the electoral commission, the judiciary, the government of President Mohammed Morsi, the post-coup government—show clear evidence of moving the country forward toward these goals.

But efforts to invoke Tahrir and extend its meanings into changing situations are not limited to mere argument about whether the revolution is continuing. In July, less than five months after the Tahrir Square uprising ended, the Police Officers Coalition requested that the handful of security police who died in the uprisings be designated police martyrs, and that their families receive compensation. The term "martyr" (*shahid*) was widely used to describe protesters killed by plainclothes policemen and *baltagiyya*. The veneration of protesters who died at the hands of the state became a turning point in the uprising. Protesting for political reform against an oppressive regime that lawlessly tortured, imprisoned, and killed its opponents, they were themselves killed by the regime and thus became powerful symbols of the need for change. Despite the rhetoric and ritual that grew up around it, however, martyrdom was not an irresistible force that swept the revolution to a triumphant conclusion:

The regime and its sympathizers started generating a fog of patriotism long before Mubarak left office, and it provided ample hiding space for anyone who feared close scrutiny in the post-regime environment. The martyr inconveniently asks, "who killed me?" and true revolutionaries take up the cause, also asking, "who killed them?" in the hope that they can beat the false patriots out of the fog. (Armbrust 2012)

By asking that police killed in clashes with protesters also be considered "the injured of the revolution," the coalition and its allies in the interim government essentially reframed the logic of martyrdom, removing the villains and positioning death in Tahrir as participation in a national rite of passage regardless of who died, or at whose hands. According to this logic, Mubarak's resignation at the climax of the rite becomes a kind of expiatory act demonstrating the power of the Egyptian people, releasing Mubarak's underlings from guilt (they are all patriots, after all), and reincorporating them back into the body of the Egyptian nation—the very opposite of the meaning the martyrs hold for most of the planners and participants of the Tahrir protests.

Islamists, too, invoke Tahrir to support particular articulations of the revolution. By March 2011 the Muslim Brotherhood, having controversially announced its intention to run a candidate for president and thus broken an earlier promise not to seek to dominate both the executive and legislative branches of government, explained its decision as necessary to preserve "the revolution of Tahrir Square." Similarly, in a speech on 29 June, four days after his election, President Mohamed Morsi constructed Tahrir in heterotopic language, describing it simultaneously as revolution square, freedom square, liberty square, and martyrs' square, then linking it to "all citizens standing in all liberty squares across the homeland, Egypt, in villages, towns and cities, in all governorates of Egypt." Drawing again on this construction, he declared on 22 November that both he and the constituent assembly charged with drafting Egypt's new constitution were immune from judicial scrutiny, and proclaimed the president the guardian of the 25 January "revolution," with responsibility—and therefore authority—to carry out its goals. This premise would give the president the ultimate discretion to define the goals of the Tahrir Square revolution, decide how to achieve them, and determine when they had been met. These efforts sought to construct a revolution that had concluded—hence further protests would be unnecessary—but whose goals had not yet been reached. Reaching these goals was no longer the duty of activists in the streets but would be carried out by the new president and his appointees as the representatives of the Tahrir revolutionaries (whether or not they had voted for him, as Morsi affirmed in his 26 June speech).

Even Salafist groups—which had pointedly refused to participate in the Tahrir uprisings, often openly denounced them, and disrupted the July 2011 Friday of Unity demonstrations that sought to show that a degree of

communitas still existed among the people—managed to rhetorically position themselves within the "spirit of Tahrir." For example, in *al-Masryun*
on 8 May 2012, the Salafi leader Abbud az-Zumur published a ten-point
plan to restore the unity of the Egyptian revolution as expressed by Tahrir
Square. Most of his ten points advised Egypt's myriad factions on how to
return to a unity of purpose despite the many divisions between political
entities, so that the revolution would not fail to create a new Egypt better
than the old. According to az-Zumur, the revolution could not fail if Egyptians of all political stripes adhered to the spirit exhibited during those
eighteen days in Tahrir Square. A founder of Egyptian Islamic Jihad and
organizer of the assassination of president Anwar Sadat in 1981, az-Zumar
was not released from prison until almost five weeks after Mubarak's resignation, so he never participated in the protests at Tahrir Square. However, when unexpectedly large parliamentary election victories were followed by judicial rejection of Salafist Sheikh Abu Ismail's candidacy for
president, Salafi leaders split over whether or not to protest this action,
and az-Zumar found himself and his followers in the streets, allying with
revolutionary socialists against the SCAF and remaining NDP structures,
now framed as obstacles to national reform. He invoked the spirit of Tahrir to encourage more such "enemy of my enemy" alliances.

In a fascinating use of symbolic action as rhetoric, the military establishment used the spirit of the Tahrir protests to justify removing President Morsi from power in July 2013. In response to nationwide pro-Morsi
demonstrations, Army Chief General Abdel Fattah al-Sisi called on Egyptians to take to the streets "to prove their will and give me, the army and
police, a mandate to confront possible violence and terrorism" (Mahmood
2013). Subsequent protests provided symbolic capital enabling the army
to initiate operations against pro-Morsi demonstrators. Six months later,
General al-Sisi managed to turn the third anniversary of the Tahrir Square
uprising into a campaign rally dominated by his supporters. One man
told journalists that if Al-Sisi did not announce his presidency, people
would occupy the square until he did (Beach 2014).

I would argue that all these cases feature a rhetorical effort by particular
political agents to yoke to their specific vision of Egypt's way forward to the
sign of Tahrir Square. In doing so, they use Tahrir as a kind of summarizing
symbol (Ortner 1973) through which they can invoke the spirit of the revolution without elaborating and articulating the many things the revolution
means to different Egyptians. But in trying to move people (themselves and
others) by tying their particular articulation of the revolution to this symbol,
they are also trying to invoke the residual power of antistructure. Amid
risk, doubt, and uncertainty in the wake of the economic and political chaos

that followed the revolution, Tahrir came to invoke nostalgia for a different period of uncertainty, a time of unexpected social unity and unlimited possibilities in which real, positive changes seemed possible.

Social Drama and the Problem of Closure

I do not want to simply argue that Tahrir Square has become an important symbol and, as such, a political football to be fought over by rival political factions. This is true but incomplete. The reality is more complex because it makes us think about symbols not only as things, as bits of social structure expressed in a ritual way, but as processes, active vehicles, and agents of change within and through political-economic contexts. As Turner says, symbols and symbolic actions "not only animate and are animated by contexts but are processually inseverable from them" (Turner 1977a: 61).

One way Turner sought to express this was through the processual model of change he called "social drama." Many forms of social change, including particularly dramatic ones like revolutions, exhibit a processual structure not unlike those anthropologists have described for rituals. A crucial difference is that whereas rituals have a ritual specialist to keep liminality under control lest it spill out and endanger the wider social order, social dramas are partly defined by the fact that they are, at least initially, out of the control of any particular social actor or institution. Revolutions like those in Tunisia, Egypt, and Libya were essentially uprisings that spun out of their organizers' control (in ways that at first delighted most of these organizers). In a sense, they became revolutions *because* they spun out of control. Part of the power of Tahrir was its continuing capacity to symbolize the generative power of collective action when society's redressive and reintegrative mechanisms failed to function.[5]

Social dramas begin with a *breach* of the structures of ordinary life, such as when, in defiance of historical precedent, the protesters returned to Tahrir across the bridge in the face of police resistance and successfully occupied the square. The ensuing *crisis* ushered in a period of antistructure, in which the ordinary rules of governance and civility did not apply. During the crisis stage, sides were taken and coalitions formed, and fissures deepened and spread through various coordinated and contiguous relationships between people and groups. Throughout the crisis, various actors of many types sought to define the ends of the uprising and to decide some form of *redress* that would bring it to a conclusion. According to Turner, such redress, when it occurs, allows the society to *reintegrate* in a modified way and create some entirely new social structure, or to break apart into new factions and political orders.

The eighteen days in Tahrir fit this pattern neatly, concluding with the national celebration of Mubarak's resignation. The subsequent revolution is much harder to clarify through this processual model. As Turner himself admitted, "it is hard to tell whether what one is observing at a given moment in the series is breach, crisis, or the application of redressive machinery" (1974).

In a processual analysis, then, the first problem is one of contingency: if every event is simultaneously a product of prior events and part of the events to come, how does one know when and where to demarcate the beginnings and ends of the process? How do we know what function each protest, clash, election, judicial decision, serves in the larger whole when that larger whole currently has no clear endpoint? Rather than speaking of a revolution, perhaps it is analytically more helpful to see this process as involving as many (proto)revolutions as there are protest movements (Joshi 2011).

It is also useful to recall how contingent those original eighteen days of protest were. Many who supported the initial protests were willing to say by 29 January, when Mubarak sacked the cabinet, or 1 February, when he pledged not to run for a sixth term, or 3 February, after Suleiman's speech, that they had accomplished enough. These included active protesters at the maidan saying enough was enough, the point had been made and concessions offered, and it was time to stop the protests. I have an e-mail from a professor of literature at Ain Shams who went to Tahrir on 26 and 27 January and by 29 January was arguing that the protests had been hijacked by people with political agendas and the protesters should go home and wait for the reforms their actions would engender. Other protesters had high hopes and ambitions but at certain points felt demoralized and became willing to stop, only to be regalvanized by such events as news of fresh protests in Alexandria or Ismailia, or by Wael Ghonim's 7 February television interview. The range of opinions expressed at Tahrir Square about why people were there, what they could seriously hope to accomplish, and what they were risking—not only personally but in terms of the nation—was broad and variable. The unity of Tahrir Square was a negotiated unity continually debated and reassessed in the light of shifting events.

Only after the celebrations of Mubarak's resignation did the simple framing of the eighteen days as a clash between the regime and a rainbow cross-section of Egyptians from all walks of life unified by opposition to the president become almost universally salient. So the problem of contingency or indeterminacy, that is, of how to describe and analyze a process as it is unfolding, is an enormous problem.

Social Drama and the Problem of Agency

The second problem is a problem of agency. What control do any of these various participants, with their different fears and visions, have over the final narrative of events? How is closure collectively determined? How are the meanings of various events and actions created or constrained?

A significant aspect of the problem of agency is not only how agency is exerted in social processes and toward what ends, but also who the agents are. It is common—because it is convenient—to speak of the SCAF, the Muslim Brotherhood, the Salafis, the secularists, Shebab al-Facebook, or any other faction as a coherent group that acts in unison. In fact, however, all these groups were internally divided in ways that often switched exactly how institutions acted with regard to the ongoing uprisings. Several of President Morsi's advisers resigned when he issued his 22 November declaration. Abbud Az-Zumar proposed his ten points at a time when the fractures within the Salafist movements had become particularly evident.

An additional complication ensued from the media's being both vehicles and agents in this process. Mass media are vehicles through which struggles to appropriate the revolution proceed, actors present themselves and their visions publicly, and coherent narratives of events are offered, contested, and transformed. At the same time, the media are also active agents that create, sustain, and reject various narratives based on their own positioning within Egypt's media ecology (Peterson 2011). Meanwhile, social media have exploded with thousands of new blogs and Facebook pages, including those of current and former government officials, expressing countless possible scenarios of what Egypt "needs" to do next.

Clearly, both the revolution and the discourses that seek to comment on it and sort out its meanings remain contingent, contested parts of the larger process I have been calling "the revolution." Multiple voices struggle with various (and changing) degrees of agency to determine which narratives will form the dominant narrative that gives coherence to the whole process. Ongoing protests continue to bring about changes, but at every stage many voices, articulated through multiple media, insist that the uprising must stop here, and that further protests are unnecessary and do more harm than good.

Conclusion

When is there enough revolution? When is the disruption of the structures of everyday life too frightening and dangerous? Is it when wealthy resort owners complain of losing a million pounds a day in tourist revenues? When the police disappear and carjackings and kidnappings increase? When the prisons are opened and criminals walk free? When tour guides in Luxor and Siwa can no longer eke out a modest living? When traffic is disrupted and shops close? When people fear their bread rations may become unavailable? Is the revolution over when a new constitution is written? When a president is elected? When the SCAF returns to its barracks? When the emergency laws are finally ended? When a new normalcy has emerged?

After Tahrir Square, Egypt entered an extended liminal state betwixt the structural coherence of the former regime and whatever new normal would ultimately emerge. One defining aspect of liminal states is the tension they pose between possibility and danger, that is, hope and risk. The desire of those favoring a swift shift to order and predictability to avoid the political, social and economic risks this ambiguity posed was as real as many others' desire to keep the revolution going in hopes that a much better future Egypt was yet attainable.

Amid all this contingency, political actors used Tahrir Square as a key symbol in which to anchor their narratives of the revolution. Maidan Tahrir was appropriated by state television and other agents of the ruling military council, whose interests were best served by emphasizing the risks of the ongoing period of antistructure, and who characterized the eighteen days at Tahrir Square as the true revolution and all subsequent demonstrations, clashes, and protests as mere hooliganism not in the best long-term interests of the country. But it was also appropriated by the agents of those demonstrations, clashes, and protests. Their core interests lay in emphasizing the hopes and possibilities of the revolution, so they posited the revolution represented by Tahrir Square as incomplete and used Tahrir as a trope to justify their current actions. Meanwhile, Maidan Tahrir was also appropriated by political actors as varied as Omar Suleyman, Abbud az-Zumar, and Mohammed Morsi to reposition groups and justify activities in response to changed contexts.

As of this writing, many, perhaps most Egyptians, have had enough of revolution. The deposition of President Morsi in July 2013 and the rise of an adulatory cult around General Abdel Fattah el-Sisi in 2014 can more or less be seen as a search for a man—and it must be a man—who can conclude this interval of chaos by announcing a clear plan and moving it forward regardless of opposition. President Morsi promised to fulfill the spirit of Tahrir but failed in three important ways. First, despite his promises to be president for all Egyptians, he came to be seen as promoting an exclusively Islamist agenda. Second, he never clearly articulated a readily understandable narrative for moving forward into a new Egyptian system. Finally, even as he concentrated more and more power in his office and presented himself as a compassionate and sensitive man, he failed to persuade many that he had the strength to carry out the job. The ideal Egyptian masculinity unites courage and compassion, strength and chivalry (Peterson 2011; Ghannam 2013). In the aftermath of Morsi's ouster, Al-Sisi emerged as the public figure who most embodied these characteristics. In Turnerian language, Egypt's quest is to find a "ritual specialist" to end this period of liminality by initiating the "decline and fall into structure and law"—the new order that will replace the old. Al-Sisi's capacity to fulfill this role depends on his ability to present an authoritative narrative of order for the new Egypt—one appropriate to the spirit of Tahrir. As events continue to unfold in Egypt, Tahrir Square continues to be invoked and appropriated as these new actors rise, seeking to tie the nostalgic experience of antistructure to their specific visions of the better Egypt to come by mobilizing sentiment and giving coherence to Egypt's ongoing process of transformation.

Notes

1. He was not directly hurt by *baltagiyya* or security forces, but caught in a wild press of bodies reacting to the charge of the camels and subsequent violence.
2. Not everyone accepts this liminal/liminoid distinction as valid. Drummond, for one, argues that seeing enormously popular films *is* a collective experience, and that immersion in the viewing experience gives people access to alternate forms of symbolic configuration, social order, and social relations (not only human-human but also human-machine and human-animal)—i.e., antistructure (Drummond 1996).
3. The ephemerality of digital spaces likewise expresses the liminality of these periods of exuberance. Many of the websites set up to capture and continue the *communitas* of Tahrir, e.g., IamJan25.com and I-Am-Tahrir-the-Art-of-Revolution Facebook page have ceased to function, although others, such as the Revolution Graffiti - Street Art of the New Egypt Facebook page, still exist.
4. In treating the SCAF as a uniform actor, I am taking the liberty of overgeneralizing to push my narrative forward. A complex, internally divided organization, the SCAF at this time included at least one general with strong ties to the Muslim Brotherhood, as well as some who were sympathetic to secular revolutionary groups. And its control over state media was far from absolute, especially in the first months after Mubarak's resignation.
5. On ritual processes that spin out of control, see Hüsken (2007). One of the problems facing Egypt in the aftermath of President Mubarak's resignation was the continued failure of institutions that could otherwise have operated as redressive and reintegrative measures for cooperation, due partly to apparent bewilderment and uncertainty, and partly to a struggle between agencies that sought to shape outcomes to their respective liking. The revolution was "unfinished" and long-lasting because the failure of

redressive and reintegrative mechanisms often produces the fundamental social divisions that Bateson (1958) named *schismogenesis*, and although new social units can be created from the social, political, and ritual when parties split off from a previously unified social unit, "in modern territorial states it is extremely difficult to 'split off'" (Thomassen 2012: 689).

References

Agrama, H. A. 2012. "Reflections on Secularism, Democracy, and Politics in Egypt." *American Ethnologist* 39 (1): 26–31.

Aguilar, F. V., Jr. 1999. "Ritual Passage and the Reconstruction of Selfhood in International Labour Migration." *Sojourn: Journal of Social Issues in Southeast Asia* 14 (1): 98–139.

Armbrust, W. 2012. "The Ambivalence of Martyrs and the Counter-revolution." In *Cultural Anthropology*, "Hotspots: Revolution and Counter-Revolution in Egypt a Year after January 25th," edited by Julia Elyachar and Jessica Winegar. Series posted at http://www.culanth.org/?q=node/491.

Bateson, G. 1958. *Naven*. Stanford, CA: Stanford University Press.

———. 1972. *Steps to an Ecology of Mind*. New York: Ballantine.

Beach, A. 2014. "Egypt Violence: Army General Al-Sisi Turns Anniversary of Tahrir Square Uprising Into Presidential Rally." *The Independent*, 26 January.

Burns, G. 1992. "The Repatriate Theme in Philippine Second-Language Fiction." *Philippine Studies* 40 (1): 3–34.

Colla, E. 2011. "The Poetry of Revolt." *Jadaliyya*, 31 January. http://www.jadaliyya.com/pages/index/506/the-poetry-of-revolt.

Demerdash, N. 2012. "Consuming Revolution: Ethics, Art and Ambivalence in the Arab Spring." *New Middle Eastern Studies* 2. http://www.brismes.ac.uk/nmes/archives/970#more-970.

Drummond, L. 1996. *American Dreamtime: A Cultural Analysis of Popular Movies, and Their Implications for a Science of Humanity*. Lanham, MD: Littlefield Adams.

El Zein, R., and A. Ortiz. 2011. *Signs of the Times: the Popular Literature of Tahrir Protest Signs, Graffiti, and Street Art*. Shahadat, April. http://issuu.com/arteeast/docs/shahadat_january25_final?mode=embed&layout=http%3A%2F%2Fskin.issuu.com%2Fv%2Flight%2Flayout.xml&showFlipBtn=true.

Findlay, Cassie. 2012. "Witness and Trace: January 25 Graffiti and Public Art as Archive. *Interface: a journal for and about social movements* 4 (1): 178–82.

Fox, J. 1987."Southeast Asian Religions: Insular Cultures." In *The Encyclopedia of Religion*, vol. 13, edited by M. Eliade. New York: Macmillan.

Geertz, C. 1973. "Thick Description." In *The Interpretation of Cultures*. New York: Basic Books.

Ghannam, F. 2013. *Live and Die Like a Man: Gender Dynamics in Urban Egypt*. Palo Alto, CA: Stanford University Press.

Ghoneim, W. 2011. *Revolution 2.0: The Power of the People Is Greater Than the People in Power: A Memoir*. New York: Houghton Mifflin.

Hafez, S. 2012. "No Longer a Bargain: Women, Masculinity, and the Egyptian Uprising." *American Ethnologist* 39 (1): 37–42.

Hirschkind, Charles. 2012. "Beyond Secular and Religious: An Intellectual Genealogy of Tahrir Square." *American Ethnologist* 39(1): 49–53.

Hüsken, U., ed. 2007. *When Rituals Go Wrong: Mistakes, Failure and the Dynamics of Ritual*. Leiden: Brill.

Ismail, Salwa. 2011. "Authoritarian Government, Neoliberalism and Everyday Civilities in Egypt." *Third World Quarterly* 32 (5): 845–62.

Joshi, S. 2011. "Reflections on the Arab Revolutions." *The RUSI Journal* 156(2): 60–67.

Khalil, K., ed. 2011. *Messages from Tahrir: Signs from Egypt's Revolution*. Cairo: American University in Cairo Press.

Kucera, I. 2012. "Follow the Afghan War: Methods, Interpretations, Imagination." *Anthropology of the Middle East* 7 (1): 38–50.

Lindholm, C. 2002. "Culture, Charisma, and Consciousness: The Case of the Rajneeshee." *Ethos* 30 (4): 357–75.

Mahmood, F. 2013. *Evolving Civil-Military Relations: A Comparative Analysis of Egypt, Turkey and Pakistan*. Cairo: Ibn Khaldun Center for Human Development Studies. Now available at http://georgetownsecuritystudiesreview.org/2013/12/26/evolving-civil-military-relations-a-comparative-analysis-of-egypt-turkey-and-pakistan/

.Makar, F. 2011. "'Let Them Have Some Fun': Political and Artistic Forms of Expression in the Egyptian Revolution/" *Mediterranean Politics* 16 (2): 307–12.

Marcus, G., and F. Mascarenhas. 2005. *Ocasião: The Marquis and the Anthropologist, a Collaboration*. Walnut Creek, CA: Rowman Altamira.

Mead, M., and R. Metraux, eds. (1954) 2000. *The Study of Culture at a Distance*. New York: Berghahn Books.

Ortner, S. B. 1973. "On Key Symbols." *American Anthropologist* 75 (5): 1338–346.

Peterson, M. A. 2011. "Egypt's Media Ecology in a Time of Revolution." *Arab Media and Society* 13. http://www.arabmediasociety.com/?article=770.

Robben, Antonius C. G. M. 2009. *Iraq at a Distance: What Anthropologists Can Teach Us About the War*. Philadelphia: University of Pennsylvania Press.

Saad, R. 2012. The Egyptian Revolution: A Triumph of Poetry. *American Ethnologist* 39 (1): 63–66.

Thomassen, B. 2012. "Notes towards an Anthropology of Political Revolutions." *Comparative Studies of Society and History* 54 (3): 679–706.

Turner, V. 1969. *The Ritual Process: Structure and Anti-Structure*. Chicago: Aldine.

———. 1974. "Liminal to Liminoid in Play, Flow, and Ritual: An Essay in Comparative Symbology." *Rice University Studies* 60 (3): 53–92.

———. 1977a. "Process, System, and Symbol: A New Anthropological Synthesis." *Daedalus* 106 (3): 61–80.

———. 1977b. "Variations on a Theme of Liminality." In *Secular Ritual*, edited by S. F. Moore and B. Myerhoff. Assen: Van Gorcum.

———. 1982. *From Ritual to Theatre: The Human Seriousness of Play*. New York: Performing Arts Journal.

Turner, V., and E. Turner. 1978. *Image and Pilgrimage in Christian Culture*. New York: Columbia University Press.

Winegar, J. 2011a. "Taking Out the Trash: Youth Clean Up Egypt After Mubarak." *Middle East Report* 259: 32–35.

———. 2011b. "Egypt: A Multigenerational Revolt." *Jadaliyya*, 21 February. http://www.jadaliyya.com/pages/index/703/-egypt_a-multi-generational-revolt-

———. 2012. "The Privilege of Revolution: Gender, Class, Space, and Affect in Egypt." *American Ethnologist* 39 (1): 67–70.

Chapter 10

Liminality and Democracy

Harald Wydra

The Ambivalence of Democracy

Democracy means that the people are the master of their own affairs. Put differently, citizens are entitled to authorize and control those who temporarily exert domination over them. This freedom of the people within the frame of coercive state structures appears to be a contradiction in terms. Modern democracy has emancipated citizens from personalized forms of rule. Governments exercise power only temporarily. This permanent uncertainty about the place of power must be bounded and channeled. Political modernity has developed a variety of controls, including the evolution of territorial nation-states, the normative basis of constitutionalism, or civic collective identity. Yet the renewal of accountable governments is in constant tension with in-built democratic tendencies to subvert established hierarchies and structures.

Democratic emancipation includes individual rights and freedoms, extension of the franchise, the pursuit of equality, or promotion of social progress. Such emancipatory dynamics of democracy have been associated with morally engaging social achievements and noble causes. They are meant to ensure empowerment of individual citizens as well as increased scrutiny and transparency of government. Praising such achievements, democratic theory has endowed emancipation with a certain degree of objectivity and rationality. It has been less vocal, however, about the collective social conditions that made emancipatory breakthroughs possible. Desires of emancipation can be formulated by philosophers as ethical imperatives or by social groups in quest of more direct influence on the distribution of power and resources. Yet processes of emancipation can only become effective if societies undergo fundamental changes in consciousness and attitude.

The coercive character of democratic rule indicates that relationships between rulers and ruled are vertical. Democratic citizenship consists largely of moral commitment to a homogeneous people that complies with government. Yet a key element of the democratic imagination in the twenty-first century is states' capacity to acknowledge the pluralism of an increasingly diverse populace and to extend the rights and freedoms of citizens. The democratic imagination thus needs to sustain a democratic ethos under conditions of pluralism and diversity. (Connolly 1997). Often, a democratic state responds to various cultural constituencies dispersed on the same territory. Two key characteristics of the democratic imagination, for instance, are the globalization of economic life and the acceleration of speed. Their effects extend to cultural communications, social movements, population migration, military mobility, and disease transmission.

In short, states impose rules but also have to guarantee the normative promise of emancipation. Empirical studies have de-historicized the interdependent rise of processes of democratic imagination and emancipation, presenting them as timeless, uncontested goals of development. In reality, however, the emancipation of individuals and collective groups thrives on liminal conditions when people overcome binding structures of compliance. Emancipation literally means "to leave paternal authority," an act of separation that does not happen primarily at the level of doctrine or beliefs. Social anthropology has studied rites of passages as acts of separation in the concrete lifeworlds of people (van Gennep 1960; Turner 1967). For individuals, emancipation often coincides with the end of a life cycle and initiation into another part of life, as in passages from the womb into life, from adolescence to adulthood, or from life to death. By analogy, democracies actually come of age through processes of transition (Wydra 2007). Making the people—originally the poor, the many, or the socially disenfranchised—into the master has been a contingent process. The emancipation of slaves, the extension of the franchise of suffrage to women, and institutional reform in waves of democratization followed immediately upon revolutions or (civil) wars.

My proposition here is to follow recent attempts at rethinking problems of the democratic imagination through liminal interstices of historical contingency (Lefort 1986; Whitehead 2002; Dunn 2005). My argument is that the democratic imagination pivots on a fragile balance manifested in the permanent tension between democratic rule and the promise of

emancipation. Processes of democratic emancipation center on the breaking of boundaries, so the democratic imagination oscillates between autonomy and mob rule, between the order of egoism and the drive toward total
equality. In modernity, democracy does not describe a thing; it prescribes
an ideal. This utopian ideal is not a timeless developmental goal. Rather,
it has been channeled through "pre-democratic" or "non-democratic"
conditions of transgressions of boundaries. From the Athenian revolution
in 508/7 B.C. to the democratic revolutions at the end of the eighteenth
century, and from the post–World War I waves of democracy to the collapse of Soviet communism and the recent "Arab Spring," the democratic
imagination has been shaped in weak moments of the social. Classical and
early modern forms of the democratic imagination saw agonistic forms of
democracy focus on the struggle for political freedom under conditions of
relative cultural unity within bounded territory. Since the late twentieth
century, democracy has spread the promise of freedom on a global scale.
The global age has created conditions in which the democratic spirit left
the bottle. To come to terms with this internal ambivalence of democracy,
we have to understand limit experiences in which peoples' interests co-
alesce with their passions.

It is impossible to determine what democracy *is* without looking into
liminal conditions that determine what it *should* be. Values are not abstract
and timeless constants but emerge in response to historical challenges,
which are often existential in nature. Touchstone theorists of revolution
and democracy responded to radical social changes in their lifetimes. Tocqueville described democracy as a "providential force," whereas Marx
regarded revolutions as a progressive historical force, the "locomotives
of history." Schumpeter's minimalist conception of democracy was more
than an empirical, realist theory of democratic rule. Given the empirical
conditions of democracy during the war mobilization in the United States
and Britain, the publication of his seminal work *Capitalism, Socialism, and
Democracy* in 1943 was a normative prescription about the only possible
way to avoid the evils of downward spirals of mob rule. Democrats may
vastly shift their political expectations. The horizon of political expectation of equality was formulated during the radical phase of the French
Revolution. The main forward movements, however, came not from the
revolutionary collapse of the old order but from "defensive gambits by
audacious conservative politicians" (Dunn 2005: 153).

In other words, the functioning, reflexes, and "political psychology" of
democracy respond to historical challenges (Ankersmit 2002). The democratic imagination has its roots in liminal conditions of authority vacuum.
In liminal situations the two main aspects of experiences coincide in the

"objective" character of a major sudden event, and the "subjective" perspective of how this event was lived through by the individuals undergoing the changes (Wydra 2007: 51–54). As carriers of the democratic imagination, passionate interests pivot on socially comprehensive limit experiences, which transgress social hierarchies and political structures. Although such limit or borderline experiences have evolved, they share the dual paradox that democracy is a system of domination that keeps the place of power empty. In democracy, the place of power remains empty in the sense that no segment of society, no institution, no party "owns" the state.

The first paradox is the permanent dialogue between democratic order and its underlying latent authority vacuum. Democracy's condition is that the permanent interregnum needs to be bounded symbolically and performatively as well as institutionally. Revolutionary transformations not only create new institutions but also transform structures of meaning and perform new acts of authority (Weber 1980). The second paradox is that the strong anti-authoritarian impulses in democracy call for a center of authority. As Tocqueville put it, "in any event, there must always be a place in the intellectual and moral world where authority exists. This place may vary, but it must exist somewhere. Individual independence may be great or small, but it cannot be boundless" (quoted in Lefort 2007: 74). A system based on contestation and struggle by free citizens nevertheless requires a meaning-giving unity that maintains the holiness and verticality of constitutional order. After the rejection of political rule by social and birth privileges, individuals are ready "to believe the multitude . . . and opinion is more than ever mistress of the world" (Tocqueville 2000: 519–21). Faith in public opinion will become a religion, less as a doctrine of revelation than as a dogmatic belief.

The Empty Place of Power

The most comprehensive attempt at capturing the authority vacuum at the center of democracy is Claude Lefort's concept of empty place of power (Lefort 1986). Lefort's holistic conception of the political rejects the categorization of democratic politics into predictable logics of social sectors, rules, or norms. Drawing on the French Revolution, Lefort (1986: 30) identifies the democratic moment as the dissolution of "markers of certainty," which comprehended institutional, symbolic, and mental structures. The essence of democracy is not in a substance or an incorporated certainty. Rather, democracy means the permanence of an authority vacuum, where the place of power is empty and can only be appropriated temporarily. The French

Revolution introduced radical indeterminacy, and not only in the state. It was a massive dis-incorporation of structures of power affecting the psychological, economic, legal, and political dimensions. In monarchies, power was incorporated in the body of the king and the corporate social body, but democratic rule is not entitled to incorporate or appropriate power.

Democracy is built on the ruins of the old social hierarchy, from which autonomous beings do not emerge. Power in monarchies was bound to the body of the king, but power in democracy is the power of *nobody* (Lefort 1986: 28). Modern democracy is essentially ambivalent about its underlying social basis, the people. Adapting Kantorowicz's idea about the two bodies of the king, one could speak of the people's two bodies, an intrinsic double meaning of the people. Despite its fickle, competitive trend to division, the sociologically complex nature of the people appears as a politically united, densely organized whole. The empty place of power causes the fantasy of the people-as-One *(peuple-un)* to emerge as a quest for a substantial identity (ibid.: 31). In France in both 1789 and 1848, the notion of the people was associated with a "whole," an "all," or a "unity" (Rosanvallon 2006: 82). The focus on "freedom" therefore underemphasizes democracy's ideological elements. Social meanings of popular sovereignty cannot be taken for granted. Democrats are just not there; they "become" so through processes of individualization. The process of losing their social place of belonging makes people uncertain about their status, identity, and life chances. Such uncertainty was pivotal in the first and second comings of democracy during the revolutionary conditions of Athens and the late eighteenth century (Dunn 2005).

The signal event in the history of democracy was arguably the uprising of Athenian crowds against Spartan occupation in 508 B.C., which defined the nature of the subsequent democratic reforms (Ober 2004: 265). The riots broke out suddenly and reached relatively great size, intensity, and duration after the council *(boulē)* resisted attempts by Isagoras and the Spartan King Cleomenes to dissolve it. They obliged all Spartan forces to retreat to the Acropolis. The riots of 508/7 B.C. were a collective act of political self-definition in which the demos rejected Isagoras as the legitimate public authority. The victory of popular sovereignty at the Bastille in July 1789 occurred under conditions of liminal fluidity and social disorder. The National Assembly legitimated this crowd violence as a symbolic act of popular sovereignty (Sewell 2005: 225–70). Claims furthering political emancipation and empowerment of the poor or of marginal outsiders can threaten existing social relations with contestation and disorder.

Fragmentation, controversy, and struggle lie at the core of the formation of a community of equals. Governments are neither supreme rulers nor representatives of the sovereign but rather temporary guardians of an empty place. This empty place of power is the liminal space of ambivalence, intensified emotions, condensed communication. Democracies have developed rules and habits to bound the fragility of the empty place of power. Constitutionally guaranteed rules bound the uncertainty about election outcomes and thus keep conflict between political groups and citizens in equilibrium. Democratic theory has "resolved" the problem of bounding by separating the rulers and the ruled, and their respective spheres of action and knowledge. A government based on a formalized set of rules and norms commands obedience by controlling citizens' actions, behavior, and responses (Dahl 1956: 13). The minimalist conception of democracy debunked the idea of the people's self-rule as a myth and restricted the people's participation to the electoral act (Schumpeter 1976). If elections are the hinge in the political struggle for government, they are also the weak link, a tricky and delicate matter. The paradox of the electoral act is that citizens become utterly disunited just when faith in community is most needed. Social solidarities are undone as citizens become disconnected from class, status group, professional group, or religious belonging in order to be converted into an account unit (*unité de compte*). In this seemingly most precious attribute of modern democracy, the power of nobody shows its strongest ambivalence. The electoral act suspends the verticality of rule. It constitutes a limited form of social disintegration.

The constitutional imaginary of representative democracy emphasizes limits to power. Public opinion has appropriated the moral right of judgment and control by establishing mechanisms of scrutiny, transparency, and accountability. As horizontal models of governance, transparency, and accountability have gradually supplanted the vertical elements of hierarchy, democracy has become strongly depoliticized. The concept of governance essentially tends to undermine vertical ideas of inequalities of power and the relationship between authorities and subordinates (Offe and Preuss 2006).

As imperialism, dictatorship, and totalitarianism have declined, democratic states in Europe have progressively been deprived of their constitutive outsides. One major consequence is that models of democratic governance and monitory democracy have challenged ideas of vertical rule in representative democracy with more horizontal forms of partnership and negotiation (Keane 2009). The European Union, for instance, relies on the idea of solidarity, which is grounded in the mutual recognition of otherness (Offe and Preuss 2006). Legitimacy in the European polity derives from a political entity in which people have become neighbors yet remain strangers to each other. The people in Europe are essentially a people of others. The genuine political innovation of Europe is to reconcile the main attribute of an empire—multinationality and diversity of people—with an essential quality of a republic, political freedom, the latter resulting from the voluntary character of the former.

Conversely, the "power imaginary constantly seeks to expand present capabilities and may undermine or override the boundaries mandated in the constitutional imaginary" (Wolin 2008: 19). The French Revolution, besides disseminating nationalist sentiments to other parts of Europe, led to fundamental socioeconomic conflicts and irreconcilable political disagreements after 1815. Political representation in continental democracies emerged in response to a specific type of political problem: the need to avoid civil war in a strongly polarized society (Ankersmit 2002: 95–98). When social relations become porous and uncertain, political expectations may enhance the power imagination. The several "waves" of democratization in the twentieth century could only occur after world wars or revolutionary upheavals. Converting violence and conflict into representations of collective self-transcendence would entail failures in democratic experiments. John Keane's *Life and Death of Democracy*, for instance, recognizes the failed experiments with democracy in the inter-war period (Keane 2009). Keane attributes rampant nationalism and the mass murder of peoples to the pseudo-democratic doctrine of national self-determination (ibid.: 2009: 567–78). In reality, however, the emergence of democracy under conditions of collapse of empire, economic crisis, and human misery was the root cause of the problem. Many European democracies in the 1920s and 1930s had not only to secure their contested borders and accommodate substantial minorities, but also redefine collective identity. The notion "totalitarian," for instance, arose in Italy in the early 1920s to designate the Fascists' breach of election procedures in refusing to accept the majority-minority principle, instead favoring a "total" solution (Wydra 2007: 92). In the United States, the unexpected dramatic sea change of the incipient Cold War and the pandemic of McCarthyism fundamentally changed the constitutive imagination of America. During the bipolarity of the Cold War, liberal values were imagined to be absolute (Hartz 1955). Liberal absolutism effectively purged New Deal values of social democracy from the national power imaginary. Liberalism made democracy coterminous with the "good society" and supporting dictatorships in the name of democracy.

Democracy and the Sacred

Democracy's "ultimate" values draw on conflicting types of knowledge as well as reflective and deliberative practices that thrive on debate and scrutiny. They reject transcendental truths. This "secular" frame of democratic politics conceals that democracies require awe before rituals and values that are impervious to contestation. As Tocqueville lucidly saw, the fragile equilibrium of the empty place of power makes democracies more dependent on ritualized formalism than any other kind of regime. Democratic citizens are left with the authority of the greatest number to guide them, that is, common opinion (Tocqueville 2000). Representative democracy is a formidable system for resolving conflicts, except for the incapacity of questioning the conditions of its own democratic source (Ankersmit 2002).

How can "democratic source" be understood? One possibility is to look at the various ritualistic practices found in democratic communities. In common understanding, ritual is the type of action that responds to sacred things. Yet during situations of authority vacuum, new ritualistic forms may become carriers of consensus and community spirit. They separate the realms of the sacred and the profane. Ritual is the very process by which a new model for the community is established—a new symbolic center of the sacred that will become the focus of the worship of authority. Rites of passage, for example, are a universal feature of human and social life. Their sequential order consists of a three-phase process. The first phase, that of separation, releases initiands from their former condition as participants in a social group and identity (van Gennep 1960). It opens up the second phase, where the actual initiation takes place. This is a liminal period in-between, a no man's land where people are temporarily without affiliation or identity, often in complete reversal of their former roles. The third stage leads to a new affiliation with a group identity that usually differs in kind from the original condition. Guided by initiated masters of ceremonies, republican rituals such as France's Bastille Day or the inauguration ceremonies of U.S. presidents are strictly formalized performative acts. Yet they are rooted in culturally creative performance, which Don Handelman has conceptualized as events-that-model (Handelman 1990: 22–57). Distinguishing them from "events that present the lived-in world" and "events that re-present the lived-in world," events-that-model are dramatic contexts in which people assign meaning and purpose to their actions in ways other than those prevailing in rationalistic conceptions of democratic autonomy, state modernization, or individualism. The purpose of ritual is to advance the fundamental objective of making a living species, group, or community flourish and prosper.

A second possibility to grasp "democratic source" is to look at the creative role of violence in democratic communities. Democratic societies are in constant dialogue with the constitutive role of "originary" violence in revolts. Sacrifice is both life-denying and life-affirming, destructive and creative. The sacrality of symbols is the way in which the object is more than the mere sum of its parts and points to something beyond itself. Democracy thus conveys images of cultural unity organized around ideas of freedom, rule of law, and collective choice of accountable rulers. This dialogue is visible in the constitutive claims of the rule of law and the collective imagination by which a democratic people defines itself. The self-representation as a democratic people appears only once "origins of democracy" are remembered and performed by the citizenship as "founding moments" of integration and reconciliation. This urge to transcend domestic conflict has been a permanent feature in democracies, despite substantial changes over time. In Athens and the United States, collective sacrifice of citizens symbolically expressed the self-confidence of a democratic community. Thucydides' version of the funeral oration made by Pericles on behalf of the first fallen in the Peloponnesian War describes ancestral ritual customs in preparation for the funeral ceremony. Pericles claims the uniqueness of Athenian democracy—"we are rather a pattern to others than imitators ourselves" (Thucydides 1997: 95)—even as he implores listeners to imitate the dead, who offered their lives as the most glorious contribution to Athen's democracy: "These take as your model, and judging happiness to be the fruit of freedom and freedom of valor, never decline the dangers of war" (ibid.: 99). Abraham Lincoln's Gettysburg address of 1863 likewise linked the prospects of freedom to commemoration of the self-sacrifice of U.S. citizens. The sacrifice of soldiers on the battlefield would become the cornerstone for turning the divisive, violent conflict into a sacred origin of American democracy.

Democratic communities still profess a collective identity, a moral commitment to the constitutionally defined demos in a cultural space that is determined against the outside. Political citizenship, for instance, is always constituted in conjunction with the identification of others as strangers, outsiders, or aliens. Constitutionalism and the rule of law protect the autonomy of individuals but cannot be rationally constructed. They are based on the coding of memory, which harks back to moments of transgression but has become a constitutive mythology over time. Inexplicable fundamentals are irreducible to communication with words. As Joseph Weiler put it, the constitutional ethos of democracies, for instance, "celebrates a supposed unique moral identity, wisdom, and, yes, superiority of the authors of the constitution, the people, the constitutional demos, when it wears the hat of constituent power and, naturally, of those who interpret it" (Weiler 2009: 108). Perhaps as in no other country, presidential campaigns in the United States appear clearly as a ritualized duel between candidates whose desperate attempts to distinguish themselves can become the fiercest rivalry. After this first phase of warlike enmity, however, the act of voting has usually integrated the nation in its totality behind the winner to show unanimous support and reverence toward the president. Constitutionalism can provide awe-inspiring stability in the case of undecided elections. The U.S. Supreme Court's Bush v. Gore decision halted the presidential election process in 2000 by stopping a recount in Florida and effectively selecting the winner (Levinson 2007). The Bush v. Gore ruling in 2000 not only reflected the justices' contempt for Congress, it also revived faith in constitutional fundamentals and gave unprecedented scope of action to what Levinson called the papalist nature of the Supreme Court, which could draw on the American public's strong approval of providing definite resolutions to contentious issues (ibid.: 122–24). Despite the predictions of many, the Supreme Court's approval ratings soon returned to the highs it enjoyed before the decision. Institutional loyalty predisposed most Americans to view the decision as based on law and therefore legitimate.

Domestic violent conflict is impure and taboo. It works as the abject that sustains the awe-inspiring holiness of the democratic order in the first place. Individual freedom and rights are in conflict with collective obedience to the law. The certain death of individuals is compensated by the promise of immortality and transcendence for a social and political collective. The specter of the sacred "always haunts the law" (Sarat, Douglas, and Umphrey 2007: 1). Modern legality requires representations of founding moments, interpretations of constitutional texts as "sacred," and assertions about the status of law more generally as a kind of civil religion. The rule of law and the anti-ritualistic impulses of democracy both recall its liminal sources.

Cleisthenes' reform in 508/7 B.C. was grounded in his skillful interpretation and sensitive reading of the riotous uprising of the demos against the archon Isagoras (Ober 2004: 281–83). In the liminal moment of a popular revolt, Cleisthenes recognized that mass action had created a new political, if not existential, fact. The "democratization" of the first democracy relied upon *isonomia*, an order of equality of citizens that did not draw on equality before the law or the individual liberty of opportunities but rather consisted in seeing political activity as the only possible sphere where unspecialized citizens could excel in public. Thus the Greeks could only become *citoyens* because they were not bourgeois (Meier 1993: 203). The Greeks coined the term democracy to describe their already existing form of government.

The emergence of modern democracy drew on the numinous experience of the revolt after 1789. The French Revolution replaced the divine right of kings with what Edgar Quinet called a "people-God." Establishing the people-God in the fiction of the people-as-One required the mobilization of a belief (if not a cult) of the impossible in people's minds and hearts. According to Rousseau, gods are actually needed to validate man-made laws, which require the inspiration of an awesome, almost mystical authority (Arendt 1984: 184). Before the French Revolution *"le peuple"* was semantically ambiguous. Unlike the English word "people," the ambivalent *peuple* connoted plebs, the vulgar mob, and canaille. *Le peuple* could refer to the whole of the population of France, but it also meant the ordinary people, commoners, the poor, and the vulgar as opposed to nobles and the clergy. The self-definition of the members of the Third Estate on 17 June 1789 as the *Assemblée Nationale* was preceded by an act that expressed the members' terror and awe before the *"presque totalité"* of the population. Emmanuel Sieyès, operating with statistical evidence, suggested that the gathered delegates represented 96 percent of the population. Despite this evidence of sovereignty expressed by the raw pressure of numbers, the assembly to come was named after the nation, not the people. The French nation was the origin of everything. "Its will is always legal. It is the law itself. . . . The Nation is always the master of every reform to its constitution" (Sieyès 2003: 136).

After divisive conflict, fractures within political communities require interpretive shifts that allow citizens to celebrate victimhood as the source of consensus and reconciliation. The Spanish transition to democracy, for instance, has often been hailed as model of peaceful transition. Franco's death in November 1975 threw the country into liminal uncertainty. The brutality and self-destruction of the Spanish Civil War now underwent a profound reinterpretation (Edles 1998) as a profane descent into hell, and conversely, the new beginning after Franco's death was interpreted as its sacred symbolic opposite. National reconciliation and *convivencia* inaugurated a widely shared consensus on democracy, rejecting civil strife and fratricidal conflict. The transfer of meaning in this ritual process is summed up in many Spaniards' conclusion that "we have met the enemy, and the enemy is us." The Spanish transition can be seen as a ritual process "in a space in and outside time," developing four core representations: "new beginning," "democracy," and "national reconciliation" with its symbolic opposite, "civil war." In South Africa, the Truth and Reconciliation Commissions (TRC) were not just a legal instrument to ascertain human rights violations: above all, they were a forum where speech acts—about experienced suffering by victims, and about inflicting torture and maltreatment by perpetrators—were performed before localized audiences throughout the country. The conflict-ridden, destructive period of Apartheid thus acquired a quality that clearly distinguished it from the new period of a democratic nation. The TRC reinterpreted stories of suffering in order to endow the new South African citizens with sacred qualities of equals.

To become a community of equals, social communities need to convert profane, destructive, and nondemocratic practices into sacred representations of heartfelt allegiance to a community (Wydra 2015). Modern law is based on a tension that "concerns less the existence of the sacred in law than the proper relation one ought to exhibit toward the law as it is expressed in sacred moments, objects, or regimes of meaning" (Sarat, Douglas, and Umphrey 2007, 10). Democrats need to "feel" that they are tied together by an idea of common origin and a common purpose. This idea is indispensable for sharing a common political destiny.

Democracy's Passionate Interests

The subversive promises of the democratic imagination and the ritualistic power of balancing the effects of political emancipation are complementary suppliers of democracy's lifeblood. At the same time, however, they constitute democracy's Achilles' heel. In an age of growing interconnectedness, speedy communication through internet and social media, and porous boundaries, liminality has become a defining feature of the global age. Nevertheless, democracies continue to require forms of the social sacred, which, given the fractures of identity in authority vacuums, cannot be the mechanical solidarity attached to the cultural unity of a people, nation, or society. Durkheim's dogmatic postulation of a social sacred as a preexisting invisible authority that predetermines people's attachment to the community does not stand up to empirical scrutiny. The container of democracy, be it its bordered territory or the self-evident rules of belonging to citizenship, may become porous.

Democracy "has altered its meaning so sharply since Babeuf because it has passed definitely from the hands of the Equals to those of the political leaders of the order of egoism" (Dunn 2005: 160). Variants of democratic individualism and socialist versions of democracy alike put citizens' autonomy at their core (Held 1987: 268–70). Autonomy is usually associated with self-determining citizens who form their judgments without significant external constraints on their actual conduct. According to James

Madison, private self-interest should control the political system. Various offices "may be a check on the other; that the private interest of every individual may be a centinel over the public rights" (Wolin 2008: 281). Madison's remedy against factionalism and the tyranny of the majority lay, amongst other things, in personal self-interest. The idea of autonomy as the individual's capacity to act on the basis of self-interest is a fundamental axiom of liberal thought. Albert Hirschman's work separates the passions from the interests as a function of modernity (Hirschman 1977). In this view, capitalist behavior did not evolve from a religious quest for salvation alone, as in Max Weber's tradition. It is also traceable to an equally desperate search for a way to avoid society's ruin. Methodological individualism is based on the assumption that individuality is predetermined by our preferences, which are ontologically stable.

However, democratic society is better conceived as based on a radical existential pluralism that takes seriously the unsocial sociability of human beings (Wydra 2011: 101–2). Conceiving of people in unitary terms joins the biological-instinctive sphere to the meaning-giving, symbolic sphere of human life. Preferences are never stable but must instead be identified with regard to the models that have shaped the trajectory of a specific leader, citizen, or nation. Sociability is the accidental, contingent expression of an infinite number of interactions and relations between individuals. The collective whole relies, in principle, on contingent and undetermined constellations and associations of these single units. The idea here is that intentions and interests of human beings are subject to reciprocity. According to anthropologist René Girard, the contagious nature of mimetism can help to account for the manner in which communication processes, even the most rational ones in economic exchange or political decision-making, rely on forms of what Girard calls "interdividual psychology" (Girard 1987: 281–431).

The order of egoism in democracy is in tension with a diffuse, urgent hope that social life is more a matter of committed personal choice than of enforced compliance (Dunn 2005). This hope is not a timeless normative constant but has been played out and performed across limit experiences. Rather than appearing as an irreducible quality of an individual rationality, "interest" expresses a relationship. Etymologically, "inter-esse" designates the space in-between, the mediation between two entities. The illusion of authenticity is well illustrated by Jean-Jacques Rousseau's distinction between *amour de soi* and *amour propre* in social order (Rousseau 1993: 75–76). For Rousseau, *amour propre* results from envy and desires produced by social order, whereas *amour de soi* suggests a situation uncontaminated by these social products. Contrariwise, Adam Smith's concept

of self-love includes the reciprocity of passions and interests. In constant
need of help of his fellows, man cannot rely simply on the benevolence
of others. Rather, "he will be more likely to prevail if he can interest their
self-love in his favour, and shew them that it is for their own advantage
to do for him what he requires of them" (Smith 1998: 22). Concerned with
the "great mob of mankind"—that is, the behavior of the average person—Smith defined self-interest as the craving for honor, dignity, respect,
and recognition. Genuine self-interest, therefore, cannot exist in a radically plural world. Rather, individualism is better grasped in its existential
desire for difference (Wydra 2011).

The radical existential pluralism characteristic of democratic societies
makes people attractive to each other. Unlike in an aristocratic or a caste
system, democratic society allows everybody access to everything. Here,
the imitation of others' desires of is paramount, allowing for rivalry, conflict, and intense competition. As Tocqueville put it:

> Democratic communities have a natural taste for freedom. . . . But for equality,
> their passion is ardent, insatiable, incessant, invincible: they call for equality in
> freedom; and if they cannot obtain that, they still call for equality in slavery. . . .
> All men and all powers seeking to cope with this irresistible passion, will be
> overthrown and destroyed by it. (Tocqueville 2000: 619)

Tocqueville's point underscores that citizens' intentions are shaped by
affective and passionate interests. It is rather doubtful, therefore, that
self-enclosure can substantiate democracy. People's legitimation of their
voluntary association with a system of domination is based on the idea
that everybody rules by means of the others. According to Rousseau, the
democratic paradox is that the higher, overarching social spirit of citizenship is in a dialectical relationship with the constitutional framework of
good laws. If an emerging people are to follow rules, the effect—which
he understands as the social spirit—has to become the cause—which as-
sumedly would be good laws—and the cause (the good laws) would have
to become the effect (the social spirit). This paradox can be resolved by
accepting that in models of authority, invisible bonds often tie members of
democratic communities together. Authority relies on a double process of
recognition (Popitz 1992: 29). On the one hand, the superiority of others as
those who set the measure as the marker of certainty must be recognized.
On the other hand, people desire to be recognized by those who set the
markers and thus receive signs that demonstrate their worth. This is not
a closure of the individual but an opening up toward others via mutual
recognition of other human beings, and eventually also toward the transcendental realm beyond the profane reality of day-to-day politics. Such

processes of mutual recognition also occur in concrete sites of dramatic performance, to be interpreted and culturally remembered. Abstract reasoning and cool deliberation are trumped by heartfelt emotions.

The central ritual of democracy—namely, the act of election, of performing the fundamental act of voting—is a site where inter-individual psychology is ritualized. Theories of social choice focus on the rationality of voter "preferences." They limit meanings of "rationality" to choice driven by self-interest. In a liberal view, markets are social settings where consumers nurture their *amour propre* (self-love) through a focus on the *amour de soi* (pursuit of genuine self-interest). It is true that in the vacuum of Election Day, citizens can be seen as one-dimensional and isolated individuals (Lefort 1986). Yet disunity and solitude in the ballot box coincide with a strongly regulated, ritualistic, community experience that usually exhibits measure, restraint, and civility. The constraint is in the ritualistic celebration of peacefully doing the same thing. According to Rousseau, the general will need not be unanimous. But it is absolutely essential that all votes are counted, as any exclusion breaks the generality. Elections show that the rationality of the vote lies less in the individual choices than in the ways people perform their allegiance to a transcendent whole. The reality of ritual is independent from the consent of the individual. The crucial element is not the individual's view but the serious, public disposition of the community celebrating the ritual, which is no theater, exercise, or game. Rituals are not only performances during transitions; they also create these transitions in the first place.

At crucial junctures of democratic thought, thinkers such as Plato, Aristotle, Alexis de Tocqueville, and Joseph Schumpeter recognized "bad" imitation, mob rule, and the downward spiral of equality. Democratic institutions can all become prey to contagion with passions. The democratic institutions of Athens condemned Socrates to death. The "rampant liberalism" characteristic of the McCarthy era illustrated how the justice system can be hijacked by logics of persecution and existential fear of an enemy (Hartz 1955). Writing in the aftermath of the 1968 student revolts in Paris, Mary Douglas (2007: 160) identified "anti-ritualism" as the "idiom of revolt". Revolts against oppression challenge rituals of hierarchy, differentiation, and power. By imposing their own cosmology of outsiders and deprived, revolutionaries can produce terror, warfare, vengeance, or retaliation. Facing deep crisis and despair, individuals reject their autonomy and seek their highest goal in the vigor of a mass movement (Hoffer 1964: 57–62). Madison recognizes this sacrificial logic when he says that "a pure democracy . . . can admit no cure for the mischiefs of faction . . . and there is nothing to check the inducements to sacrifice the weaker party or an obnoxious individual" (Madison, Hamilton, and Jay 1987 126). A full-fledged democracy would be a regime in which the majority could carry through its will against any minority. In Montesquieu's words, "the principle of democracy is not only corrupted when the spirit of equality is lost but also when the spirit of extreme equality is taken up" (Montesquieu 1989: 112).

The contagious nature of imitation means that even the most rational and reflective communication processes, such as in economic exchange, public policy, or international conflict, rely on forms of interdividual psychology. Everyday democratic politics may look like an arrangement of autonomous beings based on individual self-interest, but this is only half of the story. According to Hayek, competition draws on the affective forces of imitation. The few who are skillful at taking appropriate measures to achieve their ends will make gains in competition, thus obliging others "to emulate them, in order to prevail." Thus, rational methods will progressively be developed and spread by imitation. It is not rationality that makes competition work; rather, competition produces rational behavior (Hayek 1979: 75–76). However, within the bounded space of democratic states, irrationality not only resides in the electoral body of the "people" but can lie at the very center of "interest" politics. As Bent Flyvbjerg has argued in his study of the Aalborg project (the design, planning, and political implementation of a bus terminal), power defines both reality and the type of rationality by which this reality can be kept under control (Flyvbjerg 1998: 36). As an indicator of power in democracy, the absence of rational arguments and factual documentation in support of certain actions is just as important as the arguments and documentation produced.

Indeed, contemporary discourses of democracy are driven by attempts to re-enchant a demoralized world. On a planetary scale, the master narrative of democracy has been simultaneously attractive and subversive. The verb "to democratize" has progressively turned from a reflexive verb (doing something to oneself) into a transitive verb (doing something to others). Democratization now is applied to make other states and societies democratic, sometimes by means of force. The subversive power of the democratic imagination was most powerful in the collapse of Soviet communism and the failure of Arab authoritarianism. The revolts that led to the speedy dismantling of authoritarian systems in the "Arab Spring" projected expectations of democratic freedoms.

Democratic freedom, however, is measured by standards that are often incompatible with dynamics of democratic emancipation. Democratic participation requires some degree of democratic consciousness. According to Macpherson, changes in social inequality and consciousness require a prior increase in democratic participation, and democratic participation cannot grow further without prior changes in social inequality. (Macpherson 1977: 100). In the global age, participation and consciousness have changed considerably. Amin Maalouf's gripping metaphor compares globalization to an immense arena, open on all sides, in which thousands of oratory duels occur simultaneously. In these thousands of fights, anyone can come in with his or her own tune or own arsenal in an untamable cacophony (Maalouf 1998: 146). Maalouf's suggestion points to the impossibility of framing, limiting, or ordering forms of boundless communication.

The triumphalist mood of the post–Cold War era projected the "global convergence" of democracy. Acknowledgment of human rights and reckoning with totalitarian legacies were central features of this mood. Following the world wars and genocides of the twentieth century, the triumphant self-representations of "the people" in the frame of nation-states gave way to a new transcendence of humanity, that is, a new moral purpose linked to humanity as a transcendent quality (Canto-Sperber 2010). Collective ideological foundations of anti-racism and the protection of victims created a secular sacred. Today, in the early twenty-first century, the moral duties of democracy have changed considerably. Atrocities such as ethnic cleansing or suicide terrorism have become the demonic outside that democrats are committed to categorically rejecting. The classic foundations of democratic thought in the eighteenth century, such as the Declaration of the Rights of Man and the Bill of Rights, protected citizens from tyrannical governments. But in an age of genocide and concentration camps, the dehumanization of people prompted calls for a secular refoundation of natural law. Beyond protection from oppression, the new sacred of the early twenty-first century requires the untouchable nature of humanitarian reason (Fassin 2012) based on moral imperatives of atonement, reconciliation, and human rights.

As promises of democratic emancipation are carried onto a global level, the democratic imagination has become increasingly liable to negative imitative effects. The democratic peace thesis, for instance, draws on current theories of international morality designed to perpetuate the supremacy of the dominant Anglo-American power (Barkawi 2006: 52–53). The ruling dogma in liberal democracies holds that regular armies' killing of innocent noncombatants is legitimate, whereas terrorism is a sign of barbarism. Suicide bombing amongst civilian noncombatants generates particular horror in Westerners (Asad 2007: 90–92). Its brutality and speed eludes the dialectics between crime and punishment, loss and restitution, that are so central to the functioning of modern law. Within the mental frame of the rule of law, the public performance of suicide bombing is utterly disruptive. Suicide bombing leaves perpetrator, victims, and witnesses alike without redemption. It thus makes apparent its own constitutive outside, which is the "limitless pursuit of freedom, the illusion of an uncoerced interiority that can withstand the force of institutional disciplines" (ibid.). Therefore, one might even plausibly suggest that suicide terrorism (like a suicidal nuclear strike) is constitutive of liberalism's self-identification. The "liberal" side can thereby quickly become the dark side of democracy. The end of communism was an ideological triumph of liberal monism, imposing democracy in a quasi-mythical way and as a politically non-negotiable goal (Wydra 2008). The Bosnian catastrophe, however, symbolizes how the discourse of democratic humanism upheld by Western democracies was powerless to prevent genocide, ethnic cleansing, and civil war. This case stands representative for other more recent conflicts, notably the Syrian civil war and the implosion of the authority of the Iraqi state. The normative ideology of democracy proves inadequate in liminal conditions of a global age.

The increased vulnerability of powerful states in liminal globality shows the ambivalence of the liberal foundations of democratic states. Liberalism was born in the struggle against absolute kings. The liberal dogma of the prohibition of torture became an enforceable norm against a set of background expectations that aimed to limit the power of the state over individuals. But the post-9/11 environment substantially changed the way rights are conceived. In a time of terrorist attacks against innocent, noncombatant citizens, individuals' protection may be subordinated to a state's need to secure its territorial integrity. Suicide bombing and the vulnerability of sovereign space have become major forces driving constitutional democracies to protect themselves by returning to sacrificial practices. When states become terrorist targets, the background expectations change (Kahn 2008: 74). Now it is the state that needs protection from individual terrorists, and democratic states have made recourse to practices they condemn.

Conclusion

According to Rousseau, it is against the natural order for the many to govern and the few to be governed (Rousseau 1993: 237). Democracy's continual tendency to change to another form makes it fragile and prone to civil war. Precisely because democratic rule comes down to a permanent interregnum, social divisions and fragmentation need to be transcended. Any meaningful claim to popular sovereignty requires ritual initiation and the interweaving of affective bonds of solidarity, social spirit, and meanings of shared experiences and shared destiny. Neither the collectivist ontology of popular sovereignty in the name of the public nor the particularistic ontology underpinning methodological individualism can account for the fragile equilibrium that democracy has sustained over time. The empty place of power is thus not only a historically unique and unrepeatable event but must be conceived as a specific socio-structural condition of in-betweenness, fluidity, and fracture in the political community. The notion that "the people are the master" is a myth, but as Paul Ricoeur has indicated, the myth of the collective will is indispensable for a working democracy (Ricoeur 2004).

Despite its status as a traditional concept, democracy has been porous and susceptible to shifts in meaning (Koselleck 1985: 82). After the eighteenth century, it became equivalent to a new organizational form typical of the modern state. In the wake of the social transformations in the nineteenth century, it increasingly became associated with a state of expectation. To justify its own meaningfulness to citizens, democracy had to satisfy the needs created by political emancipation. In the twentieth century, democracy replaced "republic" and consigned all other constitutional types of rule to illegality. Still, claims to equality are not limited to representation. Equality of conditions—far beyond legal-constitutional prescriptions or a principle of social hierarchies, entitlements, and political rights—also provides human relationships with horizons of meaning. Even though many inequalities persist in social reality, equality becomes irreversible at the level of aspirational goals. Psychologically, revolutionaries and ordinary people lack clearly defined and potentially viable projects, having only alternative imaginations. If the twentieth century was the democratic age par excellence—witnessing four major waves of democratization—it was also a revolutionary age. The revolutions in Russia, China, Cuba, Turkey, and Iran, whether communist, secular revolutionary, or anti-colonial, all proposed different variants of equality.

More recently, this noncontingent and transcendent value of democracy is reflected in the popularity of "unpolitical" theories of democracy. Deliberative approaches to constitutional democracy have suggested that the value and worth of deliberation rest in its ability to wean democracy from its politicizing inclination (Urbinati 2010). Unpolitical democracy wards off the permanent threat of demagoguery and populism. It also reduces the possibility of the irrational (i.e., partisan and biased) outcomes that representative bodies and citizens' votes tend to reflect and facilitate. This rise of international tribunals and courts, the boom in legal NGOS and human rights advocacy, and the increased importance of constitutionalism have heralded the "displacement of the political into the legal" (Comaroff and Comaroff 2006: 23). The politics of regret have increased a sense of dialogue and reconciliation (Olick and Coughlin 2003: 56). Though the growing importance of international law and practices of reconciliation undoubtedly haave integrative effects, they are also problematic, in that the "democratization of memory" introduces multiple histories and contested narratives about identity.

The will of the people cannot be known and is never really respected by rulers. However, everybody in democracy is supposed to abide by it. The point is not whether we can cognitively "prove" the existence of a general will or a public good. Very few people believe that rulers in a democracy represent the collective will. Quite the opposite, rulers obviously pursue particularistic wills. Yet this is exactly the point. The constant competition to occupy the empty place of power temporarily requires an invisible "agreement," some form of unanimity. But alongside the profane aspect of the electoral procedure and the accountability of representatives, this unanimity also has a sacred element that surpasses categorization and rational analysis. In a global age of democracy, the democratic imagination may not only lead to more integration but may also undermine the emotional and affective bonds of civic identity in political associations.

References

Ankersmit, F. 2002. *Political Representation*. Stanford: Stanford University Press.

Arendt, H. 1984. *On Revolution*. Reprint Edition. Harmondsworth: Penguin.

Asad, T. 2007. *On Suicide Bombing*. New York: Columbia University Press.

Barkawi, T. 2006. *Globalization and War*. Lanham, MD, and Boulder, CO: Rowman and Littlefield.

Canto-Sperber, M. 2010. *La Morale du Monde*. Paris: PUF.

Comaroff, J. and J. Comaroff (eds). 2006. *Law and Disorder in the Postcolony*. Chicago and London: University of Chicago Press.

Connolly, W. 1997. "Debate: Reworking the Democratic Imagination." *Journal of Political Philosophy* 5 (2): 194–202.

Dahl, R. 1956. *A Preface to Democratic Theory*. Chicago and London: The University of Chicago Press.

Douglas, M. 2007. *Natural Symbols*. London: Routledge.

Dunn, J. 2005. *Setting the People Free: The Story of Democracy*. London: Atlantic Eooks.

Edles, L. 1998. *Symbol and Ritual in the New Spain*. Cambridge: Cambridge University Press.

Fassin, D. 2012. *Humanitarian Reason: A Moral History of the Present*. Berkeley and London: University of California Press.

Flyvbjerg, B. 1998. *Rationality and Power: Democracy in Practice*. Chicago and London: University of Chicago Press.

Gennep, A. van. 1960. *The Rites of Passage*. Chicago: University of Chicago Press.

Girard, R. 1987. *Things Hidden Since the Foundation of the World*. Baltimore, MD: Johns Hopkins University Press.

Handelman, D. 1990. *Models and Mirrors*. Cambridge: Cambridge University Press.

Hartz, L. 1955. *The Liberal Tradition in America*. New York: Harvest.

Hayek, F. 1979. *Law, Legislation, and Liberty*, vol. III: *The Political Order of a Free People*. Chicago and London: University of Chicago Press.

Held, D. 1987. *Models of Democracy*. Stanford: Stanford University Press.

Hirschman, A. 1977. *The Passions and the Interests*. Princeton, NJ: Princeton University Press.

Hoffer, E. 1964. *The True Believer*. 6th printing, New York.

Kahn, P. 2008. *Sacred Violence: Torture, Terror, and Sovereignty*. Ann Arbor: University of Michigan Press.

Keane, J. 2009. *The Life and Death of Democracy*. London: Schuster and Schuster.

Koselleck, R. 1985. *Futures Past. On the Semantics of Historical Time*, translated by K. Tribe. Cambridge, MA and London: The MIT Press.

Lefort, C. 1986. *Essais sur le politique*. Paris: Seuil.

———. 2007. *Complications: Communism and the Dilemmas of Democracy*. New York: Columbia University Press.

Levinson, S. 2007. "Our Papalist Supreme Court: Is Reformation Thinkable (or Possible)?" In *Law and the Sacred*, edited by A. Sarat, L. Douglas, and M. M. Umphrey. Stanford: Stanford University Press.

Maalouf, A. 1998. *Les identités meurtrières*. Paris: Grasset.

Madison, J., A. Hamilton, and J. Jay. 1788 (1987). *The Federalist Papers*. Edited with an introduction by I. Kramnick. London: Penguin.

Macpherson, C. B. 1977. *The Life and Times of Liberal Democracy*. New York: Oxford University Press.

Meier, C. 1993. *Athen. Ein Neubeginn der Weltgeschichte*. Berlin: Siedler.

Montesquieu, C. (1748) 1989. *The Spirit of the Laws*. Edited and translated by A.M. Cohler, B. C. Miller, and H. S. Stone. Cambridge: Cambridge University Press.

Ober, J. 2004. "The Athenian Revolution of 508/7 B.C.: Violence, Authority, and the Origins of Democracy." In *Athenian Democracy*, edited by P. J. Rhodes. Oxford: Oxford University Press.

Offe, C. and U. Preuss. 2006. 'The problem of legitimacy in the European Polity: Is Democratization the Answer?', in C. Crouch and W. Streeck (eds) *The Diversity of Democracy: Corporatism, Social Order, and Political Conflict*. Cheltenham: Edward Elgar.

Olick, J. and B. Coughlin. 2003 "The Politics of Regret. Analytical Frames," in J. Torpey (ed.) *Politics and the Past: On Repairing Historical Injustices*. Lanham, MD: Rowman and Littlefield.

Popitz, H. 1992. *Phänomene der Macht*. Tübingen: Mohr.

Ricoeur, P. 1984. "The Political Paradox." In *Legitimacy and the State*, edited by W. Connolly. New York: New York University Press.

Rosanvallon, P. 2006. *Democracy: Past and Future*. Edited by S. Moyn. New York: Columbia University Press.

Rousseau, J.-J. 1993. *The Social Contract and Discourses*, trans. and intro. G.D.H. Cole. London: Campbell Publishers.

Sarat, A., L. Douglas, and M. M. Umphrey, eds. 2007. *Law and the Sacred*. Stanford: Stanford University Press.

Sièyes, Emmanuel J. 2003. *Political Writings*, ed. Michael Sonenscher. Indianapolis and Cambridge: Hackett.

Schumpeter, J. 1976. *Capitalism, Socialism, and Democracy.* 3rd ed. New York: Harper.

Sewell, W., Jr. 2005. *Logics of History.* Chicago and London: University of Chicago Press.

Smith, A. (1776) 1998. *Wealth of Nations.* Oxford: Oxford University Press.

Thucydides, 1997. *The History of the Peloponnesian War.* Ware: Wordsworth Classics.

Tocqueville, A. 2000. *Democracy in America.* Edited by J. Epstein. New York: Bantam Classic.

Turner, V. 1967. *The Forest of Symbols.* Ithaca, NY: Cornell University Press .

Urbinati, N. 2010. "Unpolitical Democracy." *Political Theory* 38 (1), 65–92.

Weber, M. 1980. *Wirtschaft und Gesellschaft.* 3rd edition. Tübingen: Mohr.

Weiler, J. 2009. "Human Rights, Constitutionalism, and Integration: Iconography and Fetishism." In *An Identity for Europe: The Relevance of Multiculturalism in EU Construction,* edited by Riva Kasturyano. Basingstoke: Palgrave.

Whitehead, L. 2002. *Democratisation: Theory and Experience.* Oxford: Oxford University Press.

Wolin, S. 2008. *Democracy Incorporated: Managed Democracy and the Specter of Inverted Totalitarianism.* Princeton, NJ: Princeton University Press.

Wydra, H. 2007. *Communism and the Emergence of Democracy.* Cambridge: Cambridge University Press.

———. 2008. "Revolution and Democracy: The European Experience." In *Revolution in the Making of the Modern World,* edited by J. Foran, D. Lane, and A. Zivkovic. London: Routledge.

———. 2011. "Passions and Progress: Gabriel Tarde's Anthropology of Imitative Innovation." *International Political Anthropology* 4 (2): 93–111.

———. 2015. *Politics and the Sacred.* Cambridge: Cambridge University Press

Chapter 11

Liminality and Postcommunism
The Twenty-First Century as the Subject of History

Richard Sakwa

> The 21st will be either a century of total exacerbation of our mortal crisis or a century of purification, spiritual convalescence, and an all-round renaissance.
>
> —Mikhail Gorbachev (Gorbachev and Ikeda 2005: 145)

A s we enter more deeply into the twenty-first century, it is appropriate to reflect on what are becoming the distinguishing features of not only our century, but also the beginning of the new millennium. What does it mean for a century to be considered "the subject of history"? A first answer is to suggest that in the grand movement of time, a period is imbued with certain characteristics that become fully discernible only long after, but whose key features can be identified and challenged by contemporaries. Thus, from a macro-historical perspective the twentieth century was essentially the working out of the dreams and projects of the nineteenth century. More than that, the twentieth century from this perspective exhausted and destroyed those hopes, leaving the twenty-first century with a remarkably impoverished terrain, given the earlier "utopian" dreams and aspirations to transcend the given, the actual, and the apparently all-too-solid real. The eschatological impulse that sustained so many projects for progressive improvement of humanity's lot has apparently been exhausted in the debris of so many utopian dreams gone so horribly wrong.

Notes for this chapter begin on page 224.

A second response is to suggest that periods of time can be narrated in different ways, focusing on fundamental themes such as state development, economic modernization, or power relations. Besides these material aspects of the historical approach, there are also cultural aspects with a deep structure, above all the spiritual bases of human community and consciousness as an evolving subjectivity in which humans appreciate the contingent nature of fate and fortune. Events at particular junctures cause certain issues to become ever more insistent, as when the communist systems fell in 1989–91, or when capitalism entered into profound financial and economic crisis in 2008, throwing into question not just the ethical bases of contemporary capitalism but also the spiritual bases of the political community as a whole. The foundational search encompasses the fundamental challenge of finding new forms of political community in a post-secular era, as well as giving valance to a broader constellation of political subjects. The modernist aspiration to marginalize religious life, for example, is challenged by a new wave of religiously inflected political actors. Universal themes resonate differently and take on various hues in light of the particularity associated with distinctive historical epochs. Each generation reinterprets and appreciates universal concerns in the light of its own experience.

Temporality, Crisis, and Liminality:
The Dilemmas of Postcommunism

Reinhart Koselleck (1988) notes how the critique of the eighteenth century provoked a crisis whose first major symptom was the French Revolution. The meta-cycle of critique and crisis is subdivided into smaller cycles occurring in the following series: aspiration, fulfillment, disappointment, and reaction. Crisis denotes a special type of "epochality" in which the inner cycles have reached the stage of reaction and disappointment. In certain respects the meta-crisis identified by Koselleck continues, but postcommunism as an era is trapped in the smaller cycle of disappointment and reaction.

At the present time, three types of postcommunist crisis intersect. First is the thirty-year crisis of globalization and its focus on banking deregulation and financialization beginning in the mid 1970s, which ultimately provoked the meltdown of the international financial system as of August 2008. The disappearance of the communist alternative allowed capitalism to weaken the regulatory regime that had accompanied the postwar welfarist bargain, which had in part been generated in response to the communist threat. Various individualistic and market rationales have challenged the rationale for state action, above all protection of social security. Second, there is a crisis of governance including, above all, a crisis of democratic legitimacy. Its features are sometimes described as "postdemocracy," a situation where the technocratic rationale of governance undermines both accountability and responsiveness to popular concerns. The decline of the mass political actors of an earlier era has produced an increasingly insulated ruling class (Crouch 2004).

Finally, the disintegration of bipolar bloc politics has provoked a geopolitical crisis. Russia in particular is involved in a new "twenty-year crisis" that began with the collapse of the communist system in 1989–91. Europe, if not the world, faces problems provoked by the disintegration of the Soviet pole in the international system, all of them unresolved. Early hopes that extending the existing instruments of European security (NATO) and solidarity (Council of Europe) and broadening the remit of common security bodies like the Organization for Security and Cooperation in Europe (OSCE) would adequately respond to the new circumstances were soon disappointed. Instead, both NATO and the OSCE became sources of conflict rather than instruments for building an enduring post–Cold War security system. The European Union (EU), putatively at the heart of a working peace system for Europe, was unable to project its transcendent values into the post-Soviet area (even the Baltic states and Moldova became sites for cold peace conflicts).

The postcommunist era remains liminal in two complementary ways. The first concerns the immediate impact of the fall of communism, above all the fact that no stable new order, in economic, political, or security terms, has been established to substantiate the hegemony of the putative victors at the end of the Cold War. In terms of security, the hegemony of the West has encountered numerous points of resistance no longer couched in the classical language of class or the struggle against bourgeois imperialism. On the other side, meanwhile, none of the so-called rising powers maintains a consistent critique of the hegemonic system. Russia is certainly not a full-fledged revisionist power. Its new assertiveness is not based on an attempt to change the normative basis of the existing world order, but rather on the claim that its equal participation in that system has not been fully acknowledged. China's claims are somewhat different, and though it does not yet position itself as an alternative to the West, its assertiveness has deep cultural and civilizational roots.

A more profound element in the contemporary crisis is that the new twenty-year crisis has emerged out of the very nature of the anti-revolutions of 1989–91. These revolutions repudiated the logic of what went before, and not just the facts of the previous era. The postcommunist era is based on a fundamental asymmetry between active repudiation of one set of principles and passive acceptance of another. The asymmetry itself provoked a permanent crisis in post-Soviet Eurasia, which has become a new area of contestation between the four major powers of our time: Russia, China, the United States, and the European Union. Geopolitical contestation, as during the Cold War, is accompanied by struggles to impose sympathetic regimes in the absence of an ontological basis for a new "normality." Russia, since 1991, has tried to adapt to a normality that is itself in crisis. Russia represents a parallel sphere where the conscience and bad faith of our era are played out. Disappointment with the utopian aspirations to emancipatory socialism has given way to a reaction that repudiates not only the communist system but also the intellectual terrain from which the movement sprang (Gray 2009).

The second arena of postcommunist liminality emerges out of the collapse of long-term eschatological projects that have been the characteristic feature of modernity (Sakwa 2006). The "epochality" of the fall of communism derived from repudiation, at the social level, of revolution as an emancipatory act. By epochality I mean the eschatology of endowing parochial events with universal significance. The eighteenth-century emergence of a discourse of progressive social change based on a universal model of rationality and development applicable to all societies was clearly an event of epochal significance. This ideology, in the hands of some Enlightenment thinkers (but certainly far from all), was combined with a revolutionary approach to social change, so that the act of rupture itself had a liberating and progressive political effect. For want of a better term, this can be called "Enlightenment revolutionism." In the nineteenth century, this idea of political revolution was combined with a social agenda, above all by Karl Marx, based on the idea that through an act of political rupture, society could achieve emancipation not only from oppression but also from subordination to contingency in the very broadest sense.

This combination, termed emancipatory revolutionism, was the project that Lenin and Stalin sought to implement in one way or another in Russia and post–World War II Eastern Europe. By the late twentieth century, however, the notion of emancipatory revolutionism had lost whatever popular resonance it once might have had in countries that claimed to be building communism. A residual emancipatory revolutionism remains in the thinking of Slavoj Žižek and some other philosophers like Alain Badiou, but their popular resonance is minimal. Thus the events of 1989–91, when one Eastern European country after another shook off its communist power system, represented both the overthrow of a specific regime

type and the repudiation of the social philosophy of emancipatory revolution on which such regimes were based. This, as much as the geopolitical rearrangement of the international order they entailed, rendered these
events epochal.

Epochal thinking since the ancient world has been characterized by a
sense of the unfolding of time, which in the modern era became allied to a
progressive understanding of social change. The Russian (October) revolution was the first large-scale attempt to implement Marxist revolutionary
theory by building a society based on the rejection of the forms of Western
modernity while trying to fulfill the substance of that same modernity,
stripped off the former class contradictions. In this utopian project, as it
is now called, pragmatic reason in political discourse was displaced by a
political practice that generated closure and exclusivity. The pursuit of
transcendent and universal (epochal) goals undermined appreciation of
the particularism of the raw human material and national specificity of the
country where the revolutionaries had to work. In practice, communism
everywhere assumed national forms, but the tension between universal-
ism and particularism did not disappear (Brudny 1999). During the period
of perestroika (restructuring, 1985–91), Soviet leader Mikhail Gorbachev
attempted to extinguish revolutionism while retaining the emancipatory
core of Marxism, but this combination (which harked back to the Prague
Spring of 1968) ultimately failed.

The Displacement of Temporality, or the Timelessness of Time

The postcommunist era is associated with endings, collapse, and crisis.
Other than in the most primitive Hegelian triumphal form, it lacks a sustained collective vision of what the ancients called "the good life." The
absence of a basis in contemporary epochality intensifies structural demands on the past as a source of legitimacy and ordering principles for the
postcommunist present. Because these demands have provoked attempts
to revalorize important aspects of the communist past, struggles over history textbooks and the politics of memory have become critical elements of
postcommunist public discourse. The broader problem has been explored
by Sergei Prozorov (2009), who reinterprets Hegelian notions of the end
of history through the prism of Giorgio Agamben's philosophy. Prozorov
argues that with the demise of the communist order, Russia entered a post-
historical terrain where the teleological dimension of politics has been de-
mobilized. In his view, the 1990s in Russia were a period of "timelessness,"
and postcommunism in general can be characterized as a paradoxical

"time out of time," when the ordinary flow of temporality is disrupted and lack of the teleological dimension provokes an exaggerated political praxis oriented to the maximization of the present (Prozorov 2008).

Expectations of an easy transition from one type of historicity to another were disappointed. The temporality of the so-called transition in Russia ran aground on the realities of spatiality. Instead of conforming to the ready-made political praxis devised elsewhere, Russia entered into a period of intensified liminality that, though generated by its own civilizational identity, also reflected the broader crises of our epoch. For many generations Russia has acted as the canary in the coal mine of modernity. At the boundaries of European civilization, Russia—an uncomfortable member of the club of European powers—has endured a type of permanent liminality waxing and waning in intensity ever since the reforms of Peter the Great (Malia 2000). The fall of communism signaled the onset of a period during which, in the absence of a normality to which to adapt, Russia's inherent liminality rose to the surface, indicating a condition of permanent *krisis* (see below). Some societies find themselves in a liminal state for quite some time, and in Russia's case, the journey from the anti-revolution of 1989–91 to crisis was a short one. The crisis reflects not only Russia's permanent liminality but also the liminality in the global system. For Koselleck, the crisis has become pathological but has also itself become the new normality.

Measurement of time is a way of assessing the historicity or historical quality of a particular era. Time is indeed of the essence, and the interaction between time and historical thought has insistently come to the fore, suggesting that contexts are not timeless but connected with epistemic and moral consciousness (Miller 2008). Gorbachev notes that "idolization of the future inevitably led to skepticism about the present. in which millions live" (Gorbachev and Ikeda 2005: 139). Temporality concerns the immanence of an era, an issue explored by Eric Voegelin in an essay on consciousness, where he discusses the "time-consciousness of world-immanent man" (Voegelin 1978: 14). Awareness of an event in time distinguishes one epoch from another, the before from the after. When raised to the level of philosophy, it becomes constitutive of an understanding of history as a process. From this perspective, the novelty of the twenty-first century is what could be called the "detemporalization" of time. Koselleck once argued that the more intensely a particular time is experienced as a "new temporality," the more "the demands on the future increase" (Koselleck 1985: xxiv). This may well have been the case in an earlier era, but it is no longer so. When the epochality of an era diminishes, collective demands on the future decline, and the focus is increasingly on individual strategies. Liminality of transformation has given way to liminality of change without meaning, purpose, or direction. The citizen has been privatized, purposive collective action constrained, and corporate power extended into governance while the state increasingly acts as a corporate entity in a competitive global environment where "brand democracy" seeks to assert its values in a permanent market war.

Into the Twenty-First Century

Alain Badiou (2007) has tried to characterize the twentieth century in a series of powerful vignettes. Although schooled in the thinking of Louis Althusser, Badiou has developed a peculiarly postmodernist type of structuralism without structures. The twentieth century may well have fulfilled the promise of the nineteenth, but this also, Badiou notes, also entailed the collapse of aspirations and in particular the repudiation of the idea of the transcendent power of revolution. The twentieth century, Badiou writes (ibid.: 19), "is the Real of that for which the nineteenth century was the Imaginary." The Reformation imaginary of the sixteenth century gave way to the reality of the Counter-Reformation and the Thirty Years' War in the seventeenth, whereas eighteenth-century dreams of political emancipation, along with the nineteenth century's notions of social emancipation, had collapsed by the end of the twentieth. If liminality represents a threshold which can be both crossed and not crossed—a potential whose realization opens up new hopes—then the early twenty-first century is a most profoundly liminal period; however, its threshold cannot be crossed because it cannot be found. This is characteristic of "times out of joint," when rising dissatisfaction with the present lacks a language of the future. The grand narratives that sustained the Euro-Western mind in the era of revolution and for two millennia appear to have been exhausted (Taylor 2007). There is no "new world" to be built, so the threshold itself appears to have disappeared. What, we are forced to ask, does the "death of utopia" mean? Does it denote a new medievalism of powerful princes and petty wars, or a new humanism accompanied by a new renaissance?

The Twentieth-Century Legacy and *Krisis*

The twentieth century ultimately proposed itself as the resolution of the nihilist strain at the end of the nineteenth. Fin-de-siécle pessimism was certainly nothing new, but the twentieth fin-de-siécle was rather different than the nineteenth: the cult of violence, of revolution, of destroying the old humanity for the sake of the new, found few adherents in the Western world. The coiled spring that had suffused art and politics a century earlier had lost its energy, leaving behind the detritus of failed experiments practiced on the living flesh of humanity. This was an era that, from a Heideggerian standpoint, had a passion for the real. On this, Badiou (2007: 33) notes, "the century of revolutionary politics assembled under the equivocal name of 'communism', was barbarous because its passion for the real placed it beyond good and evil." The "real" of the twentieth century, paradoxically, took the form of powerful ideologies whose reality is mythical by definition; and though evil was real, the good became ever less tangible. The "end of ideology," if not of history, imbues the Euro-West with a mental listlessness. Yet precisely this crisis allows us to take advantage of what the Greeks meant by *krisis*: a moment of contemplation in the life of a community (the complementary term *krinein* does not quite carry this meaning).

Perhaps the best starting point from which to examine the search for a new historicity is the book of conversations between Mikhail Gorbachev, the last general secretary of the Communist Party of the Soviet Union, and Daisaku Ikeda, leader of the largest (Buddhist) religious movement in Japan. They begin with a ringing statement: "This book is dedicated to the twentieth century." Gorbachev and Ikeda were both born in the "fateful transitional period" from the 1920s to the 1930s, so both have experienced more than half of the century. They posit their talks "as an investigation into the lessons it has left us." Despite their very different backgrounds, they seek "a common spiritual basis" for understanding the events of that traumatic century. They note that although the century was characterized by world conflicts and totalitarianism, it ended with a new emphasis on "values" and "freedom." It "exposed the venom in Promethean myths, the conceit of knowledge, and the lust to dominate Mother Nature," yet ended with the pressing problem of "the right to live the lives granted us by heaven and nature, and the need to preserve the spirit of liberty and freedom of thought and faith" (Gorbachev and Ikeda 2005: vii). The wide-ranging discussions trace their own biographies against the events of their respective countries, but the key theme is whether the experience of the twentieth century could "provide grounds for the search for and construction of a 21st-century humanism," starting "where intolerant, extreme socialist humanism and the dream of communist equality ended." They condemn "ideological extremism" and rhetorically agree that if "human happiness cannot be built on violence, how do we combat evil?" They likewise agree that, "since class ethics are incompatible with morality, what can we find to replace them?" Gorbachev and Ikeda end by noting that whereas perestroika put an end to the Cold War, it is not clear what sort of world political system would replace the former bipolar system (ibid.: viii).

The discussion throws a powerful light on the self-understanding of the twentieth century by two of its most intelligent, thoughtful partici-pants. Replete with moral warnings and emphasis on spiritual values, the text reflects the journey from materialist conceptions of the historical process at the beginning of the twentieth century to thorough disillusion-ment with large-scale processes of social amelioration by the beginning of the next, when a new awareness of nonmaterial values' importance in the development of human society was emerging. However, the bulk of the discussion focuses on the negative lessons to be drawn from the commu-nist revolt against capitalist oppression, with the appropriate references to Dostoevsky's *Devils*, Lev Tolstoy, and Nikolai Berdyaev. The lessons to be drawn from Japanese militarism and its imperial ambitions, though mentioned, are overshadowed by the experience of the Soviet Union. Gor-bachev remains committed to a type of socialist humanism but is unable to generate a critique of actually existing capitalism. A powerful new ide-alism emerged from the collapse of the Soviet system, but the inevitable tendency was to naturalize the remaining (capitalist liberal democracy) system and thus to blunt the edge of critique. The book provides some powerful reflections on the *krisis* at the end of the communist experiment, but its "moralistic idealism" fails to address the problem of the new era of geopolitical competition introduced by the asymmetrical end of the Cold War, in which the structures and ideas that fought the Cold War were dis-mantled on one side but retained on the other.

This critique of a particular form of twentieth-century totalitarianism and its legacy avoids the "feeble moralizing" (Badiou 2007: 53) and dis-torted historiography that is typical of the genre (Courtois et al. 1999). It also transcends the passion for certainty that so often passes for public discourse in large parts of today's Euro-West world. In this case the re-covery of memory is accompanied by the rediscovery of thought, an un-usual combination in the contemporary world. The discussion reflects an attempt to genuinely transcend contradiction by finding some new form of synthesis that avoids a simple program of restoration. Focusing on in-dividual conscience and spiritual renewal (Boobbyer 2005), it refuses to accept that consumerist individualism could solve the problem of the ex-cesses of governmental action. The political form of the new emancipation remains unclear, and the real paradox could be that if such a collective political form based on a new historicity were found, it would nullify the emancipatory potential of the new transcendence.

The End of the Age of Revolutions
and the Epoch of the Anti-revolution

Koselleck notes a shift in the understanding of historical time. Before the eighteenth century, temporality was seen as the repeated unfolding of eternal truths.

> All variation, or change, *rerum commutation, rerum converse*, was insufficient to introduce anything novel into the political world. Historical experience remained involved in its almost natural givenness, and in the same way that the annual seasons through their succession remain forever the same, so mankind qua political beings remained bound to a process of change which brought forth nothing new under the sun. (Koselleck 1985: 41–42)

Koselleck goes on to describe historical time as imbued with a new quality resulting from "revolution" being conceptualized anew as not only circularity but overthrow and transcendence through a process of civil war. In Russia, the civil war took a very real form and ushered in seven decades of communist rule. Like the 240 years of Mongol suzerainty, the 74 years of communist power endowed Russia with a layer of historical experience that is unique in Europe (cf. Wydra 2007).

An interesting interchange between Ikeda and Gorbachev concerns the subject of the French Revolution. Ikeda, noting that Goethe, unlike Hegel, rejected the revolution "on the strength of his organic sense of life," quotes Goethe's comments on revolution:

> And, furthermore, nothing is good for a nation but that which arises from its own core and its own general wants, without apish imitation of another; since what to one race of people, of a certain age, is nutrient, may prove poison for another. All endeavors to introduce any foreign innovation, the necessity for which is not rooted in the core of the nation itself, are therefore foolish; and all premeditated revolutions of the kind are unsuccessful, for they are without God, who keeps aloof from such bungling. If, however, there exists an actual necessity for a great reform amongst a people, God is with it, and it prospers. (Gorbachev and Ikeda 2005: 37)

Numerous Russian commentators have repeated this theme. For example, Elgiz Pozdnyakov, the author of numerous books on geopolitics and the philosophy of state and law, devoted one work to the "fruitlessness of any people's attempt at substantial social changes on the basis of rational plans or ideas, ignoring the deep roots of the society and state" (Pozdnyakov 2008: 29). This argument has had broad resonance in the West in recent years (Scott 1998). Pozdnyakov developed this Hayekian theme to argue that "if the foundations of a society or state change, it is not the result of some internal upheaval, however radical it may be, but a result of lengthy and complex changes and adaptations to the changing world. Internal overturns, shocks and revolutions create only better or worse conditions for this" (Pozdnyakov 2008: 41).

In this climate, contemporary Russia is characterized by a profound anti-revolutionary spirit (Sakwa 2008: 46–47). Much Russian patriotic writing today comes close to the view, expressed most eloquently by Rudolf Kjellén (1916), of the state as an almost organic living organism, so it is no surprise that Kjellén's book *The State as a Life Form* has been translated into Russian (2008). Kjellén gives the state almost human characteristics, including (as M. V. Il'in puts it in the book's introduction), "temperament, will, character, and living features" (ibid.: 29). The tendency to anthropomorphize the state provides ready material for the international political anthropologist. Indeed, one of the best books on political anthropology in Russia claims to examine precisely "the socio-biological and cultural grounds of power, forms of social stratification and mobility" (Kradin 2004: frontispiece).

The gradualist thesis, or the evolutionary approach to social change, has now triumphed in political theory. Paradoxically, however, in political practice the whole notion of "transition" is inherently bound up with rupture and the shock transformation of societies on new principles. Whereas evolutionism developed in reaction to the terrors of the radical changes associated with the Jacobin and Bolshevik traditions; transitionism has precisely reproduced Jacobin practices. Nevertheless, the consequences of the repudiation remain to be explored. Above all, the idea of revolution, as Koselleck noted, imbued time with purpose and direction, thus inspiring generations with a sense that the flow of time was intelligible and that human intervention was purposeful and effective. A revolution marked the passage from one condition to another. For the revolutionaries, this signaled the transcendence of former inadequacies and entailed civil war, a rupture in historical development. For those of a more conservative hue, though, the outbreak of civil war destroyed the organic unity of the nation and its historical trajectory (Gorbachev and Ikeda 2005; Pozdnyakov 2008), and inaugurated a period of timelessness (Prozorov 2008, 2009). In a transition, the quality of historic time is dominated by a remedial agenda. In the postcommunist era, this agenda assumed strongly spatial forms: the future lay in "the west" rather than on some temporal horizon.

Anti-revolutionary Practices and the Cold Peace

Anti-revolutionism does not necessarily mean reaction or restoration, but it does entail an organic philosophy of history and thus of social development. With the end of the era of revolution, a fundamental problem has emerged: how to be between two states when there is no transcendence of the historical present. The concept of liminality suggests openness to the new and thus the possibility of achieving something else, but the problem appears to be the absence of "something else" besides the repetition of experiences generated elsewhere, which reflects the permanent liminality to which we have referred above. Liminality without a philosophy of history differs greatly from liminality conceived as a temporality rich with the promise of a different future. In other words, although the anthropological literature suggests that liminality acts as the portal to a more advanced state of maturity, this directional characteristic may well be absent when liminality is applied to the life of a nation. With the end of the era of revolutions has come the naturalistic restoration of temporality as the eternal changing of the seasons. The exhaustion of the idea of revolution as the positive transcendence of a given condition has allowed the return of temporality's traditional meaning: the eternal cycle of life at the mercy of the gods of fate. The practices of peacetime governance and the quality of peace are imbued with the shadowiness and ambiguity characteristic of liminal periods.

Anti-revolutionary Politics: The New Governmentality

The revolution in which the "subjects themselves become the rulers" (Koselleck 1985: 44, quoting Arendt) has now given way to a period in which the idea of "anti-revolution" permeates social consciousness (Sakwa 2001, 2006). The anti-revolution repudiates the revolutionary method of achieving social change and historical justice, but it is not necessarily reactionary. It opposes the logic of revolution (and not just the determinate features of a specific revolution), so it is more than simply a counterrevolution (de Maistre 1994: 105). Its basic spirit is well described by Gorbachev and Ikeda. Although they stress the positive spiritual charge of the new epoch, the burden of expectation has noticeably declined, and it is difficult to retrieve a sense of "genuine human history" (Koselleck 1985: 45) organized through active political engagement in the sphere of purposive action (the *Politeia*) rather than at the mercy of the Fates in the *Nomoi*, where the life of a community depends on its inherent qualities more than its self-characterization.

The features of the anti-revolution can be sketched as follows (drawing on Koselleck 1985: 46–54): (1) the deceleration of historical time; (2) evolution rather than revolution as the dominant principle, and thus repudiation of the idea of civil war as an instrument of social progress; (3) revolts or rebellions against historical injustice, subordination, or captivity that, though undoubtedly continuing to occur, have nonetheless lost their transcendental significance as emancipatory acts with some sort of universal significance, and deriving from this, (4) a great reduction, if not delegitimation, of the "utopian" element in programs of social change (belief in a "new future") because of the perceived "totalitarian" temptation inherent in all utopian projects; along with overall disenchantment with the notion of "progress," stemming from earlier scientistic and rationalistic traps that tended toward dehumanizing managerial resolutions of perceived problems; (5) a shift from material to spiritual and moral concerns, including a new awareness of "the political" accompanied by the repudiation of social revolutions; (6) spatial compression from "world revolution" to national development; and (7) civil wars that today, unlike in the epoch of revolutions when "all wars have been transformed into civil wars" (Koselleck 1985: 54), retain intense local resonance but hold little universal significance (mostly because of the absence of the escalatory threat of nuclear war that pervaded the Korean and Vietnam conflicts), and hence are increasingly protracted and intractable in nature. One act of violence succeeds another, but the international organizations established at the end of World War II lack the power or mandate to intervene effectively; meanwhile, each former superpower is preoccupied with new problems of its own. The era of the emancipation of classes and the liberation of peoples has given way to a permanent *krisis* whose liminal potential (i.e., transformative capacity) appears minimal.

Postcommunist anti-revolutionism has brought the demobilization of emancipatory movements and a new style in the management of public affairs. Its central feature is the dismantling of government in favor of governance. The underlying public choice philosophy has aggravated popular disempowerment, weakened political accountability, and intensified the power of capital over polity, including the financialization of governance and markets. The privatization of public functions goes hand in hand with their commercialization; meanwhile the *culture* (from the Latin, tilling and nurturing) of effective public participation has shriveled. Instead, the practices of Enron and WorldCom have become generalized, with disastrous consequences like those revealed in the crash of 2008.

The advance of democracy has everywhere been accompanied by the strengthening of the state in new ways (from the "coercive" to the "infrastructural," to use Michael Mann's terms) and the extension of governmental intrusion into aspects of individual daily life. Although the concept of governmentality in Foucault's works is susceptible to differing interpretations, reflecting the evolution of the concept in his thinking, it remains a rich source of insight into understanding power and authority. For Foucault, governmentality combines practices of governance and certain "mentalities" of rule that make governing possible (1991). It therefore focuses not just on the behavior of institutions but also on discursive articulations of their operation as appreciated by the subjects of governance. In a liberal democratic society, institutional practices coexist with practices and techniques that both reinforce and subvert the proclaimed principles of governance. The idea of governmentality is now also being applied to the study of international politics in an attempt to move away from increasingly sterile juxtapositions of realism versus constructivism, or other binary systems.

In advanced democracies, Wolin argues, the features of "inverted totalitarianism," generated by the development of a new totalizing power, are increasingly pronounced. Totalizing power does not rely on charismatic or personal characteristics alone but is sustained by a system whose leader is more the product of that system than its architect (Wolin 2008: 238–48, 287). Wolin talks of "managed democracy" in the United States, which focuses on "containing electoral politics" and accepts social democracy only insofar as it provides a literate, socially competent workforce for its economy and effective soldiers for its armies: "Voters are made as predictable as consumers; a university is nearly as rationalized in its structure as a corporation; a corporate structure is as hierarchical in its chain of command as the military" (ibid.: 47). An active citizenry has been replaced by an "electorate" whose support provides legitimacy for the system, and citizens are reduced to a pre-political condition. As in the Soviet system, there is "politicization without politics" (ibid.: 65): "Inverted totalitarianism reverses things: It is all politics all of the time but a politics largely untempered by the political" (ibid.: 66).

There is, as Geoff Eley (1995: 159) puts it, "a pervasive sense in our own times that the state has been passing increasingly beyond accountability." Traditional liberal-constitutional constraints on executive power grow ever weaker, while substantive aspirations to popular control and management become an increasingly distant memory. Power has not only become increasingly remote but is also, as Eley notes, ever less intelligible and susceptible to popular intervention. Gramsci's model of hegemony at least opened up spaces for resistance, however attenuated the embedded notion of revolutionary transcendence may have been. In distinguishing between coercion and consent, the latter provided an arena for counter-mobilization against the hegemonic power system. The residual idea of revolutionary transcendence may well have been superfluous, but it provided inspiration for a politics of popular empowerment. The capitalist state has never been homogeneous and has traditionally allowed for sites of contestation and incorporation.

In Gramsci's reading these sites were intelligible, well signposted, and focused on reasonably demarcated institutions of state power, although even formal institutions were understood to be embedded in networks of impersonal relations. By contrast, in Foucault's model of dispersed infrastructural power it is unclear how and where patterns of resistance can be generated. Although power may be diffuse and take weakly institutionalized and structurally undifferentiated forms, any theory of domination that lacks a modality by which to articulate strategies of counter-domination ultimately becomes an accessory to that domination. This is not, however, to suggest that this is the outcome of Foucault's analysis of the decentered patterns of contemporary capitalist domination. Foucault's late notion of "care of the self," an attitude of autopoiesis, provides insight into how strategies of personal spiritual resistance can begin to articulate a way of overcoming the modern apparatus of subjectivization. Once existing patterns of domination are exposed, they can begin to be challenged, thus perhaps restoring the cycle of revolution anew (Foucault 1980, 1991, 2004).

From Cold War to Cold Peace

Badiou's study of the twentieth century returns repeatedly to the problem of war. The century, in his view, "unfolded under the paradigm of war," with the endless but variously formulated invocation that only another war could put an end to war; therefore, "between 1918 and 1939 peace was the same thing as war" (Badiou 2007: 34). In certain respects, we once again find ourselves in a type of interwar period of no war and no peace— that is, in a cold peace pregnant with renewed conflict (Sakwa 2012).

Gorbachev stresses that the Cold War was ended by "new thinking" in the Soviet Union, noting that "the Cold War was contrary to the interests of humanity." However, he is well aware that on its own, "the abrogation of ideological conflict did not lead automatically to a general, definitive peace." The threat of nuclear catastrophe may have decreased (though even this is not certain), but new threats had emerged. As Gorbachev puts it: "The Cold War froze numerous geopolitical, national, and ethnic conflicts, not all of which were connected to the Cold War itself. . . . The Cold War quasi-stability created a reassuring impression that the post-conflict world order was predictable" (Gorbachev and Ikeda 2005: 57; cf. Westad 2005). He goes on to stress that the ending of the Cold War made our world no safer. Today many people are beginning to look on total Westernization as they once did on the threat of total, forcible communalization. Apparently, the West is incapable of dealing in a reasonable way with the results of the new thinking that freed the world from bloc politics and total confrontation. (Gorbachev and Ikeda 2005: 147)

Gorbachev laments that the fruits of the new thinking are "withering away before our eyes," and that even though Russia has "rushed toward the West with open arms and the best possible will," the West has not reciprocated. The West has been incapable of "working out either a new doctrine of collective security or a new ideology of peaceful development. Today the fate of the world is in the hands of institutes [*sic*] formed during the Cold War." The European process has been sacrificed, in his view, to the eastward expansion of NATO, and the "possible untoward consequences of this mechanistic approach to the problem of European and global security are overlooked" (ibid.).

While there is no new world to be built, the principles of the old world are aggressively advanced. Gennady Zyuganov, the leader of the Communist Party of the Russian Federation, said in his report to the thirteenth party congress on 29 November 2008 that "with the destruction of the Soviet Union war has again become a legitimate policy instrument for the leading imperialist powers" (2008). Liminality turns in on itself, and the threshold becomes the world, with movement backwards and forwards constrained. Permanent liminality no longer permits novelty and innovation but imposes formlessness and disorientation as a technique of governmentality. There is permanent change but never transformation. As Wolin (2008: 96) puts it: "Change suggests a modification that retains a prior 'deeper' identity. Transformation implies supersession, or submergence, of an old identity and the acquisition of a new one."

The wars of the twentieth century were essentially provoked by the incommensurability of conflicting temporalities. It is worth quoting Badiou at length:

Ultimately, the problem of the century is to exist in the non-dialectical conjunction of the theme of the end and that of beginning. "Ending" and "beginning" are two terms that, within the century, remain unreconciled.

The model for the non-reconciliation is war—total and definitive war, which displays three main features:
(a) It puts an end to the possibility of the bad war, the useless or conservative war whose model is the war of 1914–18.
(b) It must uproot nihilism, because it advocates a radical commitment, a cause, a true face-to-face with history.

(c)   It will lay the foundations for a new historical and planetary order. (Badiou 2007: 37)

This new war, in his view, "generates a new type of subject; a war that is also the creation of its combatant. In the end, war becomes a subjective paradigm" (ibid.: 37). What does all this mean? War became constitutive of the century, but the nature of war changed. No longer just bodies of armed men, war became internalized in the operative codes of society. This is more than the dominance of the "military-industrial complex" and even deeper than the reflexive confrontation of the Cold War years, which itself was an emanation of passive civil war (within states) between classes and alternative ideas about social systems. Rather, it is a profound militarism that became apparent in the crusader mentality of the "war on terror" and changed to "the long war" in the late Bush years—a war without end, formless and pervasive, but constitutive of Anglo-American societies and their allies. This militancy is diffuse but generates enemies as required. This immanent logic became apparent at the time of the Ukraine crisis in 2014, when the Atlantic security community quickly remobilized itself against Russia (Sakwa 2015).

Wolin (2008: 37) notes the process of "anticommunism as mimesis: the character of the enemy supplied the norm for the power demands that the democratic defender of the free world chose to impose on itself." Wolin defines a "superpower" "as an imaginary of power that emerges from defeat unchastened, more imperious than ever" (ibid.: 40). The "war" in the abstract has been declared, while the reality of great power rivalry is occluded (ibid.: 31). War is inevitable; the only questions are how the conflict will become manifest, how intense the fighting will be, and what consequences it holds for human survival.

These theoretical considerations gave rise to profound practical consequences in the postcommunist world. The tensions characterizing foreign policy were clear from the outset. Russia's first foreign minister, Andrei Kozyrev (1994: 3), aimed to combine two apparently contradictory principles. On the one hand, he sought to "guarantee the rights of citizens and the dynamic socio-economic development of society"; on the other, he insisted that Russia was "a normal great power, achieving its interests not through confrontation but through co-operation." By late 1993, Kozyrev had adopted a more sharply defined empire-saving strategy, insisting that Russia had the right to intervene to prevent it from "losing geopolitical positions that took centuries to achieve" (*Izvestiya*, 8 October 1993). The attempt to make Russia a democracy and a great power became the central principle of Russian policy as of early 1993, but these aims (typical of the essential ambiguity of Russian policy) were not entirely compatible. Kozyrev now argued that Russia could be a democratic post–Cold War great power pursuing a non-ideological definition of national interests while accepting that this could sometimes entail elements of competition with the West. This tough approach was vividly manifested in Brussels in November 1994, when Kozyrev refused to sign documents already agreed upon with NATO concerning the Partnership for Peace program. As Yeltsin explained a month later at the Budapest summit of the OSCE in December 1994, the West's attempts to discredit Russia's pursuit of "normal" great power interests by forever raising the specter of a Cold War revival threatened to lead precisely to the emergence of a "cold peace" (Kozyrev 1995).

From the late Putin years onward, Russia's behavior was undoubtedly more assertive. Whether this was simply a greater affirmative stance derived from economic recovery, political stabilization, and a prolonged commodities boom that poured resources into the Kremlin's coffers; or whether it signaled a more aggressive, possibly bellicose approach to advancing its perceived interests remains a matter of considerable controversy. The era of overwhelming U.S. hegemony in the postwar years was a historical exception unlikely to be maintained in the long run. Ironically, the collapse of the communist-oriented "second world" in 1989–91 cleared the way for the emergence of a number of potential market-based "third world" challengers, and this has already become the key theme of the twenty-first century. The threat is typically posed less in geopolitical terms than in the language of a clash of values. This is, as Badiou (2007: 4) notes, "politics without an alternative"—which means intellectual constriction, since no alternative can be thought. Thus late-capitalist modernity turns in on itself and precludes the generation of the ideas that can ensure its own sustainability over the long haul. It was this same involution that ultimately put paid to the communist experiment, which become a sclerotic closed system with weak potential to adapt to emerging challenges. "Victory" in the Cold War now threatens the victors with a similar fate. Paradoxically, many of the most avid apostles of the new militancy—the American neoconservatives—had absorbed a virulent strain of Trotskyist revolutionism in their youth and now transformed the "permanent revolution," in an inverted form, into a "permanent war" to reshape the world under the banner of freedom and democracy. John Gray (2007) comments on this when he argues that eschatological hopes did not die with the Enlightenment's rejection of Christianity but returned in the form of projects for universal emancipation, latterly in the form of American neoconservatism, the legacy of Carl Schmitt and Leo Strauss.

Relations between Russia and most western powers remain locked in cold peace liminality. Russia considers the United States sly and mendacious, and United States returns the compliment by relegating Russia to a group of semi-authoritarian states and regarding it as bent on restoring not only its prestige but also some form of neo-imperial relationship with its post-Soviet neighbors. Unlike in the original Cold War, there are no rules to manage the new relationship and no framework with which to limit ambitions. While the Soviet Union existed, there were accepted spheres of influence, but the liminality of the post–Cold War era removed these limits. The territory of the former Soviet Union became a new arena of contestation, as seen most vividly in the Russo-Georgian war of August 2008 and the struggle over Ukraine from 2013. NATO enlargement itself became a threat. As Rose Gottemoeller (2008: 7) puts it,

> The Russians, in fact, are threatening to remobilize against NATO, which undoes the good accomplished at the end of the Cold War and merely extends the twentieth-century European security nightmare into the twenty-first. Surely we can do better than that.

Instead of a Conclusion

Voegelin (1978: 8n) describes the "amusing incident" when Sir Leonard Woolley, writing a section of the UNESCO book *History of Mankind*, noted that it was impossible to rank works of art in terms of a single linear pattern of an improvement in quality, and hence raised the question of restrictivist notions of the development of mankind. Notions of progress and development, those icons of the twentieth century, may have been challenged by postmodern approaches (as well as by social anthropologists, long ago), but a healthy skepticism, if not relativism, is no substitute for a substantive analysis of the interaction of cultures and peoples. In his *New Science of Politics*, Voegelin suggests that transcendence may offer a basis for political order (quoted in Trepanier 2007: 7). Elsewhere, Voegelin (1978: 23) proposes, drawing on Plato and applied allusively, the distinction (and indeed, tension) between *Politeia*, the conscious attempt by peoples to manage their common destiny, and *Nomoi*, a more spiritually charged sense of the common destiny of a community, which may lie in the hands of the gods. Combining the two is indeed the central politico-spiritual question of our liminal age, as formulated by Gorbachev and Ikeda. On this, Voegelin (1978: 65) takes an open-ended approach, insisting that there can be no a priori rules:

The criterion of rightly ordered human existence, however, is the permeability for the movement of being, i.e., the openness of man for the divine; the openness in its turn is not a proposition about something given but an event, and ethics is, therefore, not a body of propositions but an event of being that provides the word for a statement about itself.

References

Badiou, A. 2007. *The Century*. Translated by Alberto Toscano. Cambridge: Po ity.
Boobbyer, P. 2005. *Conscience, Dissent and Reform in Soviet Russia*. London: Routledge.
Brudny, Y. M. 1999. *Reinventing Russia: Russian Nationalism and the Soviet State, 1953–1991*. Cambridge, MA: Harvard University Press.
Courtois, S., et al. 1999. *The Black Book of Communism: Crimes, Terror, Repression*. Cambridge, MA: Harvard University Press.
Crouch, C. 2004. *Post-Democracy*. Cambridge: Polity.
de Maistre, J. 1994. "Supposed Dangers of Counter-Revolution." In *Considerations on France*, edited by J. de Maistre. Cambridge: Cambridge University Press.
Eley, G. 1995. "War and the Twentieth-Century State." *Daedalus* 142 (2): 155–74.
Foucault, M. 1980. *Power/Knowledge: Selected Interviews and Other Writings 1972–1977*. Edited by Colin Gordon. New York: Pantheon Books.
———. 1991. "Politics and the Study of Discourse." In *The Foucault Effect: Studies in Governmentality*, edited by G. Burchell, C. Gordon, and P. Miller. Chicago: University of Chicago Press.
———. 2004. *Society Must Be Defended*. Harmondsworth: Penguin.
Gorbachev, M., and D. Ikeda. 2005. *Moral Lessons of the Twentieth Century: Gorbachev and Ikeda on Buddhism and Communism*. London: I. B. Tauris.
Gottemoeller, R. 2008. *Russian-American Security Relations After Georgia*. Washington, DC: Carnegie Endowment for International Peace.
Gray, J. 2007. *Black Mass: Apocalyptic Religion and the Death of Utopia*. London: Allen Lane.
———. 2009. *Gray's Anatomy: Selected Writings*. London: Allen Lane.
Kjellén, R. 1916. *Staten som lifsform*. Stockholm: Hugo Gebers Förlag (in Russian: Rudol'f Chellen. 2008. *Gosudarstvo kak forma zhizni*. Moscow: Rosspen).
Koselleck, R. 1985. *Futures Past: On the Semantics of Historical Time*. Translated by Keith Tribe. Cambridge, MA: MIT Press.
———. 1988. *Critique and Crisis: Enlightenment and the Pathogenesis of Modern Society*. Oxford: Berg.
Kozyrev, A. 1994. "Vneshnyaya politika preobrazhayushcheisya Rossii." *Voprosy istorii* 1: 3–11.
———. 1995. "Partnership or Cold Peace?" *Foreign Policy* 99: 3–14.
Kradin, N. N. 2004. *Politicheskaya antropologiya*. 2nd ed. Moscow: Logos.
Malia, M. 2000. *Russia under Western Eyes: From the Bronze Horseman to the Lenin Mausoleum*. Cambridge, MA: Belknap.
Miller, T., ed. 2008. *Given World and Time: Temporalities in Context*. Budapest: Central European University Press.
Pozdnyakov, E. A. 2008. "*Umom Rossiyu ne ponyat . . .*" Moscow: Voslen.

Prozorov, S. 2008. "Russian Postcommunism and the End of History." *Studies in East European Thought* 60: 207–30.

———. 2009. *The Ethics of Postcommunism: History and Social Praxis in Russia*. Basingstoke: Palgrave Macmillan.

Sakwa, R. 2001. "The Age of Paradox: The Anti-revolutionary Revolutions of 1989-91." In *Reinterpreting Revolution in Twentieth-Century Europe*, edited by M. Donald and T. Rees. London: Macmillan.

———. 2006. "From Revolution to Krizis: The Transcending Revolutions of 1989-91." *Comparative Politics* 38 (4): 459–78.

———. 2008. *Putin: Russia's Choice*. 2nd ed. London: Routledge.

———. 2012. "The Cold Peace: Russo-Western Relations as a Mimetic Cold War." *Cambridge Review of International Affairs* (4 September). ID: 710584 doi:10.1080/09557571.2012.7105 84.

———. 2015. *Frontline Ukraine: Crisis in the Borderlands*. London: I. B. Tauris.

Scott, James C. 1998. *Seeing Like a State: How Certain Schemes to Improve the Human Condition Have Failed*. New Haven, CT and London: Yale University Press.

Taylor, C. 2007. *A Secular Age*. Cambridge, MA: Harvard University Press.

Trepanier, L. 2007. *Political Symbols in Russian History: Church, State, and the Quest for Order and Justice*. Lanham, MD: Lexington Books.

Voegelin, E. 1978. *Anamnesis*. Translated and edited by G. Niemeyer. Notre Dame, IN and London: University of Notre Dame Press.

Westad, O. A. 2005. *The Global Cold War: Third World Interventions and the Making of Our Times*. Cambridge: Cambridge University Press.

Wolin, S. 2008. *Democracy Incorporated: Managed Democracy and the Specter of Inverted Totalitarianism*. Princeton, NJ: Princeton University Press.

Wydra, H. 2007. *Communism and the Emergence of Democracy*. Cambridge: Cambridge University Press.

Zyuganov, G. 2008. "Political Report of the CPRF Central Committee to the 13th Party Congress." 29 November. http://kprf.ru/party_live/61739.html.

Chapter 12

The Challenge of Liminality for International Relations Theory

Maria Mälksoo

Introduction

The concept of liminality favors a broad interpretation, lending itself easily to disciplinary contexts outside of the original framework of cultural anthropology. Developed by Arnold van Gennep (1960) and Victor Turner (1969) while exploring rites of passage, liminality points to in-between situations and conditions where established structures are dislocated, hierarchies reversed, and traditional settings of authority possibly endangered. The liminal state is a central phase in all social and cultural transitions. It marks the passage of the subject through "a cultural realm that has few or none of the attributes of the past or coming state" and is thus a realm of great ambiguity, since the "liminal entities are neither here nor there; they are betwixt and between the positions assigned and arrayed by law, custom, convention, and ceremonial" (Turner 1969: 80–81). Yet, as a threshold situation, liminality is also a vital moment of creativity, a potential platform for renewing the societal makeup.

There is substantial, yet unrecognized, potential for the application of liminality across a range of International Relations (IR) problems, from the study of the preeminent IR concepts—power, security, sovereignty— to the analysis of the agent-structure relationship, state formation and recognition, war and political violence, structural transformation of the international system, extraordinary politics at times of transition, and the

---

Notes for this chapter begin on page 240.

constitution of political identities. Applied to IR theory, liminality introduces an emancipatory research agenda, revealing the radical promise political anthropology holds for the study of International Relations.

The logic of transfer for applying the concept of liminality—whether to the study of individual and small-scale communal human experiences or to analysis of full-scale societal systems—stems from the underlying rationale of political anthropology, which neither plays on the opposition between the individual subject and the state, nor separates the international from the domestic sphere, or the "political" from the "social." Instead of assuming an isolated "international political realm" with a functionally defined "logic of anarchy," as has been the rule in many disciplinary traditions of IR, liminality questions the very meaning of such an opposition. Contra the hierarchical setup of traditional levels of analysis in IR, liminality shares political anthropology's assumption about the inherently political nature of "man," connecting it to the deepest, unalienable element of personhood (Szakolczai 2008b: 280). As "being human" means inseparable ties between individual subjects and political communities, liminality as a fundamental feature of the human condition could be legitimately applied to the analysis of International Relations as well.[1]

Yet the application of liminality in IR has been modest at best because, as is suggested below, the concept of liminality goes against the grain of many traditional models of thought within IR theory. Liminality creates fundamental uneasiness for traditional IR theory as it disrupts, by definition, essentializations and foundational claims. Defying set-in categories, liminality disturbs the ingrained "level of analysis" thinking in IR by emphasizing the fundamental ontological interconnection between the "high" and the "low," the "center" and the "periphery," the domestic and the international. It questions the urge for the static crystallizations typical of much positivist-rationalist IR theory, highlighting instead the processual nature of all international life, with a particular interest in the study of social change. It entails a cyclical rather than progressive understanding of international politics, and a relational rather than absolute conception of power. Or as Turner put it, liminality implies that "the high could not be high unless the low existed, and he who is high must experience what it is like to be low" (Turner 1969: 83).

Resisting binary opposition, liminality allows for extended conceptualization of a political subject (i.e., self-liminal-other). This has fundamental implications for the traditional categorization of actors (i.e., state and non-state) in international relations generally as well as for the dynamics of the politics of belonging, becoming, and recognition in Europe and elsewhere. Based on the premise that we are unlikely to grasp the workings of the core without understanding what is happening at the limit,[2] liminality takes an active interest in boundary zones and peripheries (traditionally conceived) rather than the established centers of international politics. Liminality respects the fundamental polyvocality of the world, instinctively resisting attempts to overtly unify political processes and subjects by forging them into a hierarchical order. As such, it also has implications for the normative agenda within IR theory. Finally, the concept of liminality enables IR as a discipline to seek active intellectual exchange and build mutually beneficial channels for knowledge transfers with postcolonial studies, cultural theory, international political theory, semiotics, and critical geopolitics, which have appropriated the related notions of hybridity, interstitiality, creolization, marginalization, and carnivalization (cf. Bhabha 1994; Bakhtin 1968). Liminality could become a "bridge concept" by which to deepen the interdisciplinary theoretical dialogue between these fields.

Yet despite its interdisciplinary origins and the relational bent of its title, the discipline of IR traditionally has hardly focused on what falls between neat, clean-cut categories and concentrated instead on the construction of rigid formal dichotomies. This is particularly striking, considering that most of international politics happens precisely *in between* different political subjects that are themselves inevitably "happening" as a result of multiple relational links to others. Apropos, *betwixt and between* could serve as a slogan for IR as a field of thought and practice between scholarly and practical knowledge in general—that is, if we subscribe to the argument of all political concepts inhabiting a liminal space between theory and practice. It is inherently difficult to utterly suspend essentially political concepts from politics and distil them into perennial categories, though that has been the urge of IR theorizing more often than not. Epistemologically and methodologically, we should rather recognize the intrinsic *inbetweenness* of political categories (e.g., "security," an essentially contested concept between theory and policy), and consequently engage the contradictions and normative implications of the contextual definitions of these notions (Ciută 2009). The curious absence of liminality from most theoretical elaborations of IR demonstrates no less curiously the limits of the contemporary political imagination.

This chapter seeks to rectify the situation by building a concise case for serious engagement with liminality in IR theory. The argument is advanced in four sections. After taking stock of the general implications of engaging liminality in IR theorizing, the discussion moves to explicate the value added by liminality against the backdrop of similar claims raised by scholars writing from the critical tradition in IR. Next, it sketches out the structure-generating potential of liminal conditions in international politics and liminality's analytical utility in studying war. The chapter concludes with reflections on the normative ramifications of embedding liminality deeper in IR theorizing.

Implications of Engaging Liminality in IR Theory

Liminality, as applied to IR theory, has two major consequences for the traditional ontology and epistemology of international politics. First, what it makes central to the investigation of the workings of world politics are not prefixed categories at clearly separable levels of analysis (state, international system/society) and their deterministic interaction, but rather their complex emergence, factual and discursive, via socialization into (and occasional resistance against) historically embedded rules and structural contexts (cf. Kurki 2008: 245–88; Neumann and Wigen 2013; Neumann 2014). Ontologically, then, global political reality is understood as constituted of multiple "products-in-process," entities neither here nor there but always becoming different, without any teleological implications (cf. Wight 2006: 7; Der Derian 2009: 254). That is, liminality does not share an idea of history underlined by the belief in progress.[3]

Second, having rejected attempts to objectify, reify, and temporally fix the multiple states of being, the inquiry should rather focus on genealogical exploration of the processes of becoming, and the intersocietal dimension of social change. Disregarding IR's intrinsic fetish of structure, liminality emphasizes the historical evolution of both the modern international system and the concepts used to describe its operation (cf. Walker 2001: 321–23). The stress on processuality, relationality, and differentiation, and the rejection of essentialization set liminality sharply in opposition to not only positivist/rationalist IR but also many conventional constructivist and Marxist approaches to the study of world politics. Liminality offers a fundamental critique of IR's conventional onto-spatial imagination and its traditional focus on policing the "sensible boundaries" of statehood, sovereignty, international system, identity, and security (Vrasti 2008: 300). Instead, it reveals their contested history, recognizing the inevitable intertwining of logical classifications and hierarchies with social and political ones (see further Durkheim and Mauss 1963).

While mainstream IR theory from classical realism to contemporary neoliberalism has sought universal laws of international politics, liminality seeks to capture the particular, contingent, and idiosyncratic, always aiming at a sensitive grasp of the context. True, liminality also draws on universals (e.g., the ubiquitous rites of passage), but these are based on observation of human experience, not on the rationalizations of detached analysts constructing abstract notions of universality. Liminality is an intellectual manifestation of an attempt to transform the structuralist understanding of the world into a vital field of immanence where there is no "outside" (cf. Negri 2007: 109–15), but rather a continuous flow between different forms and ways of being. Intriguingly, as Giorgio Agamben reminds us, many European languages express the notion of the "outside" with a word that literally means "at the door" or "at the threshold." Accordingly, the outside is not another space residing beyond a determinate space, but rather a passage (Agamben 2005a: 67–68). Thus, in the light of the distinctively in-between quality of liminality, IR's standard topographical division between what is happening inside and what outside of the sovereign state loses its persuasive force.

To accept liminality as a fundamental feature of political subjectivity in IR is to radically depart from reliance on concrete classifications, which seek to control the subject through the very "attack" of naming it in a particular way. All classifications, including the distinction between the inside and outside of the sovereign state, nurture the hope of successful management of a situation, as if inability to classify would signify open recognition of humans' fundamental helplessness in the face of the world (see Szasz 1970: 97–98). The metaphysics of modern security (or rather the lack thereof) demonstrates states' growing inability to use the traditional instruments of "national security" to neatly organize their safety and well-being into distinct spheres of internal and external security. It is as if the whole phenomenon of security has become liminal—quite like a Möbius strip, continually on the threshold of either one state or the other—thus eroding the traditional topology of security along with the distinction between the local, national, and international (Bigo 2001: 115). Unlike IR, with its penchant for seeking ontological safety in the certainty of timeless categories, liminality recognizes discontinuities and ruptures in world politics as the standard rather than exception. Understanding that liminality is a central fact of international political life implies concurrent recognition of our exposure to the open and de facto acknowledgement of the inevitable chaos of a world without lines of distinction (Edkins 2007: 90–91).

What value, then, does liminality add, considering that scholars writing from the critical tradition in IR have raised similar claims without making explicit use of the notion? In my reading, no other social scientific concept better drives home the old truth of the connection between how we look and what we thus see. By illuminating the flow between different states and forms of being, liminality helps us reimagine the ways we think about and relate to the international political reality. It requires us to accept disorder along with the fact that there are limits to what we can possibly know, for in liminality the outcome is never certain. Liminality allows for deeper understanding of what happens during "constitutive" or "axial" moments in national and international politics, and enables specification of the effects of these critical experiences. It embraces both the spatial and the temporal dynamic of international life, and captures the ultimate unresolvability of the agent-structure problem in IR. Though poststructuralists have long argued for a relational understanding of identity and its complexity beyond a simple self-other dichotomy, they have yet to grasp liminality's potential to explain the "problem of difference" in the construction of identities and the related processes of securitization (cf. Hansen 2006; Rumelili 2012).

A number of distinctly liminal states cropping up in the realm of international politics deserve further exploration. These include the ritual liminality of the processes of political transition; the suspended, or even permanent, liminality emerging from the ordeal of a prolonged state of political ambiguity; and the physical liminality experienced by political subjects living on the border. Understanding societal reactions to liminal experiences, or the ways political communities are shaped by liminality, permits further insights into the foregrounding of agency against set-in structures. Just as classical anthropological works studied liminality from both chronological and spatial angles, IR could equally address the possible uses of the notion as a temporal and a spatial category, as well as a characteristic experience accompanying transformative situations and transitions in international politics. These transitions can be sudden, as is the case with riots and revolutions, or prolonged, as in wars or states of enduring political instability.

Liminality helps to illuminate and understand multiple practices of global politics, from the study of political dissidents, participants of social movements, refugees,[4] stateless people, ethnic or sociopolitical minorities, and (illegal) immigrants to the analysis of states and spaces of exception in the contemporary juridical-political order of world politics (cf. Agamben 1998; Huysmans 2006). For example, it could be applied to analyze power, violence, and resistance in the context of the long "War on Terror," practices of security-political global governmentality, and acts of commemorative politics as expressions of temporal liminality (see, e.g., Edkins 2003). Critical IR scholars' recent burst of interest in Giorgio Agamben's ideas of bare life, sovereign power, and the state of exception as the biopolitical paradigm of contemporary international politics has yet to spark an imaginative leap connecting these notions to the concept of liminality. Just as the liminal state proper—the state of exception, as described by Agamben—is a space devoid of law, a zone of anomie in which all previous determinations and distinctions are deactivated (Agamben 2005b: 50), periods of broad-sweeping anomie and crisis in international relations are marked by the collapse of normal social structures. In crisis, social functions and roles can break down to the point where culturally conditioned behavior is completely overturned, and all previously relevant social relations and customs suspended and altered (Agamben 2005b: 65–66).

In the course of a prolonged liminal experience, the liminal ordeal is likely to become incorporated into and reproduced in the "permanent structure" of a society. Hence the idea of "perpetual liminality" emerges as a condition characteristic of societies that have long lived "on the limit" and thus proven quite unable to conclusively surpass the experience, in spite of their apparent entrance into the phase of societal reaggregation. This development could be most intriguing from the perspective of IR, as it would enable a culturally deeper and thicker analysis of a whole gamut of societies and states going through crisis or dissolution and collapse of a previous order. Recognizing the radical propensities generated by the liminal experience, and thus liminality's potential to bring about historical change from mere discontinuity to revolutionary rupture, touches the crux of the notion's analytical utility for IR.

Naturally, there are also clear limits to and modalities of applying the concept of liminality to societies writ large. First, there is the peril of determinism—of making the hyperbolic claim that liminality is to be found essentially everywhere. That would be a logical conclusion drawn from reading Agamben, for instance, who claims the state of exception has become the utmost biopolitical paradigm of contemporary international politics. Accordingly, a condition of permanent crisis has emerged as the new normality of international political reality, as if liminality has turned in on itself and the threshold has consequently become the world, with movement back and forth constrained (see Sakwa this volume). Still, failing to distinguish between modalities of liminality would totalize and trivialize the concept and thus diminish its analytical usefulness for IR. The acknowledgement that we live in times and a world of change, or the recognition of modernity as itself "permanently liminal" (Szakolczai 2000: 215–27), should be accompanied by close-up contextual analyses of liminal moments and situations of different degrees and types in global politics.

Second, the limitations of stretching the notion from small-scale communities to societies writ large should be clearly acknowledged in each case. Unlike the Ndembu rites of transition that provided the context for the term's original anthropological usage, large-scale societal liminal conditions lack a clear time span, obvious entrance and exit points, and authoritative "masters of ceremonies" to guide the members of the society through the liminal ordeal (Bauman 1994: 17). Therein lies the danger of the conceptual inflation of liminality through overtly metaphoric usage of the term outside of its context of conception. As scholars and practitioners of IR, we should steer clear of simply piling up new empirical evidence from our field to extend the anthropological model and forgoing critical engagement with and substantive enhancement of the original idea of liminality.

Yet another point of contestation, when applying liminality to full-scale societies undergoing dissolution or collapse of the previous order, is the actual subject who experiences the liminal ordeal on a wider scale. Is it just the society's elites, or more or less everybody—or is it really something that can only be a post hoc determination by the analyst? Put differently, how should the connection between liminality and *communitas* (i.e., the community going through a liminal experience) be understood in larger political communities (see Thomassen this volume)? Why do some types of *communitas* emerging from liminal moments turn out aggressive, full of resentment and hatred, instead of bolstering positive solidarity among group members and thereby increasing their potential for further political mobilization?[5] And what if the ritual passages of whole-scale societies go wrong and produce effects of most undesirable kind—as infamously happened with the communist regimes of the twentieth century?[6] To elucidate these problems, the engagement with liminality still needs to be substantiated by empirical studies in different fields and theoretical traditions of IR. The "Arab Spring" and the popular reactions to the debt crisis in Europe would be interesting examples to explore here.

Liminality as an "Unstructured" Origin of Structure

Liminality is commonly regarded as the space of new political beginnings, a potential source of renewal for a community, or even a platform for large-scale societal change. Social and political thinkers have reflected on the relationship between liminal experiences and the establishment of permanent structures, or the "lasting effects" of answers produced in "extraordinary moments," emphasizing the extent to which "structure" and "order" are indeed always born in liminality (Thomassen this volume; Szakolczai 2000; Wydra 2001). Given the constitutive potential of liminal experiences in the crystallization of certain ideas and practices, we should acknowledge that essentially new structure-like qualities emerge in liminal periods (Thomassen this volume). Although the playfulness of the period of liminality is inherently unstructured, it is nonetheless highly structuring at the same time. Liminality constitutes a formative experience for the subject, providing it with a new structure and a new set of rules. Once established, these rules will glide back to the level of the taken-for-granted. Hence the liminal phase/experience/period could, somewhat paradoxically in light of the essentially unstructured nature of liminality, constitute the origin of structure all the same (ibid.).[7] It is nonetheless essential to avoid the common tendency to retrospectively depict social processes as something whose result was inevitably "known in advance," almost predetermined. As William Connolly (1999) reminds us, the politics of becoming is really quite indeterminate, as the result that this process might lead to cannot be known in advance. The recognition of liminality's potential to create structure-like properties should not be mistaken for another claim of foundationalism.

The strength of liminality as the phase of pure possibility underscores the potential of agency in the liminal process. Instead of seeing reality as largely "given"—as is still done in some more conventional veins of constructivism, not to mention the traditional positivist IR approaches— the recognition of liminality simultaneously means acknowledging the power of agency in restructuring existing realities and creating new ones. The insiders of a defined political community generally perceive liminal figures as both alluring and endangering because such figures have the power to unsettle existing certitudes, truths, and identities. Situations of crisis and transition also have a positive, productive aspect, as the new setting emerging from these transitions can be better than the old order of things. Nonetheless, the prospect of the possible "permanentization" of liminality still emanates danger because it lacks the promise of reintegration that would reestablish the previous order. Therefore, permanent liminality writ large no longer permits novelty and encourages innovation, but rather imposes formlessness and disorientation as a technique of governmentality. The permanent change is thus indeed effected, but without qualitative transformation (see Sakwa this volume).

Hence, it is vitally important to pay close attention to how societies experiencing a large-scale social drama deal with the liminal period, and how they attempt to bring it to a conclusion. Who will be in charge of the "routinization" of extraordinary situations? Who will become the "carriers" of the new worldview that is eventually institutionalized (see Thomassen this volume)? These key sociological questions should be kept in mind when the notion of liminality is applied to the analysis of full-scale societal complexes and their interaction.

Standard structuralist approaches to the study of critical events tend to gloss over the fundamental ambiguity of liminal periods by reconstructing the events' historical path, leading up to the previously known outcome. Michel Dobry (this volume) has argued for the centrality of "fluid conjunctures" in international politics instead, emphasizing the importance of avoiding the illusion that the outcomes of a fundamental social experience summarize, mirror, or encompass the processes that produced them. Arguably, the perspective that reconstructs the logic of events according to their outcomes quite simply refuses to accept that the unfolding of a process can turn toward one outcome or another only at the margin. Following the logic that the outcome essentially ascribes its meaning (retroactively) to the event, this position cannot admit that "tiny causes" can often result in "great effects" or may even reverse "structural trends" (ibid.). The contingency of the results of such liminal processes as large-scale crises, revolutions, and wars thus emerges as an important shared epistemological assumption behind the concept of liminality and poststructuralist approaches to the study of international relations. Again, liminality recognizes the freedom of agency: it emphasizes the plasticity of "structures" and their sensitivity to mobilizations and actors' tactics and moves. Drawing a beautiful analogy to matter, which can be found as solid, gas, or liquid, Dobry (this volume) calls attention to the fact that social "structures" (or institutions and social relations more generally) need not necessarily be more "solid" and "stable" than matter. Rather, despite their occasional "objectification" and institutionalization, social structures and relations can equally experience transformations of their states and therefore effectively experience different states. In light of these elaborations, it is difficult not to agree with Arpád Szakolczai (2000: 218), who declares the concept of liminality to be "potentially one of the most general and useful terms of social science," comparable to IR staples like structure and order.

War as a Liminal Situation *sui generis*

War is one of the generative diseases of world politics that the notion of liminality helps us understand. All wars are essentially liminal experiences, moments of radical contingency and uncertainty accompanying the birth and demise of eras. Recognizing war as a liminal experience sheds light on war's constitutive function for politics and societies, that is, its profoundly productive power over the structure and substance of the international system and its discontents (see Barkawi and Brighton 2011). As for liminality in general, "the final element of war's ontology is its power to remake what is unmade" (ibid.: 140). Conventional veins of social and political inquiry have understood war not as a generative force but rather as an interruption in the normal peacetime processes of society, using periodization and separation to bracket it off from the inevitable march toward liberal modernity. Conceiving of war as a liminal situation *sui generis* helps to avoid the tendency of most IR theoretical traditions to reduce war to terms of analysis derived from peacetime society, or to another social domain (cf. Barkawi 2010, 2011). Instead, understanding war through the lens of liminality underscores its unique nature among other social activities, "its own character and logic that cannot be reduced to any ordinary social dynamic" (Shaw 1988: 11).

Like liminality writ large, war is fundamentally a situation of uncertainty. War constitutes a central phase in the escalation of violence and can shake existing societal structures and international system to the core. The postwar process of reconstruction can, in turn, be conceived of as a rite of reaggregation—the beginning of coming to terms with the experience of a major collapse of the existing order, healing wounds, and moving on (Szakolczai 2000: 223). But the road of transition from war to peace is hardly straightforward or fixed. The postwar phase is often marked by a prolonged state of juridical-political limbo (as in the case of Kosovo) that can result in de facto quasi-autonomous states (e.g., Transnistria in Moldova) or the separatist regions recognized by some but not most of the international community (e.g., the dubious status of South Ossetia and Abkhazia after the Russian-Georgian war in 2008).

The American cultural historian Paul Fussell (2000) has provided a remarkable account of war as a liminal experience of its own kind.[8] Besides the strikingly spatial liminal character of World War I trench warfare, that is, the distinct liminality of no-man's-land, Fussell points to an interesting pattern in the war-fighting practice and thought processes of the soldiers in World War I. There were three separate lines of trenches in the Great War—front, support, and reserve—and a battalion normally spent a third of its duty time in each. The routine in each line was similar: the unit was divided into three groups, two of which stood down while the third kept alert. Universally applicable everywhere from artillery to submarines, the daily pattern of participating in this tripartite way of dividing things for an extended period inevitably contributed to the tendency to see "everything as divisible as threes" (ibid.: 125). The magical threes of traditional myth and ritual further donated some of their meanings and implications to "military threes." As a result, the military triad took on a mythical or prophetic character that elevated military action to the level of myth (ibid.). This course is further supported by the essentially threefold conception of the military training process: first preparation, then execution, and finally critique. War memoirs replicate this process accordingly, matching the war experience of moving between the line, battle, and recovery to the existential dimensions of quest, death, and rebirth (ibid.: 130–31).

Being quite clearly distinguishable and therefore largely symmetrical with the tripartite structure of ritual processes as described by the anthropologists quoted above, these three zones of war were characteristic of the so-called traditional, or conventional, wars of the twentieth century. The Cold War, with its recurring rupture points between war and peace, and today's asymmetrical, protracted conflicts, such as the current Western war in Afghanistan, vividly illustrate the idea of permanent liminality — a prolonged condition of being stuck in the in-between zone of war and peace. Western soldiers fighting the Taliban and al-Qaeda—and perhaps equally so vice versa—find that the nature of contemporary conflict forces them to face the condition of ultimate, protracted liminality: they live in a perpetual potential war zone, in persisting tension that could burst into a life-endangering confrontation any given moment. Moreover, modern-day terrorism leaves us with hardly any "reserves" in the traditional sense of the term, as any civilian could find her- or himself at the hottest "front" of the conflict if caught in the midst of a suicide bomber's attack. Modern international conflict has turned the condition of perpetual liminality into a universal experience.[9]

The cyber component of modern conflicts further illuminates the liminal nature of contemporary warfare. Following Turner by understanding liminality as essentially becomingness, we could regard the virtual space of waging war as liminal *par excellence*. Slavoj Žižek (2003: 9) has addressed Gilles Deleuze's notion of the virtual as "pure becoming without being," which is "always forthcoming and already past" (Deleuze 1990: 80) but never present or corporeal. The virtual is a liminal space constituted only by its state of becomingness; it is not an actual being or object to become. It exists as pure becoming that suspends both "sequentiality and directionality," being a passage without a concrete line of passage (Žižek 2003: 9-10). Standard IR approaches, as Der Derian's work (2009: 255) has evocatively shown, are not equipped to explore the "interzone of the virtual, where simulacra reverse causality, being is simultaneously here and there, and identity is deterritorialised by interconnectivity." In this context, it is hardly surprising that modern security organizations like NATO are struggling so hard to accommodate cyber attacks within the traditional framework of understanding an "armed attack," and to determine whether this type of warfare could also invoke the collective defense provision of Article 5 of the North Atlantic Treaty with a legitimate case for the use of force. Cyber warfare is by definition a liminal activity: it is difficult to track down, has no clear entrance or exit points, and last but not least may be a transition to or a phase accompanying full standard warfare.

Regardless of the "new" or "old" nature of contemporary wars, the concept of liminality holds obvious analytical purchase for the reinterpretation of major crises such as political revolutions, or for studying war's impact on the rise of the modern world by considering its institutional structure as being essentially the product of liminal crises (Szakolczai 2008b: 278).

The Return of Play to the Scholarship and Practice of International Politics

Raising liminality's status as an epistemological category for the study of international politics is a critical move with fundamental implications for responsible scholarship and ethical practice of international relations. The ubiquity of liminal situations and phenomena in international politics, which this chapter has aimed to illuminate, calls for recognizing, rather than negating and suppressing, ambivalence as a constant fluctuation between different ways of being. The concept of liminality acknowledges the complexity of ambivalent situations, allowing for improved analysis of the modalities of various kinds of conflicts by genealogically tracing their conditions of emergence. Because liminality embraces difference without assuming or imposing hierarchy, it has clear normative appeal for transcending the "problem of difference" that allegedly pervades international society as a tendency to interpret difference as inferiority, destining it thereby to eradication (Inayatullah and Blaney 2006).

It would only be empirically relevant and normatively rewarding to view international politics as a "giant fugue of interweaving themes and voices, of subject and reply" (cf. Symes 2006: 317). The notion of liminality calls for recognizing an entire constellation of different "voices" of international political reality, and for reading them contrapuntally, as always engaging with each other. As outlined by Edward Said, the contrapuntal approach envisions cultures not as pure, distinct, monolithic beings, but as largely overlapping and interdependent entities in which patterns of power and domination are always accompanied by resistance and subversion, thus constituting a flow of points and counterpoints (ibid.). In a similar spirit, world politics could be regarded as made of processes and crossings rather than clearly distinguishable blocs; as a combination of fragile and mixed identities, of different figures inhabiting different edges of the international reality, of ambiguities, frustrations, and uncertainties. Instead of attempting to draw rigid boundaries (and be thus destined to continually police them) in order to represent international reality as made up of distinct entities and structures, we would benefit epistemologically by recognizing the pervasiveness of liminality in international political life.

Bringing liminality to the conceptual center of IR strongly resonates with Naeem Inayatullah and David Blaney's suggestion to revise and redesign IR as a theory of intercultural relations, or the study of differences (2006: 17). Traditional IR's inability to make a unique contribution to social theory has arguably stemmed from its persistent avoidance and denial of the problem of how to handle cultural difference. Accordingly, traditional IR theory shares the spirit of modernization theory, which attempts to establish human commonality, or universality, by employing two binaries: the spatial demarcation of inside/outside, and a developmental sequence from tradition to modernity (ibid.: 94–97). The potentiality that liminality is loaded with, however, is a powerful celebration of the claim that cultural difference offers not merely problems but also opportunities. Conceiving of human existence primarily as potentiality, or possibility, opens up the space of extended movement for subaltern agencies, recognizing their transformative capacity. Furthermore, dialogue between those holding different visions and experiences of the world can catalyze self-reflection amongst the bold and powerful of this world as well, leading them to introspect the "other" within "themselves" (ibid.: 158). Greater sensitivity to the numerous manifestations of liminality in international politics thus also enables greater awareness of our own selves and our own frames of thinking and interpretation. As in music, where the counterpoint marks a supplementary melody as distinct from the main theme, applying a contrapuntal approach in IR scholarship would essentially mean writing against the mainstream. Bringing liminality to the discipline's conceptual center could turn out to be empowering for exploration of previously unsought avenues of thought, as the study of liminal conditions in international politics brings the examination of potentiality to the fore of the study of international actuality (cf. Edkins 2007: 77).

The fact that liminality is full of potency and potentiality, as well as creativity, experiment, and play, has major implications for the scholarship and practice of IR. It calls for polyvocality in both the politics and scholarship of IR, for indeed:

There may be a play of ideas, a play of words, a play of symbols, a play of metaphors. In it, play's the thing. Liminality is not confined in its expression to ritual
and the performative arts. Scientific hypotheses and experiments and philosophical speculation are also forms of play, though their rules and controls are
more rigorous and their relation to mundane "indicative" reality more pointed
than those of genres which proliferate in fantasy. One might say, without too
much exaggeration, that liminal phenomena are at the level of culture what
variability is at the level of nature. (Turner 1979: 466)

Hence a normatively exemplary IR scholarship could function as a special
kind of a liminal-like or liminoid genre aimed at exposing the injustices, in-
efficiencies, immoralities, and alienations generated by mainstream modern
economic and political structures, processes, and ways of thinking about
them (ibid.: 494). As a discipline, IR has innate potential to become a critical practice of a very special kind, always aiming to provide clear-headed,
engaged analysis of the established order of international politics.

Notes

This chapter is a reprint of M. Mälksoo's (2012) "The Challenge of Liminality for Inter-
national Relations Theory," originally published in *Review of International Studies* 38 (2):
481–94. Initial research for the essay was supported by the European Union through the
European Social Fund's (ESF) Doctoral Studies and Internationalization Programme
DoRa, the ESF's Mobilitas postdoctoral program, and the Humanities in the European
Research Area (HERA) *Memory at War* project.

1. For the application of the notion of liminality to the study of liminal experiences of
   societies writ large, see Eisenstadt (1995); Szakolczai (2000, 2003, 2008a); Wydra (2001);
   Norton (1988). In IR, the concept of liminality has been put to use in different empirical
   contexts by Neumann (1999, 2012); Rumelili (2003, 2012); Morozov and Rumelili (2012);
   Kuus (2007); Mälksoo (2009, 2010, 2012); Stoicescu (2012).
2. Along with many poststructuralists in IR, anthropologist Abner Cohen (1969) has vividly demonstrated the significance of boundary maintenance in the development of
   political distinctiveness.
3. Cf. Walter Benjamin's work on passages and his idea of nonlinear time in *The Arcades
   Project* (1999).
4. Cf. Lebow's (2012) captivating account of the initial psychological state of the German
   scholars who emigrated in the United States in the 1930s.
5. This problem is further analyzed in the context of the contemporary "memory wars" between Russia and its former satellite states in Central and Eastern Europe in Mälksoo (2012).
6. Arpád Szakolczai (2000: 223) has described Soviet communism as a specific kind of
   permanent liminality, as under this regime "the Second World War never ended."
7. Turner often pointed to liminality as an "original state" of a kind, the formless reality
   out of which new forms emerge, the zone of new beginnings. He touched on the crux of
   the matter in his famous essay "Betwixt and Between" (1967: 97) as follows: "Liminality

may perhaps be regarded as the Nay to all positive structural assertions, but as in some sense the source of them all, and, more than that, as a realm of pure possibility whence novel configurations of ideas and relations may arise."

8. I am grateful to Prof. Richard Ned Lebow for pointing me toward Fussell's work.
9. Drone warfare is yet another example of doing away with the traditional boundaries between war and peace, as the populations under the surveillance and potential attacks of drones live in a zone of constant possibility of being killed. See further Ansorge (2012) and Gregory (2012).

References

Agamben, G. 1998. *Homo Sacer: Sovereign Power and Bare Life*. Translated by D. Heller-Roazen. Stanford: Stanford University Press.
———. 2005a. *The Coming Community*. Translated by M. Hardt. Minneapolis and London: University of Minnesota Press.
———. 2005b. *State of Exception*. Translated by K. Attell. Chicago and London: University of Chicago Press.
Ansorge, J. T. 2012. "Orientalism in the Machine." In *Orientalism and War*, edited by T. Barkawi and K. Stanski. New York: Columbia University Press.
Bakhtin, M. M. 1968. *Rabelais and His World*. Cambridge, MA: MIT Press.
Barkawi, T. 2010. "On the Limits of New Foundations: a Commentary on R. Harrison Wagner, War and the State." *International Theory* 2 (2): 317–32.
———. 2011. "From War to Security: Security Studies, the Wider Agenda and the Fate of the Study of War." *Millennium: Journal of International Studies* 39 (3): 709–16.
Barkawi, T., and S. Brighton. 2011. "Powers of War: Fighting, Knowledge, and Critique." *International Political Sociology* 5 (2): 126–43.
Bauman, Z. 1994. "After the Patronage State: A Model in Search of Class Interests." In *The New Great Transformation? Change and Continuity in East-Central Europe*, edited by C. G. A. Bryant and E. Mokrzycki. London and New York: Routledge.
Benjamin, W. 1999. *The Arcades Project*. Cambridge, MA, and London: Belknap Press.
Bhabha, H. K. 1994. *The Location of Culture*. London: Routledge.
Bigo, D. 2001. "Internal and External Security(ies): The Möbius Ribbon." In *Identities, Borders, Orders: Rethinking International Relations Theory*, edited by M. Albert, D. Jacobson, and Y. Lapid. Minneapolis: University of Minnesota Press.
Ciută, F. 2009. "Security and the Problem of Context: A Hermeneutical Critique of Securitization Theory." *Review of International Studies* 35 (2): 301–26.
Cohen, A. 1969. *Custom and Politics in Urban Africa*. Berkeley and Los Angeles: University of California Press.
Connolly, W. E. 1999. "Suffering, Justice, and the Politics of Becoming." In *Moral Spaces: Rethinking Ethics and World Politics*, edited by D. Campbell and M. J. Shapiro. Minneapolis and London: University of Minnesota Press.
Deleuze, G, 1990. *The Logic of Sense*. New York: Columbia University Press.
Der Derian, J. 2009. "Virtuous War/Virtual Theory." In *Critical Practices in International Theory: Selected Essays*. London and New York: Routledge.
Dobry, M. 2015. "Critical Processes and Political Fluidity: A Theoretical Appraisal." In *Breaking Boundaries: Varieties of Liminality*, edited by A. Horvath, B. Thomassen and H. Wydra. New York and Oxford: Berghahn Books.
Durkheim, É., and M. Mauss. 1963. *Primitive Classification*. Translated by R. Needham. Chicago: University of Chicago Press.
Edkins, J. 2003. "The Rush to Memory and the Rhetoric of War." *Journal of Political and Military Sociology* 31 (2): 231–50.

———. 2007. "Whatever Politics." In *Giorgio Agamben: Sovereignty and Life*, edited by M. Calarco and S. DeCaroli. Stanford: Stanford University Press.

Eisenstadt, S. N. 1995. "The Order-Maintaining and Order-Transforming Dimensions of Culture." In *Power, Trust, and Meaning: Essays in Sociological Theory and Analysis*, edited by S. N. Eisenstadt. Chicago: University of Chicago Press.

Fussell, P. (1975) 2000. *The Great War and Modern Memory*. Oxford: Oxford University Press.

Gennep, A. van. 1960. *The Rites of Passage*. Chicago and London: University of Chicago Press.

Gregory, D. 2012. "Dis/Ordering the Orient: Scopic Regimes and Modern War." In *Orientalism and War*, edited by T. Barkawi and K. Stanski. New York: Columbia University Press.

Hansen, L. 2006. *Security as Practice: Discourse Analysis and the Bosnian War*. London and New York: Routledge.

Huysmans, J. 2006. "International Politics of Exception: Competing Visions of International Political Order between Law and Politics." *Alternatives: Global, Local, Political* 31 (2): 135–65.

Inayatullah, N., and D. L. Blaney. 2006. *International Relations and the Problem of Difference*. New York and London: Routledge.

Kurki, M. 2008. *Causation in International Relations: Reclaiming Causal Analysis*. Cambridge: Cambridge University Press.

Kuus, M. 2007. *Geopolitics Reframed: Security and Identity in Europe's Eastern Enlargement*. New York: Palgrave Macmillan.

Lebow, R. N. 2012. "German Jews and American Realism." *Constellations: An International Journal of Critical and Democratic Theory* 18 (4): 545–66.

Mälksoo, M. 2009. "Liminality and Contested Europeanness: Conflicting Memory Politics in the Baltic Space." In *Identity and Foreign Policy: Baltic-Russian Relations in the Context of European Integration*, edited by P. Ehin and E. Berg. Aldershot: Ashgate.

———. 2010. *The Politics of Becoming European: A Study of Polish and Baltic Post-Cold War Security Imaginaries*. New York and London: Routledge.

———. 2012. "Nesting Orientalisms at War: World War II and the 'Memory War' in Eastern Europe." In *Orientalism and War*, edited by T. Barkawi and K. Stanski. New York: Columbia University Press.

Morozov, V., and B. Rumelili. 2012. "The External Constitution of European Identity: Russia and Turkey as Europemakers." *Cooperation and Conflict* 47 (1): 28–48.

Negri, A. 2007. "Giorgio Agamben: The Discreet Taste of the Dialectic." In *Giorgio Agamben: Sovereignty and Life*, edited by M. Calarco and S. DeCaroli. Stanford: Stanford University Press.

Neumann, I. B. 1999. *Uses of the Other: "The East" in European Identity Formation*. Manchester: Manchester University Press.

———. 2012. "Introduction to the Forum on Liminality." *Review of International Studies* 38 (2): 473–79.

———. 2014. "The Semantics of Early Statebuilding: Why the Eurasian Steppe Has Been Overlooked." In *Semantics of Statebuilding: Language, Meanings and Sovereignty*, edited by N. Lemay-Hébert, N. Onuf, V. Rakić, and P. Bojanić. Abingdon, Oxon, and New York: Routledge.

Neumann, I. B., and E. Wigen. 2013. "The Importance of the Eurasian Steppe to the Study of International Relations." *Journal of International Relations and Development* 16 (3): 311–30.

Norton, A. 1988. *Reflections on Political Identity*. Baltimore: Johns Hopkins University Press.

Rumelili, B. 2003. "Liminality and Perpetuation of Conflicts: Turkish-Greek Relations in the Context of Community-Building by the EU." *European Journal of International Relations* 9 (2): 213–48.

———. 2012. "Liminal Identities and Processes of Domestication and Subversion in International Relations." *Review of International Studies* 38 (2): 495–508.

Sakwa, R. 2015. "Liminality and Postcommunism: The Twenty-First Century as the Subject of History." In *Breaking Boundaries: Varieties of Liminality*, edited by A. Horvath, B. Thomassen and H. Wydra. New York and Oxford: Berghahn Books.

Shaw, M. 1988. *Dialectics of War: An Essay in the Social Theory of Total War and Peace*. London: Pluto.

Stoicescu, M.-R. 2012. "*Communitas* and Forms without Foundations: Romania's Case of Interlocking Liminalities." *Review of International Studies* 38 (2): 509–24.

Symes, C. 2006. "The Paradox of the Canon: Edward W. Said and Musical Transgression." *Discourse: Studies in the Cultural Politics of Education* 27 (3): 309–24.

Szakolczai, A. 2000. *Reflexive Historical Sociology*. London: Routledge.

———. 2003. *The Genesis of Modernity*. London: Routledge.

———. 2008a. *Sociology, Religion and Grace: A Quest for the Renaissance*. London: Routledge.

———. 2008b. "What Kind of Political Anthropology? An External Insider View." *International Political Anthropology* 1 (2): 275–82.

Szasz, T. S. 1970. *Ideology and Insanity*. New York: Anchor.

Thomassen, B. 2015. "Thinking with Liminality." In *Breaking Boundaries: Varieties of Liminality*, edited by A. Horvath, B. Thomassen and H. Wydra. New York and Oxford: Berghahn Books.

Turner, V. W. 1967. "Betwixt and Between: The Liminal Period in Rites de Passage." In *The Forest of Symbols: Aspects of Ndembu Ritual*. New York: Cornell University Press.

———. 1969. *The Ritual Process: Structure and Anti-Structure*. Harmondsworth: Penguin Books.

———. 1979. "Frame, Flow and Reflection: Ritual and Drama as Public Liminality." *Japanese Journal of Religious Studies* 6 (4): 465–99.

Vrasti, W. 2008. "The Strange Case of Ethnography and International Relations." *Millennium: Journal of International Studies* 37 (2): 279–301.

Walker, R. B. J. (1989) 2001. "History and Structure in the Theory of International Relations." In *International Theory: Critical Investigations*, edited by J. Der Derian. Houndmills, Basingstoke, Hampshire, and London: Palgrave Macmillan.

Wight, C. 2006. *Agents, Structures and International Relations: Politics as Ontology*. Cambridge: Cambridge University Press.

Wydra, H. 2001. *Continuities in Poland's Permanent Transition*. Houndmills, Basingstoke, Hampshire and London: Macmillan.

Žižek, S. 2003. *Organs without Bodies: Deleuze and Consequences*. New York: Routledge.

Contributors

Peter Burke (born 1937) was educated at St Ignatius's College, Stamford Hill, London, and St John's College Oxford. After seventeen years at the University of Sussex, he moved in 1979 to Cambridge, where he became Professor of Cultural History. He retired from the Chair in 2004 but remains a Life Fellow of Emmanuel College. He has been a visiting teacher or researcher in Berlin, Brussels, Canberra, Groningen, Heidelberg, Los Angeles, Nijmegen, Paris (the EHESS), Princeton, and São Paulo. He is a Fellow of the British Academy and Member of the Academia Europea; Ph.D. (honoris causa), Universities of Lund, Copenhagen, Bucharest, and Zurich; and Honorary Fellow of St John's College Oxford. He has published twenty-six books, and his work has so far been translated into thirty-one languages.

Michel Dobry is Emeritus Professor at the Department of Political Science at the Sorbonne (Université Paris I), where he has taught politics and sociology since 2001. He has published widely in the area of political transitions, political and social legitimacy, and international war and security. His major publications are *Sociologie des crises politiques* (Presses de la FNSP, 3rd ed. 2009), *Democratic and Capitalist Transitions in Eastern Europe: Lessons for the Social Sciences* (editor) (Kluwer Academic Publishers, 2000), and *Le mythe de l'allergie française au fascisme* (Albin Michel, 2003).

Bernhard Giesen is Professor Emeritus at the University of Konstanz. He has taught regularly at Yale University and been Visiting Professor at Stanford University, University of Chicago, NYU, the European University Institute in Florence, and elsewhere. He has published books in seven languages, among them publications on collective trauma (*Triumph and Trauma*, Paradigm Publishers, 2004) and German collective identity

(*Intellectuals and the Nation: Collective Identity in a German Axial Age*, Cambridge University Press, 1998). His latest book deals with inbetweenness (*Zwischenlagen*) as the foundation of social order. He recently co-edited (with Jeffrey Alexander and Dominik Bartmanski) a book on visual sociology, *Iconic Power: Materiality and Meaning in Social Life* (Palgrave, 2012).

Agnes Horvath is a founding editor of the peer-reviewed journal *International Political Anthropology*, which has run a yearly IPA Summer School in Italy since 2008. Based in Florence, she is an Academic Affiliated Visitor in Sociology at Cambridge University. Her publications include articles and chapters in Hungarian, English, Italian, and French. She is the author or co-author of eight books and thirty-five articles, most recently *Reclaiming Beauty* (co-editor) (Ficino Press, 2012), *Modernism and Charisma* (Palgrave, 2013) and *Statesman: The Politics of Limits and the Liminal* (co-editor) (Tivoli, 2013).

Maria Mälksoo (Ph.D. Cantab.) is Senior Researcher in International Relations at the University of Tartu. She was a visiting postdoctoral fellow at the Helsinki Collegium for Advanced Studies (2012) and a member of the HERA-funded international collaborative project *Memory at War. Cultural Dynamics in Russia, Poland, and Ukraine* (2010–2013). She is the author of *The Politics of Becoming European: A Study of Polish and Baltic Post–Cold War Security Imaginaries* (Routledge, 2010). Her work has appeared in *International Political Sociology*, *Review of International Studies*, *European Journal of International Relations*, *Security Dialogue*, *Communist and Post-Communist Studies*, and several edited volumes.

Stephen Mennell is Professor Emeritus of Sociology at University College Dublin. His books include *All Manners of Food: Eating and Taste in England and France from the Middle Ages to the Present* (1985), *Norbert Elias: Civilization and the Human Self-Image* (1989), and *The American Civilizing Process* (2007). He holds the degrees of Doctor in de *Sociale Wetenschappen* (Amsterdam) and Doctor of Letters (Cambridge). He is a member of the board of the Norbert Elias Foundation of Amsterdam, the Royal Netherlands Academy of Arts and Sciences, the Royal Irish Academy, and Academia Europaea.

Mark Allen Peterson is Professor of Anthropology and International Studies at Miami University. He is the author of *Connected in Cairo: Transnational Popular Culture and the Making of the Cosmopolitan Class* (Indiana University Press, 2011) and *Introduction to International Studies: An Interdisciplinary*

Approach to Global Issues (Westview, 2013). His first book was *Anthropology and Mass Communication: Media and Myth in the New Millennium* (Berghahn Books, 2003). He has published articles in many journals, including *Anthropology Today*, *Childhood*, *Contemporary Islam*, *New Reviews in Hypermedia and Multimedia*, *Journal of Consumer Culture*, *Anthropological Quarterly*, *Research in Economic Anthropology*, and *Arab Media and Society*.

Camil Fransisc Roman is a Ph.D. Candidate in Politics and International Studies at the University of Cambridge. His latest publications are a book review essay (2014), two book reviews (2013), and a co-authored study of Romanian security and defense policy from 1990 to 2006 (2007). He has also published widely as a regular columnist in the Romanian mainstream press (2011–2012). Camil was a Ratiu Family Foundation Scholar (2011), winner of the PAIS Scholarship of the Department of Politics and International Studies at the University of Warwick (2008–2009), and Scholar of the Romanian Ministry for Education and Research (2002–2006).

Richard Sakwa is Professor of Russian and European Politics at the University of Kent and an Associate Fellow of the Russia and Eurasia Programme at Chatham House. He has published widely on Soviet, Russian, and postcommunist affairs. Recent books include *Russian Politics and Society* (Routledge, 4th ed. 2008), *Putin: Russia's Choice* (Routledge, 2nd ed. 2008), *The Quality of Freedom: Khodorkovsky, Putin and the Yukos Affair* (Oxford University Press, 2009), and *The Crisis of Russian Democracy: The Dual State, Factionalism, and the Medvedev Succession* (Cambridge University Press, 2011). Two of his books came out in 2014: *Putin and the Oligarch: The Khodorkovsky-Yukos Affair* (I. B. Tauris) and *Putin Redux: Power and Contradiction in Contemporary Russia* (Routledge).

Arpad Szakolczai is Professor of Sociology at University College Cork since 1998. Previously he taught at the European University Institute in Florence and was Visiting Professor at the Universities of Bologna, Konstanz, and Milan. He is the author or editor of seven books: *The Dissolution of Communist Power: The Case of Hungary* (Routledge, 1992, co-authored with Agnes Horvath), *Max Weber and Michel Foucault: Parallel Life-Works* (Routledge, 1998), *Reflexive Historical Sociology* (Routledge, 2000), *The Genesis of Modernity* (Routledge, 2003), *La scoperta della società* (Carocci, 2003, co-edited with Giovanna Procacci), *Sociology, Religion and Grace: A Quest for the Renaissance* (Routledge, 2007), and *Comedy and the Public Sphere: The Re-birth of Theatre as Comedy and the Genealogy of the Modern Public Arena* (Routledge, 2013). He has published articles in *Theory, Culture and Society*,

International Sociology, American Journal of Sociology, British Journal of Political Science, Current Sociology, History of the Human Sciences, the *European Journal of Social Theory, European Sociological Review,* and *International Political Anthropology.*

Bjørn Thomassen is Associate Professor at the Department of Society and Globalisation, Roskilde University. He is co-editor of the journal *International Political Anthropology.* Recent books are *Liminality and the Modern: Living through the In-Between* (Ashgate, 2014) and *Global Rome: Changing Faces of the Eternal City* (edited, Indiana University Press, 2014). He has published in journals across the social sciences, including *Comparative Studies in Society and History, European Journal of Social Theory, Anthropological Theory, Journal of the Royal Anthropological Institute, History, and Theory, Social Anthropology, Europæa, Journal des Europeanistes, Journal of Modern Italian Studies,* and *International Political Anthropology.*

Harald Wydra is a Fellow of St Catharine's College at the University of Cambridge, where he has taught politics since 2003. He held visiting fellowships at the École des Hautes Etudes en Sciences Sociales in Paris and the Australian National University in Canberra, and was Visiting Professor at the Université Paris Ouest Nanterre La Défense. He is a founding editor of the academic journal *International Political Anthropology* (www.politicalanthropology.org). His books include *Continuities in Poland's Permanent Transition* (Palgrave, 2001), *Communism and the Emergence of Democracy* (Cambridge University Press, 2007), *Democracy and Myth in Russia and Eastern Europe* (co-editor) (Routledge, 2008), and *Politics and the Sacred* (Cambridge University Press, 2015).

Index

Adam, 67
Adams, John Quincy, 114
Adorno, Theodor, 68
adulthood, 17, 18, 50, 170, 184
Agamben, Giorgio, 209, 230, 232
agency, 29, 42, 46, 52, 64, 178, 231, 234, 235
aggression, 122
alchemy, 4, 72–4, 78–9, 81–84, 87, 89–90
ambivalence, 2, 4, 22, 23, 29, 34, 53, 55, 61,
      62–67, 183, 185, 188, 200, 238
      sociology of, 62
American Indians, 115
anti-revolutions, 207
anti-structure, 132, 164
Apartheid, 194
arena, 64, 101, 102, 103, 172, 199, 208, 218, 223
Aristotle, 11, 19, 34, 84, 197
art, 3, 7, 29, 47, 63, 79, 84, 171, 212, 223
Athena, 64, 70
Athenian revolution in 508/7 B.C., 185
authority vacuum, 6, 185, 186, 190, 194
      fractures of identity in, 194
      liminal conditions of, 185
Axial Age, 51

Babeuf, Gracchus, 194
Babha, Homi, 61
Bachelard, Gaston, 98
back regions, 131
Bacon, Francis, 32, 67
Badiou, Alain, 208, 211–213, 219–222
Baltic states, 207
barbarism, 114, 115, 127, 199
Bateson, Gregory, 25–27, 158, 168
Baudrillard, Jean, 67
Berdyaev, Nikolai, 213

biological sociology, 45
bipolarity, 189
birth, 18, 20, 32, 42, 55, 64, 83, 116, 141, 186,
      235, 237
Blair, Tony, 131
Blake, William, 81
Blaney, David, 239
border, 22–24, 48, 79, 82, 90, 101, 115, 124,
      131, 171, 186, 189, 194, 231
border (and borderland),24, 48
borderline experiences, 186
Borkenau, Franz, 14, 15, 27
Brinton, Crane, 96
Bronze, 79
Bush, George W., 133, 192, 221

Calculations of Actors, 102
Camus, Albert, 141–2
capitalism, 28, 35, 125, 185, 206, 213
ceremonies, 18–9, 29, 31–2, 40, 42, 49, 50, 52,
      69, 77, 87, 147, 150, 190, 233
chaos, 12, 21, 34, 77, 82, 85, 153, 154, 157,
      175, 179, 230
chaotic historicity of social facts, 98
charisma, 15, 26, 28, 31, 34, 35, 52–4, 104,
      105, 141, 149, 158, 159, 169, 218
      as relational, 104
      situational, 104
China, 82, 201, 207, 208
Circe, 68
civil war, 1, 15, 125, 142, 144–147, 155, 156,
      158, 159, 189, 193, 200, 214, 215, 217, 221
civilization, 1, 14, 30, 48, 50–52, 69, 112, 114,
      115, 123, 124, 127, 207, 210
civilizing process, 5, 112, 119–121
Clausewitz, Carl von, 99, 100

Cleisthenes, 192
Cleomenes, 187
clowns, 35
cold peace, 5, 7, 207, 215, 219, 222, 223
Cold War, 6, 7, 127, 189, 199, 207, 208, 213,
    219–223, 237
collective action, 106, 176, 211
communism, 14, 35, 52, 54, 55, 97, 185, 198,
    200, 205–210, 212, 221
communitas, 47, 52, 165, 167–169, 171, 172,
    175, 180, 233
conjunctures, 93
Connolly, William, 234
conquest, 122, 124, 125
contagion, 64, 65, 149, 197
contingency, 39, 42, 55, 70, 97, 177, 179, 184,
    208, 235
contrapuntal approach, 238–9
conversion, 41, 79, 84, 87
copper, 79, 84
Corneille, Pierre, 133
corruption, 152
cosmology, 142, 197
Council of Europe, 207
counterrevolution, 147, 173, 216
cowboys, 115
creation, 4, 18, 21, 67, 74, 77, 78, 81
    imitation of, 78
Crete, 79
crisis, 2, 14–16, 25–28, 30, 45, 47, 53, 54, 55,
    62, 79, 83, 89, 96, 100, 104, 104, 147–149,
    151, 152, 154–8, 169, 176–7, 189, 197,
    205–210, 212, 221, 232–4
critical events, 4, 5, 92–98, 103, 235
critique, 15, 21, 25, 28, 34, 44, 88, 148, 169,
    206, 207, 213, 229, 237
Cyber warfare, 238

de Gaulle, Charles, 104
death, 17–8, 23, 30–32, 42, 63, 81, 83, 88, 132,
    141–145, 174, 184, 233
decivilizing process, 5, 120 122–3
Deleuze, Gilles, 61–62, 237
Delilah, 68
democracy, 6, 27, 28, 94, 96, 97, 118, 158, 183,
    185–191, 192–202, 207, 211, 213, 217–8,
    221, 222
    ambivalence of, 183
    Athenian, 191
    constitutional ethos of, 191
    democratization of the first, 192

first and second comings of, 187
global convergence of, 199
origins of, 187
political psychology of, 197
Spanish transition to, 193
democratic emancipation, 198–9
democratic imagination, 184–5, 194, 198–9
demonological gaze, 65–6
de-objectivation, 102
Der Derian, James, 237
desectorization of social space, 5. 103
Desfontaines, Nicolas, 133
desire, 30, 69, 76–78, 85, 89–90, 149, 179, 183,
    195–6
destiny (manifest),112, 114, 128
destruction, 20, 72, 118, 127, 143, 158, 193,
    220
differentiation, 147, 197
Dilthey, Wilhelm, 13, 14, 16, 19, 31, 46
discipline, 2, 5, 7, 8, 34, 39, 43, 44, 77, 82,
    126, 200, 228, 239, 240
divine, 6, 67, 79–81, 83, 86–88, 142, 143, 145,
    147, 149–152, 155, 158, 193, 224
    love, 86
Dobry, Michel, 4, 5, 235
Douglas, Mary, 31, 197
Dumont, Louis, 131
Durkheim, Emily, 13, 16, 25, 28, 43–45, 46,
    85, 194, 229

Eastern Europe, 208
Economic theory, 35
Egypt (modern), 164–170, 172, 174–180
eidos, 13, 15, 22, 27, 31
Eisenstadt, Shmuel, 51, 145
Election Day, 197
    vacuum of, 197
electronic communication, 166
Eley, Geoff, 218
Elias, Norbert, 5, 16, 17, 26, 28, 35, 70,
    120–128
empty place of power, 6, 186–188, 190,
    201–2
    as liminal space of ambivalence, 188
    fragile equilibrium of the, 190
epochality, 206, 208, 209, 210
equivocality, 62
Eros, 76, 90
escalation, 2, 28, 149, 236
eschatology, 208
ethnic cleansing, 2, 199, 200

etiology, 100
etymology, 19, 24
European Union, 189, 207, 208
Evans-Pritchard, E. E., 45
Eve, 67
event, 4–6, 11, 17, 30–34, 40–42, 48–9, 81, 89,
    93–101, 103, 105–107, 120, 123, 141–143,
    148–151, 155, 158, 165–174, 177–8, 180,
    186–7, 190, 196, 201, 206, 208–210, 212,
    224, 235
    autonomy of the, 99
events-that-model, 190
evil, 33, 64, 66, 67, 70, 118, 149, 152, 153, 156,
    185, 212
execution, 6, 141–143, 144–151, 153, 154–159,
    237
existential pluralism
    radical, 195–6
experience, 2, 3, 5–7, 11–20, 22, 27, 29–34,
    40–42, 47–51, 54–56, 69, 77, 89, 101,
    117–8, 122, 124, 126, 127, 132, 135, 141,
    146, 148–150, 153, 154–156, 158, 164–167,
    169–172, 180, 185–7, 193–195, 197, 201,
    206, 210, 212–214, 216, 227, 230–237, 239
    etymology of, 19
    formative, 19, 30, 51, 158, 234

Facebook, 164–5, 178
factions, 146, 158, 175–177
farming, 120, 122, 123
fear, 19, 32, 65, 80, 119–121, 127, 151, 152,
    173, 178, 179, 197
Feher, Ferenc, 142, 144, 145, 148, 153, 159
fluid conjunctures, 5, 98, 101, 102–105, 235
    theory of, 101
Flyvbjerg, Bent, 198
focal point, 104
Foucault, Michel, 13–15, 22–3, 31–2, 35, 50,
    54, 72, 86, 217–219
fragmentation, 73, 18, 200
frame, 15, 34, 43–46, 50, 52, 54–5, 65, 66, 142,
    154, 158, 174–5, 183, 190, 196, 199, 223,
    226, 237, 239
Franco, Francisco, 193
Frazer, James, 42 , 45
French political crisis of 1958, 104
French Revolution, 6, 141–143, 145–147,
    149–150, 152, 156, 158, 185–7, 189, 193,
    206, 214
front regions, 131
frontier, 5, 97, 112–128, 130–135

Furet, François, 142, 145–148, 150, 154,
    158–9

garbage, 62–64, 123
gender, 44, 49, 69, 167, 169, 170, 172
genealogy, 4, 14–5, 72–3, 90
generation, 48, 119–120, 164, 170, 206, 210,
    215, 222
geopolitics, 7, 207–9, 213–4, 219, 221–2, 228
Gettysburg address (1863), 191
Girard, René, 25, 28, 54, 81, 83, 147, 152,
    155–157, 195
Girondins, 154
globalization, 1, 184, 199, 206
gnosis, 88, 89
Gnosticism, 12, 83
Goethe, Johann-Wolfgang von, 85, 141, 214
Goffman, Erving, 5, 131
gold, 42, 78, 79, 81, 82, 84–87
Gorbachev, Mikhail, 205, 209, 210, 212–216,
    219, 220, 223
Gottemoeller, Rose, 223
grammar of war, 99
Gramsci, Antonio, 218, 219
Gray, John, 208, 222

Handelman, Don, 190
Hayek, Friedrich, 198, 214
Heidegger, Martin, 14, 72, 212
Helen, 67, 76, 79
Hermes, 23, 26, 83, 85, 87, 88
heroic fallacy, 94–96, 101
Hertz, Robert, 45
hierarchies, 2, 183, 186, 201, 226, 229
Hirschman, Albert, 195
historical anthropology, 5, 131
historical contingency, 184
    liminal intersterstices of, 184
Hollywood, 112, 125
Horkheimer, Max, 68
hybridity, 4, 61, 228

idealism, 13, 19, 33, 34, 213
identity, 1, 4–6, 18–9, 30, 64, 72–74, 76–79,
    81–83, 85, 89–90, 103, 130, 132, 167, 183,
    187, 189–190, 191, 194, 202, 210, 220, 229,
    231, 237
IkedaIkeda, Daisaku, 205, 210, 212–6, 219,
    220, 223
image-makers, 82

imaginary, 67, 145, 148, 149, 151, 154, 157, 158, 211
    constitutional, 188–9
    power, 189, 221
imagination, 5, 6, 39, 65, 67, 75, 184–186, 189, 191, 194, 198–9, 201–2, 228–9
imitation, 4, 19, 25, 26–28, 78, 82, 83, 196–8, 214
Inayatullah, Naeem, 238, 239
Inbetweenness, 4, 15, 24, 40, 62–67, 70, 228
incorporation, 43, 49, 90, 113, 125, 148, 153, 156–7, 219
individualism, 95, 117–8, 190, 194–6, 201, 213
initiation rite, 17, 18, 73, 89
inside/outside, 239
integrity, 73, 85, 90, 200
interdependence, 98, 102, 104, 119, 123
interdividual psychology, 195, 198
International Political Anthropology, 3
International Relations (IR) theory
    and agency, 228
International Relations Theory, 226
invention,72, 78, 84
irrationality, 2, 61, 88, 153, 198
Isagoras, 187, 192

Jackson, Andrew, 115
Jacobins, 152–5
James, William, 41
Jefferson, Thomas, 114
Jesus, 41
John the Baptist, 68
Judeo–Christian tradition, 67
Jung, C. G., 87–89

Kant, Immanuel 11–17, 19–20, 22, 25, 29, 34–5, 143
Kantorowicz, Ernst, 142, 143, 187
Keane, John, 188–9
King Arthur, 131
Kjellen, Rudolf, 215
knowledge, 12, 15, 17, 39, 67, 70, 73, 74, 76, 77, 79, 82, 83, 88, 89, 95, 104, 105, 107, 114, 120, 188, 189, 207, 212, 228, 230
    forbidden, 76
Koselleck, Reinhart, 15, 28, 55, 87, 201, 206, 210, 214–217
Kozyrev, Andrei, 221, 222
krizis, 210–213, 217

La Bruyère, Jean, 131

laws in history, 98, 99
Le Roy Ladurie, Emmanuel, 131
Leach, Edmund, 45
leadership, 51–54, 120, 167
Lefort, Claude, 158, 184, 186–7, 197
legitimacy, 105, 151, 188, 207, 209, 218
leisure, 7, 47, 56, 134
level of analysis, 227
Levinson, Sanford, 192
Levi-Strauss, Claude, 45
Liberal absolutism, 189
liberalism, 35, 189, 197, 200, 229
life stages, 49
liminal, 2, 4–8, 11, 18, 20–26, 28–9, 31–34, 40, 41, 43, 46–51, 53–56, 76–79, 81, 83, 87–9, 93, 112, 122, 128, 132, 134, 148, 149, 152, 154–5, 158, 167–171, 179, 184–5, 187–8, 190, 192–3, 200, 207, 210, 211, 216–7, 223, 226–8, 230–240
    acts, 133
    ordeal, 232, 233
    people, 136
    person, 135
    situation, 3, 22, 24–26, 34, 41, 50, 53, 88, 89, 185, 235, 238
    zone, 122, 134
liminality, 1–10, 14, 16, 18, 21, 23, 25–35, 39–56, 59, 67, 73, 77, 79–81, 85, 86, 89–90, 112, 116, 120, 127, 132–134, 142, 148–150, 156, 158, 165, 167–170, 176, 180, 183, 194, 205, 206, 208, 210, 211, 216, 220, 223, 226–240
    permanentization of, 54
    spatial dimension of, 48
    temporal dimension of, 48
liminoid, 47, 116, 132, 168, 169, 240
limit, 39, 44, 56, 73, 77, 80, 105, 112, 119–120, 123, 128, 171, 185–6, 188, 195, 197, 200, 223, 228, 231–2
    material limits, 23
Lincoln, Abraham, 191
Lope de Vega, 133
Lotman, Yuri, 61, 62
Louis XIV, King, 5, 130–132, 134–5
love, 12, 30, 32, 40, 50, 76, 79, 86, 87, 90, 135, 196, 197

Maalouf, Amin, 199
Madison, James, 195, 197, 198
Maintenon, Madame de, 132, 135
Mann, Michael, 217

marriage, 23, 31–3, 85, 87, 132, 135
martyrs, 164, 168, 173, 174
Marx, Karl, 14, 25, 26, 34, 35, 83, 142, 145,
    186, 208–9, 229
mask, 31, 70, 75, 76, 133
master of ceremony, 18–9, 29, 50, 52, 74, 77,
    87, 150, 190, 233
Mauss, Marcel, 25, 28, 43, 45, 156, 229
McCarthy, Joseph, 130, 189, 197
McCarthyism, 189
Meaning (s)
    horizons of, 197
    loss of, 2
    moments of, 165
    of popular sovereignty, 187
    of rationality, 193
    of shared experiences, 196
    of Tahrir square, 164
    structures of, 186
    transfer of, 193
    void of 2, 156
mechanical growth, 74
metallurgy, 73–4, 76, 78–9, 82–3, 89–90
metaxy, 15, 19
mimetic desire, 149
mimetic violence, 25
modernity, 3, 7, 28, 32, 40, 49, 51, 54, 55, 183,
    185, 195, 208–10, 222, 232, 236, 239
Moldova, 207, 236
monsters, 62–5, 79
Montesquieu, Charles de, 198
Moore, Barrington, 97
Mubarak, Hosni, 164–5, 168, 170–175, 177
multi-sectoral mobilizations, 101
Mumford, Lewis, 72, 118
museological gaze, 65
Muslim Brotherhood, 165, 174, 178
myth, 5, 26, 32, 43, 45, 53, 67, 68, 70, 76, 79,
    112, 124–128, 144, 153, 188, 191, 200, 201,
    212, 236–7
mythology, 26, 112

National Convention, 141, 143, 144, 149,
    151–2, 154
nationality, 117, 189
NATO, 207, 220, 222–3, 237
natural disaster, 40, 50
Needham, Rodney, 45, 82
neo-Kantian, 12–14
Neolithic, 24, 79
Neoplatonism, 83

Nietzsche, Friedrich, 13–16, 19
non-being, 53, 73, 74
nostalgia, 176
novel, 29, 40, 72, 126, 132, 135, 214

Odysseus, 68, 79
order, 2–4, 6, 12–3, 16, 19–22, 27, 29, 34–5,
    42, 46, 50–52, 54, 55, 61, 62–64, 67, 70,
    76–7, 79–80, 83, 85, 87–8, 112, 115,
    119, 148–9, 152–154, 156–7, 169, 172,
    176–7, 179–180, 185–188, 190, 192, 194–5,
    198–200, 207, 209, 219, 221, 222–4, 228,
    231–236, 239–40
    dissolution of, 2, 34
Organization for Cooperation and Security
    in Europe (OSCE), 207, 222
Orwell, George, 131
outcomes, 2, 3, 6, 93, 95–99, 107, 119, 188,
    201, 235
out-of-the-ordinary, 15, 28, 52, 149

parasitic, 76, 77
Paris, 43, 67, 76, 79, 130, 141, 152, 197
participation, 18, 20, 31, 166–169, 172, 174,
    188, 198–9, 207, 217
passionate interests, 6, 88, 186, 194, 196
Paul (saint), 41
people-as-One, 193
    fantasy of the, 187
people-God, 152, 193
performance, 5, 18, 47, 82, 131–133, 149, 169,
    190, 197, 199
Pericles, 191
phenomenological, 5, 94, 143, 144, 146, 148,
    150, 159
pilgrimage, 47, 48, 167
Plato, 4, 11–3, 15, 19–22, 25, 27, 30–31, 35,
    47, 73, 77, 83–4, 87, 197, 223
play, 16, 21, 29, 47, 50–51, 55–6, 69, 74, 77,
    81, 85, 113, 117, 119, 125, 127–8, 133–4,
    142, 143, 156, 195, 208, 227, 234, 238–40
poetry, 126, 169, 171
political Fluidity, 93
political legitimacy, 105
political religion, 147, 156, 159
political subjectivity, 230
political transition, 4, 231
politics of becoming, 234
Popper, Karl, 106
popular revolt
    liminal moment of, 192

pornography, 29
postmodern, 29, 34, 35, 39, 47, 98, 167, 211, 223
Pozdnyakov, Elgiz, 214–5
Prague Spring (1968), 209
problem of difference, 231, 238
problematization, 15, 32, 51, 56
Prozorov, Sergei, 209–10, 215

Quinet, Edgar, 151, 193

Rabutin, Roger de, 135
Racine, Jean, 135
Radin, Paul, 25, 44, 77
rational choice, 35, 73, 95
rationalism, 25, 29, 32, 33
regicide, 6, 141, 142, 144, 153, 154
religion, 14, 43–45, 48, 147, 156, 159, 171, 186, 192
revisionist, 142, 145, 207
revolution, 3, 4, 5, 6, 14, 30, 32, 35, 47, 49, 74, 81, 88, 99–97, 100, 103, 106, 141–159, 164–179, 184–187, 189, 197, 201, 207–212, 214–216, 218–9, 222, 231–2, 235, 238
Ricoeur, Paul, 201
rites of passage, 2, 4, 16–9, 21–3, 31–2, 42–46, 54, 73, 76, 89, 131, 132, 148, 184, 190, 226, 229
ritual, 3, 5–6, 18, 24, 25, 27, 31–2, 39–50, 52, 53, 82, 85, 89, 120, 132–4, 144–5, 149, 151–154, 156–158, 169, 172–173, 176, 180, 190, 191–194, 197, 200, 231, 233, 236–7, 240
ritual passage, 39–42, 44, 46, 49, 52, 54, 233
Robespierre, 142, 144, 153, 156
Romanticism, 126
Rotrou, Jean, 133
Russian Revolution, 209

sacred, 6, 24, 34, 48, 53, 63–66, 74, 79–81, 87–8, 143–147, 149–150, 152–158, 189–194, 197, 199, 202, 220
    symbolic center of the, 6
sacrifice , 27, 53, 79–81, 87, 144, 147, 149, 152, 154–157, 187, 191, 197, 220
    collective, 187
sacrificial crisis, 147, 149, 152, 154, 157
Saint-Just, 141, 144, 153, 156
Saint-Simon, Duc de, 13, 131, 133–135
Salome, 68
Samson, 68

savagery, 124
Scarron, Paul, 135
schismogenesis, 25–7, 29
Schleiermacher, Friedrich, 13
Schmitt, Carl, 222
Schumpeter, Joseph, 185, 188, 197
Scudery, Georges de, 133
Second World War, 55
sectoral borders, 101
    collapse of, 101
seduction, 62, 66–70
    inbetweenness of, 67
self-divinization, 80
self-constraint, 119, 120
self-reform, 55
separation, 17, 18, 43, 44, 54, 63, 79, 82, 85, 167, 170, 184, 190, 236
Serres, Michel, 61–62
sexuality, 23, 32, 33, 55
Sieyès, Emmanuel, 193
situational logic(s), 98–9, 102–3, 106–7
smith, 73–81, 89
Smith, Adam, 195, 196
social change, 176, 185, 208–9, 214–217, 227, 229
social drama, 6, 45–6, 146, 165, 176, 178, 234
social media, 39, 167, 178, 194
social, the, 44
socialism, 35, 165, 186, 208
Socrates, 197
Sophists, 12, 20, 21, 25, 73
Sorel, Georges, 29
speech act, 23, 29, 194
spiral, 73, 82, 146, 152, 185, 197
spirit of Tahrir, 165, 175, 179, 180
stamping, 14, 15, 29, 41, 88, 150
state formation, 116, 122, 125, 226
state of exception, 65, 231, 232
Stoicism, 84
stone, 23, 75, 77, 78, 84, 85, 85, 89, 90, 185
Strauss, Leo, 222
Levi-Strauss, Claude, 16, 46, 85
structure, 2–7, 12–3, 16–7, 22–25, 28–31, 34, 40, 41–43, 45–47, 49–55, 77, 83–4, 89, 94–5, 101–103, 112, 120, 124, 132, 148, 164–166, 169–172, 175–180, 183, 184, 186–7, 206, 211, 213, 218, 226, 228–9, 231–240
    plasticity of, 101
    states of, 101
survival, 105, 121, 122, 223

symbol, 15, 24, 40, 44, 46, 47, 51, 63, 67, 80, 88, 141, 143–154, 158, 159, 165, 167, 168, 170–173, 174, 176, 179, 186, 187, 190, 191, 193, 195, 200, 240
Szakolczai, Arpad, 2, 3, 4, 11, 14–5, 46, 50, 51, 53–55, 76, 112, 120, 148, 227, 232–3, 235–6, 238

Tahrir (square)
    spirit of, 164
Tahrir Square, 164–177, 179, 180
taken–for–granted, 6, 18, 28, 30, 52, 73, 234
Tarde, Gabriel, 28, 44, 88
technological growth, 72, 73
technology, 4, 72–74, 79, 81–82, 90
Teiresias, 64, 70
television, 130, 136, 167, 169, 177, 179
terror, 1, 80, 85, 96, 141–147, 155–159, 175, 193, 197, 199, 200, 215, 221, 231, 237
Thackeray, William, 132
theater, 7, 27, 133, 169, 197
thought (history of) 11, 15
Thucydides, 191
tin, 79
Tolstoy, Lev, 213
topology of security, 230
totalitarianism, 188, 212, 213, 218
totemism, 43, 44, 45
traders, 116, 117, 121
transformation, 1, 5, 27, 29, 41, 44, 47, 63, 72–74, 78, 79, 81, 82, 83, 87, 90, 94, 95, 101, 102, 148, 180, 186, 201, 211, 215, 220, 226, 234, 235
    alchemic, 74
transgression, 18, 57, 67, 151, 158, 185, 191
transition, 4, 5, 7, 14–17, 27–9, 34, 35, 42–3, 45, 48–50, 55, 61, 69, 89, 93–4, 96, 103, 106, 112, 134, 155, 184, 193, 197, 210, 212, 215, 226, 231, 233–4, 236, 238
transitology, 29, 95
travel, 39, 46, 49, 65, 79, 166, 167, 168
trial, 6, 18, 22, 79, 141–146, 148–155, 158, 172
Trojan War, 67, 76, 79
Truth and Reconciliation Commissions (TRC), 193
Turner, Frederick Jackson, 5, 115–6, 124
Turner, Victor, 3, 16, 55, 117, 131, 226
tweets, 165, 167
twenty-year crisis, 207

Ukraine, 221, 223

uncertainty, 2, 6, 39, 47, 51, 53, 62, 104, 119, 175, 176, 183, 187, 188, 193, 235, 236
unequivocality, 68, 69
United States, 5, 46, 112–115, 117, 121, 124, 127, 128, 185, 187, 189, 191, 208, 218, 223
unlimited, 12, 19, 20, 21, 22, 30, 34, 76, 77, 151, 176
utopian, 6, 31, 185, 205, 208, 209, 217

van Gennep, Arnold, 2, 3, 5, 13, 16, 17, 18, 39, 42–46 50, 51, 54, 73, 120, 148, 155, 184, 190, 226
Versailles, 5, 130–135
Veyne, Paul, 99
Victim 62, 65, 66., 69, 76, 77, 79, 81, 147, 155–157, 194, 199, 200
victimhood, 65, 193
    imagination of, 65
victimological gaze, 66
violence, 25, 29, 53, 56, 65–69, 73, 80, 99, 119–122, 124, 125, 127, 147, 148, 149, 152, 157, 175, 187, 189, 190, 212, 217, 226, 231, 236
    "originary", 190
    cycle of, 120
virginity,32, 33
Visconti, Primo, 130, 131, 133, 134
Voegelin, Eric, 13–15, 19, 27, 31, 35, 88, 210, 223
void, 2, 40, 87, 156

Walzer, Michael, 142–145, 148–150, 153, 154, 159
war in Afghanistan, 237
war on terror, 221, 231
warfare, 7, 22, 55, 69, 197, 236, 237, 238
Weber, Max, 14–16, 19, 28, 31, 34, 50–52, 54–56, 104, 105, 115, 125, 186, 195
Weiler, Joseph, 191
Wild West, 112, 125, 126
Wolin, Sheldon, , 189, 195, 218, 220, 221
World War I, 28, 185, 236
World War II, 27, 127, 166, 208, 217

Yeltsin, Boris, 222

Žižek, Slavoj, 204, 233
Zyuganov, Gennady, 220

Lightning Source UK Ltd.
Milton Keynes UK
UKHW022132070620
364529UK00009B/703